And
Blow Not
the Trumpet

And

Blow Not

the Trumpet

A PRELUDE TO PERIL

By STANLEY D. PORTEUS

PACIFIC BOOKS
Publishers

PACIFIC BOOKS

P.O. Box 558, Palo Alto, California

IF THE PEOPLE of the land take a man of their coasts, and set him for their watchman . . . . but if the watchman see the sword come, and blow not the trumpet, and the people be not warned; if the sword come and take *any* person from among them . . . . his blood will I require at the watchman's hand."

— Ezekiel 33:2–6

Of Pies and Prefaces

APART FROM their initial p's, there are quite a number of points of resemblance between pies and prefaces. In addition to the fact that both are cooked up for the occasion, so that a book without a preface or a dinner without pie would seem a little perverse, they have much in common. They can either be light or heavy, shallow or deep, tart or sweet, dry or juicy, fluffy or fruitful. Each can be made to serve a similar purpose; in case the company omits the courtesy, they give the cook a chance to invite comment on the rest of the meal. That one comes at the beginning and the other at the end of the main course does not affect the analogy. Most guests, whether comfortably or uncomfortably replete, are polite enough to accept the pie; authors, not being cheek by jowl with their readers, cannot trust people's politeness. Their only chance of getting their prefaces read is to put them at the beginning. The proof, too, of the preface is in the reading.

Psychologists, nowadays, make brave attempts at analyzing personalities through their patients' interpretation of ink-blots. How much more significant the process would be if they allowed their subjects to make their own inkblots, as authors do. The pathway from personality to paper via the arm, hand, and writing implement is a very direct one, and of all protocols, prefatory remarks are the most revealing. By their prefaces ye shall know them.

Thus we find that the urge to write indicates a certain

juvenility of temperament. To hog the spotlight of attention, to have one's uninterrupted say to the tune of eighty
thousand words, more or less, is an opportunity that any
adolescent would describe as something super. Added to
that is the prefatory privilege of unashamedly discussing
your own brain child. Possibly we have placed the age level
of authors too high. Perhaps our literary exhibitionism belongs better in the infantile or diaper stage. The psycho-
analysts would call it a scatophilic interest except that they
themselves are so fond of writing. Maybe the best analogy
is between the magnum opus and the mud pie.

Be that as it may, there are as many varieties of prefaces
as there are degrees of defiance when, as Touchstone remarked, men "quarrel by the book." There is the preface
apologetic, in which the author offers amends for having
written at all — an endless process, for the more he apolo-
gizes the more he writes. A milder form is the explanatory
preface, wherein the writer makes the plain fact that he has
muddied the waters of criticism or controversy plainer still.
There is the preface gratitudinal, the pickpocket's preface,
which includes a long list of author's authorities to prove
that if he stole at all it was from the best purses. Then there
is the perspirational preface, wherein the author canters
over the field to warm himself up for the real race, or the
preface peripatetic, in which the writer goes over the whole
ground with a magnifying glass to show there is no spot
on which he has not shed at least a drop of ink. Nor should
we forget the epistolary preface, through which the author
addresses the reader on better terms than he expects to be
anywhere else in the book. But whatever labels these prefaces bear — polemical, praiseful, or merely prattling —
they all echo the cry so common in the kindergarten play-
room: "Come, come! See what I've done!"

But this preface, at least, will offer no apologies for a
book on as important a subject as Hawaii's contributions to
national defense; it will make no acknowledgment of its

sources of information — the list would be too long — nor apologize for omitting the names of important personalities, since they are too numerous; it will offer no regrets for criticisms because they are sharp, provided they be not dull; and of admissions or disclaimers it will make but one. The author found it so difficult to write a book about the Islands without putting Hawaii on the title page that he had to go all the way back to Ezekiel, who appeared to know all about happenings like Pearl Harbor even though he had never heard of the place.

All of which merely brings us back to where we started by proving that any author who tries to make a preface different merely succeeds in making it pied.

STANLEY D. PORTEUS

Contents

Contents

CHAPTER I

Waiting for Its Hour

IT WAS Robert Louis Stevenson, inimitable teller of tales, who thought that there was a fitting relation between places and events. An old inn near Burford Bridge was one spot that impressed him with its air of expectancy. He wrote: "Within these ivied walls, behind these green old shutters, some further business smolders, waiting for its hour."

But this is a man-centered view, as if Nature cared enough about the experiences which torture or delight us to bother about arranging their setting. She does not stage-manage her own dramatic occurrences. She leaves untouched the pine that stands exposed on the pinnacle as though inviting the lightning, and splinters the tree in the sheltered valley. There is no place too bright to be exempt from tragedy. The darkest imaginings have fallen short of reality, even of those who see blood on the moon.

Nonetheless, there are places that can put a quietening finger on the restless spirit. It was green pastures and quiet waters by which walked the restored soul. But men wander everywhere and carry their wickedness with them.

Certainly no one, however foreboding, could look at Pearl Harbor and imagine its hour a tragic one. Seen from a height, its contour and coloring are satisfying. It lies midway between the bare slopes of the Waianae Mountains and the cloud-hung mass of the Koolau ranges. On the north it is bounded by a broad wash of light green — the green of growing cane — running up towards Schofield.

1

On the south it is blocked off by the blue of deep Pacific water. In between is a land mass outlined with kiawes and mangroves, into which Pearl Harbor fits comfortably, like a piece of a jig-saw puzzle. With its narrow neck and the widely branching curves of the east and west lochs, it looks exactly as if it were cut out with a fret-saw; only its color, silver grey against the kiawe forest's dark green, breaks the continuity of the picture.

If it be true that terrain makes a lasting impress on the nature of its inhabitants, then Hawaii folk should be an extremely easy-going people. Peace should go with these islands. The effect of type of scenery on imagination is reflected by Stevenson when he said that certain places cry aloud for a murder. Others call for a happy vacancy of events. Perhaps this clear brightness, this quiet of the lochs, conferred a sense of security on the minds of the sentinels, a feeling that war would be an unreasonable or impossible intrusion here. This mild air may have made it easy to forget that death lurks where it pleases.

But if the peace of Pearl Harbor contributed its share towards dulling suspicion and wakefulness — the idea is by no means fantastic — then somnolence should be the ordinary state of Hawaii's civilian population who are continually exposed to natural unruffled beauty. There are many who claim that our boasted tolerance is merely indolence and that only exceptionally powerful stimulants or irritants keep us awake.

But in spite of a happy conjunction of mountains, sea, and soft air, and regardless of the effort-delaying influence of an almost changeless climate, the people of these islands have a respectable record of accomplishment in various fields. Life can be easy here, the native Hawaiians have proved it so — life, that is, expressed in the passive sense; a sunny beach, some fish and poi, a little music and laughter may fill your days, which then so quietly round off into years. We will not stop to argue the question as to whether this kind of living is, or is not, the happiest, but for those who think that life needs the yeast of activity, Hawaii is not the place, unless they bring with them a considerable drive and enthusiasm for achievement. They must be will- ing, when the spirit flags, to apply to themselves the merci- less spurs of ambition. We may as well freely admit that here it takes more than ordinary determination to swim against the current, and that mental alertness is not our natural state, but has, by various circumstances, been forced upon us.

All these things enter into the story of the civilian de- fense of this sea frontier, and both place and events demand their share of attention. Thus the historian seeks little justification for devoting space to description, especially when story and setting bear such incongruous relations. If the pace of that description seems too leisurely and the pauses over some point of beauty or interest too long, that will provide added proof of the fact that writers who wander around these islands are inclined just to wander.

Your first view of Oahu, military and naval key to the whole Hawaiian Sea Frontier, has little of that surprising beauty of the South Seas which Stevenson declared "touches a virginity of sense." He was thinking of quiet water in the foreground, a fringe of palms, and a background of high shadowed mountains, aloof from human habitation, but keeping a friendly companionship with the clouds. On the contrary, as your ship or plane approaches Koko Head, the scene is, if anything, repellent. The land has all the harsh- ness of color and form of recent volcanic fires, even though a thousand years may easily have elapsed since these craters were active. The rains, which elsewhere bring fertility, have contributed nothing to soften the scene. They have matched violence with violence, so that each ancient crater is scored with hundreds of furrows which discharge them- selves upon a rocky platform swept bare by the sea. In a southeasterly blow every jagged tooth and headland is

marked by tumbling wash and columns of spray, the madness of waves constricted within these cliff-bound fissures.
On these bare rocks and solidified ash nothing grows, except
where in the dips of the craters some twisted kiawes find
shelter from the wind and the spray. On such a coast you
would expect nothing to happen, not even a murder, unless
a ship were the victim.

But this disorder of the seas along the Molokai Channel
makes Honolulu and its mountain background more en-
ticing. The bay between Koko and Diamond Head is sheltered, the mountains are greener and withdrawn from the
coast, and for the first time a coral reef appears, its sketchy
breakers serving to outline, like a draughtsman's light
strokes, the architecture of the island. The land begins to look
as if it had living possibilities. The kiawes, the transported
mesquite of Mexico, though they live only on the fringes of
Honolulu polite tree-society, here do their best to thicken
their foliage and cover the foreshore, hinting at the arboreal
wealth to come. Soon they break, to disclose lawns and
green fairways; spreading monkeypods appear, palms lean
over the beaches, and before you are opposite Diamond
Head you may sense a city hidden in trees.

If the visitor is unused to tropic islands he will find constant interest in the appearance of the reef. From the landward side the breakers seem running an endless relay race.
Each rears itself on the edge of the reef, holds its moment
of beauty only long enough for the succeeding wave to
catch its sparkle, and then subsides into the long ripples of
the lagoon. During the early days of the war, when Honolulu was blacked out completely, pilots of belated aircraft
had reason to bless the reef, for on the darkest nights its
faint phosphorescence is visible from the air.

The heat and bustle of the city and the commercial air
of Waikiki may set the visitor wondering where he may
find that sense of quiet and relaxation that the books so
generously promise. It does not seem to go with little

cluttered-up grocery stores and sun-warped, unpainted
wooden houses that line the streets as soon as the fine stone
buildings of the center of the city are left behind. This
might be some Figueroa Street of Southern California, half
grown, except that some of the houses are set in what might
have been once fine gardens, now represented by a bedrag-
gled palm or carelessly planted hibiscus. There is a good
deal of Honolulu's environs that is untidy and unlovely,
rather like slums that have wandered off into a garden.

Only when the visitor has left the coastal plain and
reached the residential valleys will he find any hint of good
living; but immediately he has entered one of these folds
in the hills, he finds that he has stepped into beauty, not
breathtaking nor stupendous, but affording glimpses of
something satisfying that he could live with and absorb.

This change is of course due to the mountains that have
lost their aridity and newness of aspect, taking on the appearance of an old garden wall tumbled down in spots,
where the valleys are inset. Their sides are steep, in many
places dangerous to climb, but vegetation flows down from
their summits, greening the ridges, and softening their outlines. Perhaps the most distinctive features of Honolulu
mountains are the little tributary gullies, down each of
which comes a river of kukui trees, their greyish-green
foliage in strong contrast to the dark, forested ridges that
lie behind.

It is pleasant to see that man has gone along with that
beauty, accepting these mountains as background for lawns
and gardens, fitting homes onto ledges and sidings, or spilling
them gently out upon the valley floor. Here in Manoa
Valley, for example, there must be a thousand little gardens,
each with its patch of lawn, ringed about with poinsettias,
many-colored ti plants, and the yellow and red of crotons.
Before the whites came, this was where the Hawaiians had
their house foundations and some of their stone walls still
stand, weathered and grey with lichens, shadowed closely

by tree ferns and flowering bananas. Perhaps it was from the gently flexing broad blades of the wild bananas that the hula dancers got the idea of the movements of their hands. Here is an easy land, a land that makes everything welcome, as this convocation of all the flowering trees of the world shows. For scarcely anything you see belongs here. The host has departed; the guests have overrun the place.

But this is within the city. What the visitor may find hard to realize is that Honolulu is an overgrown town among islands whose economy is entirely agricultural, with all that that fact entails. He may think that the city, with its sometimes narrow, always crowded streets, sets the key for life in Hawaii, but this is not so. The land under cultivation comprises perhaps only one-twelfth of the total area and the rest is sparsely if at all inhabited, given over to solitude and quiet.

You will appreciate this fact when you fly to Molokai across the twenty-mile strait that separates it from Oahu. As you draw level with the land, you will see at right angles to your flight some miles of foreshore, as deserted and lonely as any Robinson Crusoe's island. There are smooth rocky headlands and curving bays, behind which the land rises in red dirt slopes scored with dry runnels and sparsely covered with kiawe trees. But you will see no road nor house nor other sign of human occupancy. I suppose a man's footprint on those beaches would be as unexpected as Man Friday's.

So lonely is Molokai that here was chosen the spot for the leper settlement. You may look into Kalaupapa from above by following a crossroad that winds through dusty lantana and low trees till it reaches the edge of a two-thousand-foot cliff. A footpath angles across the face of this precipice, the single means of entry for the settlement except from the sea. From the top of the high gate that bars the trail, a wire from which tin cans are suspended runs to the guard's cottage, so that their jangling serves notice that someone goes up or down.

The settlement of Kalaupapa ("flat leaf of land") is walled in with these cliffs which meet the sea at either end, thus cutting off all landward egress except by this single trail. Into that sunken space have been crowded more suf' fering and misery than into any comparable spot in the Pacific area.

When the late sun floods into Kalaupapa as through an embrasure, the place glows with color. Possibly this an' cient beauty of their own land lapping them round about has contributed to the laughter and cheer that, incredible as it may seem, are not lacking to the inmates of this place. And strangest of all was the eager interest, vouched for by one who knows the lepers well, with which they, forever imprisoned from the world, listened to the radio reports of that world's struggle to free its peoples from the menace of aggression. Man's spirit truly needs but little space upon which to light and refresh itself. In the story of others' sacrifice and heroism these poor souls found for themselves enlargement.

This is, of course, a part of Hawaii of which we do not speak willingly, and is our saddest advertisement. I mention it solely as a reminder that there is a background of sadness and tragedy to all these Pacific islands — the extinction or displacement of its native race, a process to which leprosy has contributed its share. Unfortunately, the name Molokai has been so closely associated with the site of the leper settle' ment that many people believe the whole island is given over to the lepers instead of perhaps one-fortieth of its area.

Flying up the slot between Molokai and the neighboring island of Lanai, you will realize at once the strength and weakness of this sea frontier. There are too many beaches to defend so that an enemy could land almost anywhere he pleased, but having landed there are few places he could go. But if you can forget for a moment the human stage with its dramas of tragedy and dissension you will find this coast' line peculiarly satisfying. The water for some distance up to a quarter of a mile from land is shallow: the bottom variously white sand, mud, and coral or lava rock. Hence the sun high overhead spills color everywhere, pink, green, yellow, light blue, in pastel shades, all edged with the dark purple of deep water outside the reef. A succession of rock-walled fishponds are strung at intervals along the shore and these may be green, yellow, or pearl-grey according to the time of day.

The high end of Molokai presents the characteristic scenery of many of the islands of the South Seas. The land gathers itself into summits whose contours are generally hidden in a crumpled blanket of clouds, while the long leeward slope is scored by gulches so deep that the air scarcely stirs in their recesses. Streamers of clouds constantly reach down from the cloud rack over the valley heads to dissolve in the warm air below. The quiet will remind you of what Stevenson wrote of the Marquesas: "The face of the world was of a prehistoric emptiness; life appeared to stand stock-still, and the sense of isolation was profound and refreshing."

Where Molokai is backed up against the sea, it lifts itself thousands of feet above the breakers at its base. The face of the precipice is cut off so cleanly that it has beheaded many a small stream that must now discharge itself in mid-air, at first as a waterfall and later as a mare's tail of mist. Only at one or two places have the streams, aided perhaps by some fault of structure, cut back faster than the ocean could advance, and there they fall into deep valleys, inaccessible except in calm weather by canoe.

But the lonely isle of Molokai is not the only one which possesses a large uninhabited region. On Maui the great bulk of Haleakala is almost surrounded by a belt road and inside this ring are hundreds of thousands of acres containing no signs of human habitation save a ranger's cottage and a military observation post. Occupying its center is a huge volcanic sink, the crater of Haleakala, given over to silence since its fires died down perhaps a thousand years ago.

The mountain mass cuts off the trade winds so that the grassy slopes above the Kula road form what is normally one of the quietest spots on earth. It is a silence that can be felt, its only break the occasional songs of English sky-larks which, having been brought thus far, have adopted this place as home. But four thousand feet down, at the foot of the mountain, was an arid red waste of kiawes and prickly pear which the marines used as an artillery practice range, alight at night with green tracer bullets and the glow of exploding shells. One can imagine the mountain listening, recalling to itself its own commotion of so many years ago. Now, too, the marines have gone home and the skylarks sing undisturbed.

The West Maui Mountains too, like Haleakala, are par-tially circumscribed by a thin trickle of travel. The road begins a few miles beyond the old Hawaiian capital town of Lahaina, skirts the dry palis and rocky elbows overlooking Malaaea Bay, passes through Wailuku, and ends in what was once an old Hawaiian fishing village clinging preca-riously to the cliffs. Lahaina roadstead, protected by the islands of Lanai and Kahoolawe and ending in Malaaea Bay was once of considerable naval importance. The de-serted island of Kahoolawe became known as "Little Tarawa" because of the number of naval shellings and prac-tice assaults which it underwent, while Malaaea Bay itself was being constantly churned by waves of landing craft. The most unmistakable sign that the war was over was when the whales again came into the bay.

Planes from Honolulu frequently pass by the perimeter of West Maui, near enough for the observer to realize that here too is much unexplored or at least unexploited country. From the six-thousand-foot rim of the central crater of Eke, brown and terra-cotta ridges march down to the sea, soli-tary steeps known only to the tropic birds and the wild goats. Far away from such places seem the dissensions with which men trouble their hurried existence.

On the other side of Haleakala, across a twenty-mile strait, lies the Big Island, the island of Hawaii. If it were possible to view the whole of Hawaii at one time, the observer would note human beings scurrying to and fro like ants within a very narrow strip of territory on either side of the round-the-island road. This zone of activity might be several miles wide in places, in others no wider than a span. But wide or narrow, this strip of movement contains within its circumference a central core of silence given over to forests, lava flows, and the solitude of great heights. Perhaps a few wild sheep or straying cattle might produce some spots of action, but for the most part it is a vast stillness. In other countries such areas are watched over by kites, vultures, eagles, or buzzards, the sentinels of the air; here the sky is as empty as the land.

Now and then, in a number of years, the volcano puts on a show, and once in a generation or so a tidal wave may hit these shores the only phenomena of violence in these islands. The eruption, while it lasts, is a truly magnificent sight, with lava fountains spouting three hundred feet or more in height. There is a roar of deeply repressed forces bursting their bonds, followed by rivers of molten stone thrusting red tongues through the forests; but even this commotion, great as it is, soon subsides. The fountains decline, the roar is diminished to a fretful splattering of some residual cone; then silence, while Nature takes up her task of filling in her own ravages, hiding the earthquake cracks with vegetation, and thrusting up a fern or two in the middle of a lava flow, as earnest of her benevolent intentions.

So all this rage and turbulence is but the affair of a moment, and the quiet procession of the years resumes. This Pluto who thinks to fill the earth with his clamor is nothing but an old blacksmith working late at his forge. Presently he too banks his fires and goes back to sleep. Even the tidal wave, vast as is its destructive force, ravages only a few yards of beach before the ocean retreats to its accustomed bounds. Uproar and catastrophe are not native here.

Perhaps every country or territory has within it some spot that contains more of its essence than any place else. There is a little lake not far from Placid into which one could imagine has been crowded most of the Adirondacks' atmosphere. A single peak and mountain tarn may typify the whole of Western Canada or the American Northwest. An amphitheatre of red rocks surrounding a mulga-covered hollow bears the authentic signature of Central Australia, and a single view of red monoliths will open a whole window on Arizona. Similarly, one glance at a picture of a half-dry waterhole and a few camel-thorn trees, even though the animals standing in the sparse shade may be quite indistinguishable, and one will say — this is the interior of Africa, unmistakably.

If I were given the task of choosing some spot that is of the essence of Hawaii, I should go to Kauai, though each one who knows the Islands may have his particular preference. The place I think of is not far from where Captain Cook had his first close view of his newly-discovered islands, in 1778. It is a little bay, tucked away in a black lava coastline, where you may find in miniature all that has been written about in the South Seas.

In this expanse of broken headlands and deep rifts in the lava where the seas heap themselves in confusion, a little river has chosen to scoop out for itself a sandy cove, at one side of which, sheltered by what was once a rocky islet, it can slip out to sea. The arc of the bay is wide enough at first to accommodate the brimming Pacific rollers but they soon break into a smother of foam and finally slide up the long sands, to leave a film of water glistening in the sun.

From green lawns where coconut palms lean, tendrils of creeping vine feel their way down towards the sea. Beyond the lawns is a riot of growth, tree ferns, ginger, and tall Ironwoods, their trunks hidden for fifty feet with the great broad leaves of that strange clinger, the *monstera deliciosa* vine. Then with one of those sly digs at man's idea of harmony in color, Nature has interposed as background a cliff of red volcanic rock upon which bougainvilleas spread their most blatant purples. From that garish coloring the eye turns to the cool shade with almost a shock of contrast. Such is Lawai Beach, and many a tired flier, all keyed up and overwrought from bombing missions over Japan, who was lucky enough to spend his five-day rest period at this spot, will recognize every detail of its description. Fortunately, when Lawai Beach was sold it fell into the hands of gentlefolk who love it well. I hope that when they are done with it, it may revert to the people of Kauai, to whom by right of use and affection it once belonged.

If these things, these scenes, are typical of Hawaii, and I have tried to avoid the fulsomeness of affectionate description, what effect might they have on a people who are constantly exposed to their influence? I believe that laughter comes easily in Hawaii, so that there is rarely the appearance of extreme earnestness. Unlike many other communities we take neither our woes nor our pleasures seriously, but spread over all a light mantle of gaiety which, if it wears thin in places, can easily be replaced. The open road, the empty beach constantly invite, so that the poorest family if it can mount itself on wheels and borrow a tent or tarpaulin for the weekend can own as many shares in Hawaiian sunlight, sea, and air, as the richest. So it comes that most of our sinning is no hole-and-corner, but an out-of-doors affair.

Thus we are inclined to be somewhat irreligious, or pantheistic at best. We do not fear very greatly nor desire very ardently either the threats or the consolations of religious creeds. The missionaries' chief antagonist has not been wickedness but the climate. Even church walls have come to look like a means of restraint.

As to our human relationships, they too are lightly as sumed. We lend a ready but a very casual ear to charity. There is a plethora of organizations which we are willing to join but to which we do not really *belong*. We are shallow-rooted, so that we remove ourselves easily, but are soon homesick for the color, the breezes of Hawaii; and when we return our friends scarcely seem to know that we have been away. When the tourist receives the traditional Hawaiian welcome, he little realizes that it is our own welcome home we are vicariously celebrating, and that we really care little about him. We give him the keys of the city but the doors have no locks. Enter if you like, but you will rarely find the host at home. Thus it is that all human relationships hang loosely, which is what Stevenson meant when he said that affection among the Hawaiians is strong, but not erect.

A paganism made healthy by exposure to sunlight, an improvidence that sees no winter ahead, a lightheartedness that refuses to be dampened too long even by sorrow or disaster, a shallow but fertile soil of character, are native here. They are counteracted partially by traditions of hard labor and frugality on the part of the many, by drive, shrewdness, and money-making foresight on the part of the few. But, in all, these things are tempered by a mildness and tolerance in the surroundings which tend to blunt asperities and soften the keen edge of purpose, wherever found. Ultimately the few and the many, the leaders and the mass, are drawn together by what some call the aloha spirit and what others of shorter acquaintance may look on as devil-may-care.

If this be a true portrait of place and people, what should be their hour? Surely nothing in Hawaii cried aloud for tragedy; certainly this was the last place where one might stop and listen for the far-off mutterings of war. "Fear cometh as a storm and your calamity as a whirlwind," was written in a land of droughts and hurricanes, clouds of devouring locusts, sudden assaults by watchful enemies. Our story surely could have nothing in common with the history of the Day the Preacher wrote of hundreds of years ago, *"the day when the keepers of the house shall tremble, and the strong men shall bow themselves, and the grinders shall cease because they are few, and those that look out from the windows shall be darkened, and the doors shut in the streets; yea, they shall be afraid of that which is high, and terrors shall be in the way."*

Who pondered those words in Hawaii in December, 1941? Who had need to?

CHAPTER II

Hawaii as Advertised

NOT HERE. Not in Hawaii. Tragedy may haunt other places, other peoples, but surely not these islands and their peace-loving population. The breeding places of dissension are well known, marked as they are by the mass murders of two thousand years. The powder keg of the Balkans, those small mountain-ringed states where the flames of nationalism and racial rancor flare so fiercely that a sudden wind from any direction may set a world conflagration going; the western cockpit of Europe, in which for centuries armies have marched and countermarched, leaving behind them human blood and bodies to fertilize the field where poppies grow side by side with the weeds of ancient wrongs and unexpiated enmities; Eastern Asia, where social hatred and injustice work like a ferment; or those ill-styled republics of the New World, in which petty despotism ceaselessly brews revolution; all these are places in which to start a war, but not in Hawaii.

The place geographically does not lend itself readily to order of battle. This is no tight little island like Britain. Our islands are scattered so widely that no more than three of the eight can normally be seen at one time from any other of the group. They therefore lack the proper concentration for defense. Distance has always served them protectively. Instead of the twenty-two miles of the Strait of Dover, twenty-two hundred miles of open ocean separate us from the nearest mainland, a country that is not only friendly but covers us with its flag. To organize our defense is no light task. Even as rich a country as America cannot afford to make these islands bristle with fortifications so as to be impregnable. Eight islands with over six thousand square miles of territory and close upon one thousand miles of seacoast can hardly be made to bristle. Their size and wide dispersal through 3 degrees of latitude and $5\frac{1}{2}$ degrees of longitude make it impossible to fortify them to the degree that invasion would be impracticable. The utmost that could be accomplished for each island is to militarize strongly comparatively small and scattered areas, protect the beaches by machine-gun nests, gather the main forces inland, and then move them along a ring of highways so as to concentrate rapidly large forces at threatened points, thus using the advantage of internal lines of defense. That at least was the original plan for Oahu, but whether the experience of invading large islands held by the Japanese in the Pacific has modified this strategy drastically, only a member of the military staff could say. But in any case, a great part of the Hawaiian group is decidedly vulnerable.

The military strength of these islands was probably generally overestimated. The visitor to these islands of a few years back, having read of Hawaii as a great outpost of defense, a steel helmet upon which an enemy's offensive strokes would blunt themselves, might look in vain for the evidence that could justify this description of the Territory. It is true that as the visitor approached the harbor of Honolulu, his ship rounded the grimly menacing cliffs of Diamond Head. Looking up at these, he no doubt comforted himself with the belief that here, in all probability, was another Gibraltar. But Diamond Head commands no landlocked strait, no bottleneck of ocean commerce. Nor does it project itself onto a promontory with a low neck joining it to a featureless mainland. On the contrary, Diamond Head is a closely knit portion of the island's littoral. Moreover, it is completely dominated by high hills at its back, well within artillery range. The enemy having effected a landing elsewhere and occupied these heights, his artillery could quickly turn its crater into as terrible an inferno as ever it was in the days when Pele, goddess of Hawaiian volcanoes, staged her fireworks there.

But in the twentieth century Diamond Head does not fit the military engineer's specifications for a modern fortress. Consequently the tourists' imaginations were vain. For years it harbored nothing more destructive than a mortar battery, intended no doubt to make things uncomfortable for enemy ships attempting to enter Honolulu harbor; but otherwise its military value, except as an observation post or a fire control station, was small.

As for Punchbowl, the green crater that immediately overlooks the city, its only martial usage was to accommo-date in its shallow bowl a pistol range for the police depart-ment. So far was it removed in the public mind from war and armaments that the highest point on its rim was chosen as the place on which to plant the Easter cross. Yearly, the people of Hawaii drove slowly at night around its lower rim, to look at the reflection of the cross in the clouds, thrown there by the searchlight that illuminated it from below. Honolulu then had certainly little of the appearance of a strongly fortified city.

There were big guns of course, but these were hidden away under the coconut palms that fringed the foreshore of Waikiki, so close to the residential section that every time they were to be fired notice was given to the people in the neighboring apartments to take their crockery off the shelves lest it be broken by the concussion. But as most of the crockery in Waikiki apartments was cracked or broken anyway, usually no one took much notice of these military intentions.

The inquiring tourist, if he were so minded, could no doubt have discovered by diligent investigation more about Honolulu's defenses; but diligence was about the last thing expected of the tourist. What could a land of tropical sun-shine, and of palm trees nodding and whispering among themselves in the moonlight, a land of *dolce far niente* and soft evening skies, have to do with defense and war?

And strangely enough, these islands — with perhaps a little less emphasis on a little grass skirt in a little grass shack — were very much as advertised. It was truly Aloha Land, with all the things comfortable or comic, that the songs declared about it. Perhaps like all seaports frequented by the tourist tribe, it had become rather rapidly cheapjohn and commercialized, with a curio shop around every corner filled with Hawaiian mementos mostly made in Japan. Waikiki Beach was even in those days somewhat oversold, though it had not yet reached the stage when every square yard of beach assayed as many cigarette butts as the sand-filled receptacles beside the elevator in a Chicago hotel. It was still alluring to the eye, and most of the things to which the discriminating visitor objected, the tourist brought with him.

For those of us whose recollections go back twenty-five years, the sand beside the Moana Hotel was then a favorite spot for a quiet picnic supper. There were no crowds and no one stayed to watch the sunset colors spreading from their mixing bowl behind the Waianaes, to gild Diamond Head or throw a saffron cloak over the palms along the bay. There was no commotion, only the swish of the backwash on the sands, heard always against the constant mutter of the waves on the reef.

These were before the days of retaining walls and dis-figuring groins, so that the beaches lay unbroken to opposite the Queen's surf [1] and beyond, until the Diamond Head cliffs of hardened volcanic ash and tufa met the sea and were finally planed off to a coral bench scarcely below tide level. Now and then the marine artist scraped his canvas

[1] The various lines of surf, occasioned by the configuration of the reef, as seen from Waikiki, each have their particular designation.

and drew the scene afresh. The currents swept inshore and what was last week a golden strand was suddenly trans' formed into a boulder-strewn sea floor with raised lava platforms full of tiny pits and perforations through which the wavelets hissed and bubbled. But even if bathing were restricted by such a change in the character of the fore' shore, swimmers did not complain, for the sand was merely swept farther along the beach; the wind changed, the cur' rents set the other way and in a little while here was the sand back again, with all the pot holes filled, the scattered boulders masked, and the sound of the waves pitched to the old familiar key.

No one then was extremely critical of picturesque Waikiki. Instead of acres of apartments there were placid duck ponds and rectangular taro patches, each walled off from its neighbors by narrow mud barriers, where the family carabao stood chewing the cud of reflection in what' ever moods of reflection carabaos have. The horse trams and, later still, the cable cars provided slow but safe trans' portation from Honolulu, whose rush and bustle were soon left behind and forgotten. Typical of the leisurely pace of things was the reply of the Hawaiian policeman on duty near the post office to a visiting Englishman. "Officer," said the visitor in his most condescending Oxford manner, "I wish to go to Waikiki." The overstuffed pillar of the law looked down at the tourist with the very essence of Hawaiian good humor. "No *pilikia*," [2] he replied, "you can go." That was the way most of the Honolulu residents felt about any tourist. No *pilikia* — he could come and go, unless, as was usually the case, he came bearing letters of introduction from someone we had scarcely met, in which case we overreached ourselves in his entertainment.

I speak of the peaceful and piping twenties when, having just been freed from war weariness, everyone was possessed

[2] *Pilikia* is the Hawaiian word for trouble or annoyance of any kind. "Wahine (woman) pilikia" is a common affliction in the islands.

with the belief that the world owed him a long vacation and a good time. Soon after this idea was adopted enthusiastically on the mainland, the stirrings of unrest and get-rich-quick philosophy touched these shores. Our first attempts to attract and amuse the tourist were a little naïve. I remember one Hawaiian eating-place in a garden where there was a miniature volcano into whose rocky bowels could be stuffed driftwood, pine boxes, newspapers and a smudge pot or two of crude oil. When all this was lit and glowing with a couple of Roman candles added for lava fountain effect, hula maidens, convoyed by dusky malo-clad Hawaiian youths, appeared on a floral platform and danced in the light of the conflagration. The most incredible thing about this performance was not its innocent naïvete, but the fact that it was free. So too was the Sunday night concert at the Moana Hotel for which the banyan tree provided cover but no cover charge.

Then in the successive depressions, recoveries, and recessions of the fitful thirties came disillusionment to those who thought to ride the tourist flood to prosperity in Hawaii. A few families went on the breadfruit line, but only the most unfortunate were without their daily fish and poi. The only migrants were the golden plover and an occasional professor taking his maiden aunts to China. We would have been glad to welcome even our old-time Australian visitors-for-a-day, the men arrayed in bright blazers, which they soon discarded to disclose multicolored suspenders supporting trousers "rather tight across the shoulders," the women wearing antipodean antebellum hats and motor dusters. You met them returning to their ship, tired and hot, but each clutching a bunch of equally weary oleanders or wayside hibiscus. But "down under," they mixed droughts with their depressions and no one had money for travel. So for Honolulu there was nothing to do but revert to its former habit of rolling up the streets at eight o'clock and going to bed.

Such attractions of the Atlantic City or Coney Island type as had been provided for the amusement of the sophisticated tripper soon languished, but entertainment at a higher level was then, and is still, housed in strange places. Honoluluans have heard Paderewski play in a sun-warped ramshackle pavilion at Aloha Park, Waikiki, and, quite recently, Handel's Messiah sung in a boxing and wrestling arena, misnamed the Civic Auditorium. It was an odd situation — the walls that commonly echoed the crowd's urgings to assault and battery now ringing with the Hallelujah Chorus, while the sports promoter and proprietor walked up and down, doubtless wondering at the size of the "house" and the possibilities of combining some such attraction with his heavyweight wrestling and fistic programs.

Hawaii, after all, had good reason to settle down to ordinary conditions of pleasant monotony. What suggestion of change or instability is there in a climate where fifty-six to eighty-six degrees represent the extremes of temperature, where thunder is heard once or twice in the season and where the winds are so moderate that a gale at forty miles an hour does a very satisfactory job of tree pruning, not on account of the violence of the storm, but simply because limbs and branches are unused to any but the gentlest treatment.

The fact that each season shades so imperceptibly into the next constitutes one of life's drawbacks in Hawaii. With neither the winter to look back on nor the spring to anticipate, the years have the habit of stealing upon one unawares. We become insensitive to the passage of time until, suddenly and unexpectedly, we are old. What Stevenson wrote of another Pacific islander is also true of the people who call Hawaii home. "The Marquesan," he says, "passes to the grave through an unbroken uniformity of days." Days that are humdrum but happy are the swiftest of all.

Climate of all things is the most persistently oversold.

It is the most universally overrated, the most egregiously lied about state of affairs. No one, they say, does anything about the weather, though everyone talks about it. There are, however, notable exceptions to this statement. The people of Southern California and Florida not only talk about it but they sell it in large real estate lots, while the people of Hawaii use it as fancy wrapping for vacation trips. One would not claim for an instant that the people of these islands, for all their missionary background, are more truth-loving than their competitors in the weather-selling business, but we do lie less about it. We come nearer to the truth because we live nearer to it, Nature herself having set a lower ceiling for liars hereabouts. When floods devastate Southern California or hurricanes whip the palms of Florida to shreds, all that their local boosters can say in extenuation is that the weather is very exceptional. Hawaii has much fewer exceptions and therefore we lie less. We sell our climate on a very stable market.

So much is this the case that it takes a minimum of meteorological data and less experience and training to make a successful weather prophet here than elsewhere. Any one can foretell tomorrow's temperature within five degrees and as for the rest of the climate the same prediction will do for most of the year. "Generally fine, winds moderate, showers in the uplands" is a blanket prediction that would give the prophet a batting average of 75 per cent correct throughout the year, and that is nearer the truth than most people in the real estate business come about anything.

Such statements call for facts and figures. Though we do not need a meteorologist to predict our weather, he is useful in recording it when it arrives. It is worth noting that he is housed just above another Federal official with whom it is useless to argue — the collector of internal revenue. It has been suggested that the reason they make the weather obser-vations at the top of the Post Office Building instead of at the level of Merchant Street is to keep the prognosticators out of

range of influence of the Big Five, who are suspected by some
people of controlling everything in the islands, including the
climate.

The staff of the Weather Bureau in Hawaii come nearer
to living in an ivory tower than any other group of people in
the Territory, except that their tower is built of stucco atop
the Federal Building in Honolulu. There they work in an
atmosphere of detached serenity. The elevators will take
you up to the high level on which the United States Courts
function, but if you wish to mount still higher it must be by
your own unaided exertions. At the end of the first long
flight of stairs you come to the former location of a very
hush-hush department, the former Division of Censorship.
The tables and chairs of the lady letter-readers are still there,
row on row, but the chairs are empty, the tables bare. The
snip-and-snoop department has folded its files and stolen
away, probably about as silently as the Arabs, of whose
noisy habits while shifting encampments the poet knew
little.

You must climb two more long flights before you reach
the director's office, whose windows provide a view of the
mountains and valleys behind the town. It is a most beautiful outlook and an ideal spot for a weather man's station.
He has absolutely nothing but weather in view. The clouds
gather over the mountains, the showers drift down the valleys, the trade winds shift inconsequentially between north
and east, the sun shines most of the day, the weather man
is in his heaven, and all's well with the world. Whether the
staff ever come down to the level of Honolulu's hurly-burly,
I cannot say. For over forty years these people have battled
with the elements, using only their bare hands, a typewriter,
and an adding machine. You will find their observations
summarized in the Director's Annual Report. [3] There the
climatic assets of Hawaii are officially given as follows:

[3] Annual Meteorological Summary, 1945. Walter F. Feldwisch, Director,
Weather Bureau Office, U.S. Department of Commerce, Honolulu.

The outstanding features of the climate are the remarkable differences in rainfall over adjacent areas; the high percentage of hours with sunshine over leeward lowlands, and the persistent cloudiness over or around mountain peaks nearby; the remarkably equable temperature from day to day, and the small differences in temperature between summer and winter months; the persistence of trade winds, and the rarity of damaging storms of any kind.

Even allowing for the fact that the weather man has written for forty years substantially the same report, this is still a triumph of succinct statement — no storms, no calms, no heat, no cold, yet endless variety according to location, in clouds, in sunshine, and rainfall — in short, a more unruffled disposition than Mother Nature shows toward any other of her weather-conditioned children.

A brief summary of Mr. Feldwisch's report shows that at sea level our average temperature for forty years was 75 degrees, which is of course warm. (Only four populated places in the world touch an all-year average of 85 degrees.) But the outstanding feature of the climate is the fact that there are no extremes. July and August average about 83 degrees in maximum temperatures while January and February average 76 degrees. Hence there are only 7 degrees between our summer and winter climates. Just once in forty years has a temperature of 100 degrees been officially recorded and that was at Pahala, Hawaii, on April 7, 1931. There are many who claim that the reading was made by the cockeyed Mayor of Kaunakakai. No one, however, doubts the all-time low of 25 degrees registered at Humuula, on Hawaii, at an elevation of almost 7,000 feet. The temperature may be summed up by saying that about 85 per cent of our population suffer under extreme temperatures of 85 degrees. There were 5 days over this reading in 1945. This is uncomfortably warm but very moderate compared with midsummer heat on mainland America.

Humidity can, however, be distressing at times, with percentages between 75 and 85 quite common. In Hilo the humidity has reached 97 per cent — fortunately at night when the general temperature had fallen.

Rainfall is exceedingly variable according to location on the leeward or the windward side of the mountains, and their proximity. On Kauai they boast of 600 inches or 50 feet annually at Mount Waialeale and complain of 20 inches at Waimea, fifteen or twenty miles away. On the island of Hawaii you may find a range of less than 10 inches in the Kau desert, to over 260 inches on the slopes of Mauna Kea. Maui offers a contrast of 11 inches at Kihei and 385 inches in the West Maui Mountains. At the head of Manoa Valley on Oahu the rainfall is 133 inches, a mile and a half down the valley 70 inches, 40 inches at its mouth, and about 20 inches at Waikiki.

Liquid sunshine can be quite concentrated on the island of Hawaii. In February 1918, 32 inches fell in Honomu on the Hamakua Coast in a single 24-hour period. Honolulu has nothing like this to offer for the record, the worst being passing showers in 1917 amounting to 13.2 inches in a single day. Some of these passing showers pass rather heavily, a half inch of rain in five minutes having been recorded on more than one occasion. This, it must be admitted, is more liquid than sunshine.

As to storms, the highest wind velocity recorded in 21 years was 44 miles an hour. The year 1945, however, was a very bad year for electrical disturbances; we had no less than five, and in the worst there must have been at least six claps of thunder.

People who enjoy cold baths should stay away from Waikiki except perhaps in the month of March when the water varies from 75 to 77 degrees. In August the range is from 79 to 82 degrees. Except for the psychological effects of being undressed and a wet sensation on the skin, one could step from dry land into the water without noticing the transition. For some people at Waikiki, it is lucky the water is wet. The other effects are practically nil.

From the above figures, if the reader has leisure to study them, it is quite evident that storm warnings fly but seldom in Hawaii. The barometer of public opinion similarly points rather consistently to "Fair." Deprived of the weather as a subject of complaint, our typical citizen, looking for some-thing to grumble about, usually settles on the Big Five. Just what he has suffered at their hands he does not know. At one time he could buy a weekly newspaper to find out what his grievances were, but even that ran out of copy. Before it did so, there was some reason to suspect that someone mixed sugar with its vinegar, which made it somewhat tasteless for conversational salads. In any case it developed a weak heart and a poor circulation. It slipped easily into oblivion, giving up first its ghost writer, and finally the ghost itself.

It should be remembered that weather is what man lives by and in; it is the most ubiquitous of natural phenomena, so that there is no hour of the day or night throughout the year but what there is some of it around. It is no wonder that its inconstancy becomes the most constant topic of conversation. This conversation has become an essential part of our social ritual so that it is only after we have offered our comment on the weather in the form of "good day" or "good evening" that we proceed to inquire into the second matter of universal concern, the state of one's health. With the days and seasons so equably ordered in Hawaii, is it any wonder that we need a cause for complaint, and fall back on the Big Five?

Reference has been made elsewhere to the theory that the ease of living, engendered by mildness of climatic conditions, is at the root of another condition for which Hawaii is justly famous. Though it is idle to assert that the Islands are wholly free from the social irritations that come about through people of so many racial complexions sharing such limited living space, it would be generally agreed that we are less prone to excitement over these matters than other communities.

Various people, particularly naval officers from the deep South, are quite at a loss to understand such a complacent attitude. It is difficult for them to comprehend a situation where the presence of so many non-whites does not constitute a threat of some kind. There is no alternative of "govern or suffer" presented here, so that it is easy to be tolerant in such things as race relations.

Nowhere on earth will you find such a variegated mixture of colors, creeds, and competency. Yet, we all share the highways, the buses, the schools, the churches, or other means of public assembly. We have no damn Yankees but "damn" can be conjoined with everything else in racial stocks — Japanese, Chinese, Filipinos, Portuguese, part Hawaiians, haoles — we damn them all. In all places the froth of the melting pot bubbles over — at orchid shows or lectures at the Academy of Arts, at graduation exercises of the university, at funerals, church services, football games — the color line wobbles freely throughout. If anyone were inclined to start a race riot, who would be "it"? The different racial groups certainly do not love one another but there is no real racial hatred. We come nearer to practical Christianity of a negative type here than elsewhere, but no one has persuaded us to this largeness of view. We just grew into it, the sober truth being that there are so many racial differences apparent, that if one were annoyed by them he would surely suffer a stroke and die young. There is only one opprobrious blanket term that has been invented to describe the variegated population of these islands, and those who use it have only to establish ten years' residence and they too would be "gooks" like the rest of us.

It is foolish to believe that this place attracted to itself a peace-loving broadminded population, free from prejudice and bigotry and intolerance. Our history gives the lie to such a theory of selective immigration. For fifty years every ship that sailed from New England should have had engrossed on its manifest a cargo of earnest convictions, ranging over all subjects from slavery to original sin. The owners of these convictions, who came to settle in Hawaii, were the reverse of easygoing and tolerant. "Go ye into all the world and preach the gospel to every creature" was a command that was eagerly obeyed, and if the creature didn't like it, he was compelled to lump it. Everybody who came to these islands accepted at least half of the injunction — they were all goers even if they weren't gospelers. Whether the stock in trade were salvation or saucepans, the creature had a slim chance to develop any serious sales resistance. This was no place for slackers, whether the traffic was in sandalwood or souls.

What then was the mellowing influence? Was it the humidity that took the starch out of the clerical collar and loosened the stitches of the trader's money bags so that strife, bigotry, and greed were displaced by good humor, tolerance, and generous living? What kind of a spell does Hawaii exert so that this place, once the home of dissension, became the birthplace of such idealistic organizations as the Pan-Pacific Union and the Institute of Pacific Relations? Here is indeed an interesting psychological puzzle.

The writer was present at the inception of the I.P.R., that magnificent if finally futile gesture of good will, proffered by the West to the East. The procedure was entirely typical of Honolulu, which has more committees, councils, and conferences than any other place of equal size and talkativeness. This planning committee was presided over by a local clergyman whose interracial sympathies were liberal to the point of unctuosity, and was called to arrange an agenda for the first I.P.R. conference. He proceeded in true Y.M.C.A. fashion. Taking chalk in hand, he made an announcement. "Let us," he said, "write down on this blackboard all the questions that anyone can think of which might cause misunderstanding or antipathy between oriental and occidental peoples."

Soon we contributed an imposing list ranging from cartels

to contraception, through miscegenation to missions, and which would have ended in Japanese Zeros, if we had known they had any. Then after considerable argument "about it and about," our leader took a duster and erased the lot, after which we all went home, satisfied with our contribution to interracial understanding. And this is exactly what the Conference, when it was held, accomplished. Surely nowhere else in the world could such things happen; while we spread resolutions besprinkled with whereas's on our minute books, time takes the duster and erases our problem. At least, that is what in our blindness we thought would always happen in Hawaii. Being tolerant and good humored ourselves, how could anyone treat us otherwise?

Had statehood come to Hawaii ten years ago my suggestion for a suitable coat of arms would have been an Aloha shirt, supported by two gecko lizards, pregnant, and carrying the motto "No Pilikia."

But fortunately this was not the real Hawaii, even though it did come close to that earthy elysium which the advertisements promised. Underneath the velvet there was some steel; behind all the goodwill was a considerable realization that this was still an untrustworthy and vindictive world; that racial pride and arrogance were not exclusively the white man's attributes, and that both our oriental exposure and military innocence invited attack. It is paradoxical but true that in Hawaii's day of crisis, it was not the civilian population that was caught napping. Due to some remarkable, unlooked-for prevision and planning, it was but a short step forward that Hawaii's population had to take to be in the forefront of participation in total war. Perhaps the old militant spirit of the missionaries was not dead; perhaps the old Yankee trading shrewdness had not lost its cutting edge; in any case a combination of these or other factors summoned up enough resolution for the playing of a part of which we are not ashamed, even in a world where courage and steadfastness became commonplace.

CHAPTER III

The Tolerant Trades

A VERY BRIEF review, even though it be merely in the nature of a sideglance into history, will show unmistakably what a change of environment will do to a people. The Hawaiians, as is well known, are that group of Polynesian seafarers who wandered farthest from their ancestral home of Hawaiki, or Havai'i, in the Society Islands, making the two-thousand-mile voyages in their double outrigger canoes. The nearest habitable island to Hawaii is Midway, which lies along a chain of islets and reefs extending northwest, but beyond Midway is a vast expanse of empty sea. Directly south of Hawaii is a group of islands variously called the Equatorial or Line Islands and which include Christmas, Fanning, Washington, and Palmyra, with Howland and Baker Islands lying off to the side. These were the only stepping stones for the Hawaiian migration.

But the nearest of these, Palmyra, lies over a thousand miles in a straight line from Hawaii. What was accomplished by the early explorers who first crossed these seas can hardly be imagined. Their ships were outrigger canoes lashed together in pairs, with pandanus mat sails and deep-sea paddles as means of propulsion, green coconuts and fish their provender, and Orion's Belt as their guide. What really drove them on was courage and a high spirit of adventure, with probably over-population as the initial push.

After discovery of these islands came settlement, and for several hundreds of years, according to tradition, voyages to and from the homeland took place, during which the taro, the Hawaiian dog, pigs, and fowl were brought here, and, probably, the coconut palm, breadfruit, and other plants as part of the cargoes. But about the thirteenth century these visits ceased with the overseas journeys of Paao, the priest of Raiatea who was credited with introducing heiaus or temples, human sacrifices, and the red feather mantles peculiar to royalty. The paper mulberry was also imported for making Polynesian bark cloth or tapa. Hence the Hawaiians began the business of bringing plants and trees to this country, a procedure enthusiastically adopted by later immigrants.

But after Paao, the ties with the homeland of Hawaiki were severed. "The urge for deep sea adventure decreased," says Buck, "and interest narrowed to the coastal seas. Voyaging canoes ceased to sail out from the channel of Ke Ala-i-Kahiki (Road to Tahiti), and trim their course for the Equator. The long sea voyages of the northern rovers had ended — Hawai'i had become home." [1]

But settling down on the land involved changes in the character of these hardy seafarers. One of the reasons for the discontinuance of these voyages of high adventure was the geographical area of Hawaii. With so much space, overpopulation and internecine wars no longer provided the centrifugal force that originally thrust the wanderers out over these far Pacific horizons. For the small Society Islands and atolls, each with a few score miles of beaches, the newcomers to Hawaii exchanged several thousands of square miles of territory with corresponding lengths of coastline. Such a hinterland of depth and variety of climate was not to be found anywhere else in tropical Polynesia. However, the Hawaiians, like later migrants, found it convenient to settle in a narrow coastal belt below five hundred feet altitude, so that all their villages were within sight of the sea.

[1] Buck, Peter H. *Vikings of the Sunrise.* Frederick Stokes Co., New York, 1938.

This fact, and the Hawaiian's love of fishing, together with occasional inter-island visits for pleasure or fighting or both, kept up a friendly association with the sea. But he was no longer the great ocean adventurer, the Pacific Viking, that his foreparent was.

Gradually the Hawaiian became a landsman, attaching himself as a feudal retainer to the high chiefs, spending his time tilling his taro patches or tending his pigs, with occasional excursions inland to cut koa trees for war or fishing canoes, or in search of obsidian for the fashioning of his stone adzes. Occasionally he took part in bloody struggles between various island chiefs or kings, but these were not very man-consuming, warfare having become a rather highly stylized affair, in which the high point in defeat was not the loss of thousands of warriors, but the fall of some noted chief. There was slaughter at times, as witness a house near Pearl Harbor whose containing fence was said to have been built of the thigh bones of the slain. Generally speaking Hawaiian warfare was no bitter-end struggle claiming thousands of victims. Their cruelties, such as they were, were tempered by the provision of cities of refuge to which the vanquished could escape. Wars that ended in wholesale slaughter of the common people would have resulted in making the *alii* or Hawaiian aristocracy turn to labor as a means of sustenance, a type of activity to which they were constitutionally averse.

The influence of environment on temperament and disposition, whether national or individual, is undoubted. The only scientific disagreement with regard to the matter is how much should be attributed to heredity and how much to nurture, as formative factors. The writer is one who maintains that both Nature and nurture vary in their influences, though endowment is the primary factor. Nevertheless, the physical background refuses to stay there, but constantly edges itself forward until it becomes part of the foreground,

and enters into the warp and woof of personality or character.

To make this plain demands a short biological excursion.
Consider for a moment what is called protective coloration
in the animal world. The stripes of the tiger are merely the
sharp shadows of jungle reeds and high grass indelibly etched
on the exterior of the animal. The blotches of the giraffe are
likewise the dappling and splashes of sunshine and shade
from lightly-foliaged African vegetation. The skin of the
animal is sensitive like a photographic plate, but the time
exposure must extend over almost countless centuries. To
this end certain inner urges contribute greatly, such as
sexual selection, which can hardly be a hit-and-miss affair,
but goes along with the current of environmental effects on
appearance and structure.

Hence what is called protective coloration is really a har-
monization of the foreground of structure with its physical
background, involving mental tendencies, which of course
depend on structure. For it must always be remembered
that it is not the color or marking that is itself protective,
but the merging of reaction and appearance that counts.
A certain type of mentality and consequent reaction goes
with a particular type of structure or appearance. The
covey of quail must not only match the color of their surroundings but, in order to remain invisible, their behavior
must match the immobility of the ground. Put them in
motion and the screen of invisibility is swept to one side.
No spider or insect in the type of reaction which is called
"shamming death" — a very common type of behavior —
ever thinks to itself, "If I stay quite still I shall appear to be
dead," for it does not know what death is. The behavior
is entirely instinctive. So too the elephant joins itself to the
forest tree, the tiger to its reedy covert, before either is concealed in that remarkable fashion that every hunter knows.
On all sides we see the adaptation of structure to use. Birds
and fishes are stream- or air-lined. The burrowing animals

do not need to be taught to make holes that exactly fit their forms. Incidentally, probably much of the restlessness of wild animals confined in zoos is due to their inability to adapt their behavior to the corners of their rectangular cages. The right angle is one of man's inventions. He alone delights in corners and triangles.

In human beings our subconscious satisfactions become closely related to a familiar environment, and when we migrate, our happiness may depend on our ability to fit in with the changes. The tall, long-striding, tough, and narrow-hipped mountaineer can hardly be similar in character to the alert, restless, nervous brush-dweller, whose small size and quick mobility give him not only the hunting form but the hunting temperament. Neither would adjust very well to the other's habitat.

As regards the native people of Hawaii, the effects of environment are apparent. Sunshine and ease of sustenance have given them big frames, excellently adapted for putting on excessive weight in middle age, which finds them slug-gish, good-humored, and slow moving. Though athletic in youth and at all times capable of sudden feats of strength, they are averse to long-continued, uneventful exertion. Their emotions are labile, their attitudes non-resistant rather than actively opposed to change. They show a lively interest in the new, provided its acquisition does not demand excessive effort.

We are told that the iron in the soil of Hawaii is not readily available as plant food and certainly little of it has entered into the soul of the Hawaiian. He is neither a bitter nor a cruel adversary; he cannot be said to have been defeated by the whites —he merely succumbed. Missionary domination was accepted almost gratefully, the only pro-tests coming from non-missionary whites. At no time did the native offer violence, not even when the new teachers denounced his ancient religion and its priests in the most condemnatory terms. Consequently there were no martyrs

among the missionary folk even though one or two deserved
to be. The Hawaiians actually accepted the emasculation
of their language at the hands of their teachers. The letters
r, *t*, and *v*, were dropped from the printed word, which of
course made printing easier but left the poor Hawaiian in
confusion to this day. He is still uncertain whether he
should say Hawaii or Havaii. The report of the nine missionaries who carried on the purging is expressed in laxative
terms. Here is an extract from their report. "L, though
two pills have been given to expel it, is to remain to do
its own office and that of its yoke fellow R." If instead of
giving it such strong medicine they had partially disem-
voweled the language, the task of Hawaiian orthography
would have been easier. In early days, it was much simpler
to go without a wash than to ask for the *ipuauau* or wash-
basin; especially when every vowel must be separately
enunciated.

It is somewhat surprising that the only organized resistance the natives showed against the whites was at the time
of Captain Cook's death at Kealakekua Bay on Hawaii.
This minor battle claimed the lives of five whites, including
Cook, and possibly thirty Hawaiians. But even this conflict
was the result of a sudden fit of rage at the threatened
seizure of the old King, and the outbreak was soon over
and repented. Thereafter, there were several killings of
sailors from visiting ships, but these were merely incidents.
Nothing approaching a war between natives and whites
has ever taken place. This was not due to any lack of
opportunity to secure firearms. The traders would have
sold the Hawaiians anything from billiard tables to gun
carriages, and in fact did so. Kamehameha's fort at the
foot of Fort Street once mounted over forty cannon.

How different the experience of the whites with another
branch of the Polynesian race, the New Zealand Maoris.
The ancestors of these people turned their canoe prows
southward and made their way in successive voyages to "The

Land of the High Mists," which is what these natives from low atolls called this place of snow-covered mountains wrapped in clouds.

The first encounters with the whites disclosed a different temper in the Maoris than in the easy-going susceptible Hawaiians. There was no dearth of courage in either group, but the Maoris added determination to physical hardihood. The cold climate and more difficult living conditions put a premium on mental energy and foresight. Moreover, these warriors did not fail to recognize the superiority of the white man's weapons and lost no chance to acquire muskets and other guns, though ammunition was generally scarce. Hence when the white settlers and their government attempted encroachment on native lands through the breach of treaties, the native population took up arms and in two bitterly-fought wars earned an honorable peace, respected to this day.

Two battles which proved the Maori mettle will be cited here. Three successive attempts at assault by a white force of well over a thousand men failed against Maori earthworks at Orakau, and the troops were reduced to using the methods of sapping and mining, approved for the reduction of strongly-fortified places in Europe. When an interpreter called on the natives to surrender, their answer was, "We will fight ake, ake, ake" (forever and ever). Only after being without water for two days and having suffered heavy losses did the small force of 300 defenders march out and calmly, under the heaviest fire, break through the cordon of whites to abandon their position. The British 65th Regiment so admired the courage of the Maoris that they erected a tablet to those who fell. This was a chivalrous action, but the last words of the inscription, "I say unto you, love your enemies," were rather ambiguous. There seem to be better ways of showing affection for your enemies than killing them. This happened in 1864, when the British in New Zealand had 22,000 men under arms.

Another battle more damaging to white prestige was that of the Gate Pa at Tauranga, the same year. A force of 70 officers and 1,616 men assaulted the Maori position after shelling it for eight hours with thirteen large guns. The troops, supported by the guns of three warships, entered the fortification that seemed deserted except for a few wounded men. Suddenly a fierce fire from hidden rifle pits was directed against the soldiers. Ten of the officers fell, and the men tumbled incontinently out of the breach in panic. Reports of the battle, though conflicting in some respects, all agreed in praising the unexampled bravery of the native defenders. As a result of their stead-fastness and courage, the Maoris never were forced to sue for peace, a fact of which they are justly proud.

All of this points the contrast in temperament between the two branches of the same race, both of them equally adventurous; but one people settled in a land where the climate was bracing and existence arduous, the other found a home in low latitudes where conditions of climate and terrain were far more pleasant and sustenance considerably easier. Nowhere has human plasticity been better demon-strated than in Hawaii. The physical effect of the Hawaiian environment has been shown by Shapiro, who found that island-born Japanese differed from their home-born parents in 55 per cent of the measurements taken, denoting what the investigator calls "an arresting modification," due to "the dynamic and plastic character of the human organ-ism." The greatest change was in increase of stature, which Shapiro calls "tremendous." [2]

The first showdown between the whites and the haoles in these islands took place in 1895 in the form of an insurrection against the Republic, aimed at restoring Queen Lilioukalani to the throne, an event which would also have brought the Hawaiians again to a position of political dominance. We cite this occurrence briefly because it

[2] Shapiro, H. L. *Migration and Environment*, Oxford University Press, 1937.

exemplifies not only the lack of determination in the natives, but also the way in which life in Hawaii served to dull the edge of vindictiveness in the victorious whites.

Not only was the Revolution of 1893 comparatively bloodless — one man was wounded in the whole affair — but the suppression of the counter-revolution was marked by so many remissions of penalties against its captured leaders that many thought the Republic of Hawaii lost dignity by failing to shoot a few rebels. The archplotters were a group of whites and part-Hawaiians who, for various reasons, selfish or otherwise, strove to break the rule of the missionary-business men's coalition which had set up the republic. President Sanford Dole heard of the design and ordered a raid on rebel headquarters in which one Government supporter was killed. In three days the revolt was suppressed at the cost of half a dozen rebel casualties. Farrington, the historian of these events, records that a raid on the ex-Queen's residence uncovered "a large assortment of arms — nine rifles and five pistols." His emphasis on the fact that these were "of the finest work-manship" is a little like the March Hare's insistence that what he put in the watch was the very best butter. The significance of the find is somewhat reduced by the histori-an's admission that most of the rebels did not know one end of a gun from another and that what he described as "a small arsenal" consisted mainly of coconut shells filled with giant powder.

Five of the leaders were condemned to death, but Dole commuted the sentence to thirty years' hard labor and a $10,000 fine. Next the fine was remitted and ten years taken off the sentence. Finally, within a year of the rebellion, all were fully pardoned. Though to the tough-minded all this savored of "opera bouffe," appeasement worked. The old enemies settled down together in amity, but whether the extreme mildness of the purge was due to Christian charity, political tolerance, or merely climate, we cannot determine. Hanging on to an ancient grudge may be too laborious for these latitudes. Possibly sweat-baths and blood-baths are incompatible. However, the lesson was not lost on Hawaii. "These successive remis-sions," wrote Farrington, "show with what readiness the people of Hawaii forget political differences even though those differences call for the defense of principles by resort to armed force." Perhaps the period should rightly have been placed after "forget."

Hence from this very brief excursion into our history it would seem that the Hawaiian environment does some-thing to its people, whether native or immigrant. Com-pared with their first cousins, the Maoris, the Hawaiians are more malleable, less opposed to cultural change, and decidedly less belligerent. As for the whites, they also tend to develop shorter political memories, thus lessening rancor and strife, and have a difficult time retaining the prejudices they bring with them from elsewhere. Compromise is easy here; any alertness, any sensitiveness to distant threats would seem to be so much out of character as to be para-doxical.

Incidentally, all of this apparent weakening of serious purpose or determination gives some people extreme mis-givings as to the future of Hawaii. The point of view differs according to whether our ideals of living are those of easy happiness or restless accomplishment. Perhaps the world really needs a land of let-down, a surcease from plotting and striving, a refuge from our own inventions, each of which, like the atomic research discoveries, complicates existence immeasurably. But if a contribution to the world's good and evil is expected from Hawaii, then we had better move our University, our libraries and laboratories a couple of thousand feet higher above sea level; either that or a long continued course of blood transfusions will be necesssary to keep up our mental and physical energy — so the pessimists think.

Be that as it may — the idea smacks of high treason — surely no one could have blamed us if December 7th had found us comfortably asleep. A place so calm and serene, so fortunately disposed along normally unruffled latitudes, a land of orchids and rainbows, and easy tolerance — surely here anxiety and suspicion were out of place. The setting of a watch against invasion where for a century and a half no hostile invader had set foot, premonitions of disaster where ordinarily peril never threatens, awareness of the cloud on the horizon no bigger than a Japanese hand could hardly be expected from those whose professional business it was to keep watch and ward. As to the civilian population, any advocacy of war preparedness might well have been regarded as hysteria of the most unwarranted kind.

Our feeling of natural optimism was reinforced materially by the notion of the invincibility of the American fleet. A view of the seemingly unending procession of four hundred ships of war filing past Diamond Head in 1940 sent Honoluluans home to their beds more convinced than ever that Pearl Harbor was an offensive and not a defensive base, the spot from which the bolt would be fired that would blast the presumptuous Japs clear out of the seas. We obtained quite a lot of quiet amusement out of the recurrent maneuvers in which the Navy played the game of wresting these islands from the Army. It did seem a little funny to hear of a single man with a flag landing on a beach and declaring himself a regiment of marines, and many a chuckle followed one landing rehearsal when a boatload of invaders was upset in the surf and the brave defenders had to rush to their aid and haul them to safety. Of course such a happening was not in the game, and the umpires declared the landing successful and the position taken. When, as was usually the case, the Navy's conquest of the island was announced, citizens smiled and commented that this would undoubtedly help the Army appropriations in Washington.

By common report, bolstered by the witness of a crowd

of vacationers, our island population was devoted to big business, its only diligence to fend off any external political threat that might interfere with fat dividends. The isola- tionism of the mid-West, born of long security, should have had its confirmed counterpart in Hawaii. With our back- ground we, above all, should have been imbued with the faith that somehow the war clouds would be dissolved by conferences or appeasement; conversely, to say that a com- munity which exists by compromise would have an aware- ness of impending danger, and a consuming haste for pre- paredness is to put an undue strain on credulity.

To pretend that this awareness was general would be to imply that the average man in Hawaii is endowed with a measure of foresight that he does not possess. Nevertheless, there were enough who believed that there was a chance, even if it was a long one, of crippling disaster, and were willing to take precautionary measures that went so far beyond the foreseeable future that, had they been finally proved unnecessary, would have seemed absurd.

When camping in the Kalahari desert in Africa, the writer once expressed some misgivings about danger from lions and was laughed at for his fears. "Lions are gentle- men," I was assured by our Dutch desert guide. "They never interfere with you so long as you leave them alone." But that night he laid aside his rifle and stood a shotgun loaded with buckshot against a bush near his head. "A load of buckshot," he explained, "will make a bigger hole in a lion's head at close range than any rifle bullet." "But," I objected, "you said lions never bother human beings." "Well, you see," said he, "it's always the unexpected that happens in Africa."

Here was a watchfulness born of living precariously. Perhaps the other extreme of security may have a like effect. Possibly after living so long in an atmosphere of unwonted calm, the approaching storm may have set our nerves a-tingle. In any case, while some Americans were shouting against

the embroilment of our country in the quarrels of Europe,
while other groups bitterly denounced national lethargy in
the face of a threatening world conflagration, a prescient
few in Hawaii went about their preparations against a blow
that even our professional defenders could not envisage with
any liveliness of imagination.

It is true that Generals Drum and Herron, and later
General Short, thoroughly approved of civil preparedness in
emergency, but their ideas ran to the pattern of preventing
sabotage, a word which, because of events in Europe, had
come to haunt military commanders' dreams. They thought
civilian readiness would prevent panic, and might be useful
in pre-war periods of national strain, though when the crisis
actually occurred they were all set to step in and run the
show professionally, as it ought to be run. The proclama-
tion of martial law and military dictatorship had already
been drawn up and was in the general's desk ready to be
presented to the civil governor for signature. In public
addresses before the war, General Short made it quite clear
that martial law would be the first step as soon as war had
been formally declared. Invasion, the threat of blockade,
were convenient bogeys with which to scare the civilians,
but no one with any military sense believed in such things.

In the meantime, before describing local civilian defense
organizations, it would be interesting to look at the other
peoples of the Pacific area, nations much nearer to the path
of the destroyer than this community, and discover how
they regarded the situation and what preparations if any
were being taken against impending storm.

Even if such a survey were to prove that we were the
only people not sufficiently watchful, we are hardly to be
blamed when all the experts, with the possible exception
of one group, were agreed that as far as attack from Japan
was concerned, Hawaii was unapproachable. The noteworthy exception to this unanimity of informed opinion was
of course the Japanese. As one high military authority put

it at one of the numerous inquiries after Pearl Harbor: "We knew that war was on the doorstep, but not on *our* doorstep."

CHAPTER IV

Operation Ostrich

THE STATE of the Pacific world for a few years before Pearl Harbor was that which was represented in Shakespearean plays by the inset "Alarums and Excursions." A considerable proportion of the excursions were provided by the Institute of Pacific Relations, self-initialed the I.P.R., and to a much lesser degree, some of the alarums. The latter were few because like most organizations dedicated to a noble purpose, in this case mutual understanding as between East and West, it was optimistic about its success. It consisted of the largest body of occidental experts on oriental affairs that the Pacific had seen.

By 1937 it had progressed considerably beyond its rather unctuous beginnings some years before. It had gathered representatives from the various countries together into conferences held in different parts of the Pacific basin. It had been given some thumping support, both in the way of publicity and checks. It had its own well-trained secretariat, accustomed to looking on the bright side of things, a research staff, and its own magazine, *Pacific Affairs*. This quarterly's list of contributors and reviewers included professors of history and economics, politicians, missionaries (both active and ex-), businessmen, authors, editors, and the forerunners of that loquacious and cocksure tribe, the news commentators. The last named were the people who, during the war, were to feed a whole news-hungry world on the five loaves and two fishes of censored reports. They apparently operated both before and behind the military front, so far in front that at one time the Russians, so it was rumored, had to request one leading commentator to cease broadcasting his analysis of the news for four days to enable their troops to catch up. Thus the radio commenta-tors anticipated scientific research by breaking up the atoms of news in cabled dispatches and expanding them by radio-active devices into chain reactions of words that almost deafened the rest of the world. The reason for the popu-larity of these news comminutors was that people had learned to listen better than they had learned to read.

These things were of course merely in the womb of N.B.C., though more likely it was a radio tubal pregnancy. Meanwhile, the best we had at the time was the I.P.R., which allowed nothing to go unrecorded that was thought, or at least expressed, with or without thought, on the Far Eastern situation. We may cheerfully admit that a good healthy organization for mutual understanding has value in promoting a sense of security. To many people's minds, open discussion of problems is tantamount to their solution, an attitude based on the belief that man is a talking animal, and little else. There is little doubt that this corps of inter-Pacific experts contributed greatly to allaying our mental unrest. Some congenital viewers-with-alarm were included in the crowd, but mainly as awful examples. But the inter-esting thing is that these people were alarmed at the wrong things. They resembled our military and political leaders who were so exercised in mind at the idea of sabotage, that while they hunted the mouse under the bed the lion walked in the door. But the writer must express his gratitude to the I.P.R. and its well-informed magazine, *Pacific Affairs*, without which this chapter could scarcely have been writ-ten. His observations will no doubt be characterized as a good example of hindsight or being wise after the event. This is supposedly the easiest kind of wisdom. I disagree — there is nothing so difficult. Mankind has shown itself particularly deficient in this kind of wisdom. If it were easy we would have no more religions, revolutions, wars, and depressions instead of cycles of them. "What's all this about?" is the great unanswered question of history, and if there were more certain hindsight we should have less need for guessing at the future.

Therefore, drawing heavily on hindsight with the I.P.R., we propose to examine attitudes and opinions of various people with regard to Japan's southward expansion, the policy and movement that the Nipponese called Nan-yo, or towards the South Seas. Of interest particularly is com- ment from the countries that lay directly in the path of that expansion.

The Philippines were of course in great danger, a serious matter perhaps for the Filipinos, but from the American point of view not quite so bad. The distance of Manila from Washington constituted the first and most decisive weakness of the Philippines' defense, but even if, as was readily con- ceded, that country were conquered by Japan, the event constituted no threat to us. Geography, if not the god of battles, was still on our side. America had signified her intention of practical withdrawal from the military scene upon the granting of independence to those islands. The fact of the Philippines' indefensibility was of course not overlooked by our naval and military strategists and those of other nations, including Japan.

Speaking of the prospective evacuation of the American naval base of Cavite, Bywater, the British naval expert, wrote in 1935: "I rather fancy that American strategists will breathe a sigh of relief if this proves to be the case. In a war with Japan, the Philippines would be an unquali- fied liability, impossible to defend and destined to fall an easy prey to the enemy." [1] The utmost that was expected of America in the event of war in the Philippines was a delaying

[1] Bywater, Hector C. "Japanese and American Naval Power in the Pacific." *Pacific Affairs*, June, 1935.

action that would give her time to organize her defense in depth across and through the Pacific islands. Unlike Singapore, there was little talk of the impregnability of Corregidor.

Next in line, and the richest of all prizes that the Japanese could covet were the Netherlands East Indies, producing raw materials essential to Japan's war-making potential. Among these were crude oil, the basis for the processing of gasoline, kerosene and aviation fuel, and rubber, tin, nickel ore, bauxite, manganese, and wolfram. It was not to be expected that these territories which were not only wealthy but vulnerable would have been left out of the scope of Japan's co-prosperity sphere. That the Dutch had any illusions about being left alone indicated a remarkably naïve viewpoint as to the kind of world they lived in. To abide by a policy of non-interference with others' affairs gave no guarantee of being left alone, if your nation was both rich and defenseless. The Dutch made it clear to the world that they did not want to fight, but this was no defense.

With the war clouds thickening in Europe, confidence in non-resistance began to wane and soon the people of the N.E.I. were suffering under a war of nerves in which, however, these phlegmatic Dutchmen probably came off the better. Van Mook, Minister for Colonies in the Netherlands Government and later Governor-General of the Dutch East Indies describes this war of nerves in a book which he aptly sub-titles "Battle on Paper, 1940–1941." [2] Unfortunately when the actual crisis came the resistance offered by the Dutch, though desperate, was almost as flimsy. The story is typical of the common tragedy of unreadiness that overtook the whole of the peoples that opposed Japan, and is embroidered by the fallacious expectation that good intentions and professions of national good will can take the place of armaments. "Like all peaceful democracies," says Van

2 Van Mook, Hubertus J. *The Netherlands Indies and Japan, Battle on Paper, 1940–1941.* W. W. Norton Co., New York. 1944.

Mook, "we were caught unprepared." Along with national
inoffensiveness the Dutch seemed to rely heavily on someone
else to check Japan.

Ostriches are said to hide their heads in the sand when
imminent danger threatens. Ostriches do no such thing —
they have far too much sense. But the same cannot be said
of democracies. One such head-burying sandhill in which
the Dutch took refuge was the strength of the British and
the impregnability of Singapore. Another even bigger burying ground was the determination and the ability of America
to preserve what Japan had left of the *status quo* in
East Asia. It is interesting to note the way in which the
democracies — Britain, America, and the Netherlands East
Indies — each borrowed one another's sandheaps. Probably
the largest sandhill by far, one that accommodated all the
heads at once, was the theory of Japan's utter exhaustion
as a result of the war in China. The net result of all this
head burying was a most unwarranted cheerfulness. Thus
Van Mook could speak of "a certain temporary optimism"
that was felt just before the final catastrophe befell. That
is a strange fact to record of the year 1941 when all the
world contained only two classes of people — fools and
pessimists.

There is still one interesting question that must probably
be left to historical research. Was Japanese aggression the
result of long distance planning or was it due to an oppor-
tunist policy, devised at short range to meet a series of com-
mitments that became more and more pressing, but which
were not envisaged in advance? Van Mook has no doubts
on this score. He believes that hegemony of the East had
long been Japan's considered goal. "The slowly and method-
ically moving Japanese temperament," he writes, "could
not have planned the successful campaigns in the Philippines, Malaya, the Netherlands East Indies, and Burma in a
few months, nor even in a few years." The Dutch should
be good judges of slowness of temperament.

The world economic crisis of 1929 tended to bring countries with low production costs into an improved position.
For a time the only good market was for cheap goods of
general usage, and Japanese trade and Japanese nationals
prospered in foreign countries. But these nationals formed
what Van Mook called "indigestible units." What he writes
of the Japanese in the N.E.I. applied in large measure to
Hawaii.

"They not only want their own clubs, societies, and
places of worship, but their own schools, doctors, and dentists; their own banks, shops, and means of transport; their
own periodicals and printing presses." Hawaii too knows
of Japanese language schools, the Yokohama Specie Bank,
the *Nippu Jiji* newspaper, the Mitsukoshi store, the N.Y.K.
line of steamships, the Japanese Chamber of Commerce,
etc. Van Mook derives this tendency toward a sticky
cohesiveness in the Japanese partly from their "insularity of
character and linguistic incapacity" but chiefly from devotion to their "deified Emperor." Part at least of this motivation is forever lost to them.

In the Dutch East Indies, Japanese banks, importers, shipping lines, warehouses, and retailers soon combined to
channel trade through a closed nationalistic system, supported by semi-official organizations such as the Nanyo
Kohatsu. Against this combination the Dutch took effective
measures. Import licenses, restrictions on foreign workers,
licensing of certain trades, an immigration quota for workers,
a coastal shipping law restricting rights to ply between certain ports, and a law prohibiting foreigners from fishing in
territorial waters — all of these were aimed at curbing
Japanese expansionist programs. In short the N.E.I. drew
its deadline as boldly as if she really had the strength to
back it up.

Naturally these trade restrictions became at once the
target for Japanese attacks. In February 1940, Japan opened
up the subject with a note, which was of the heads-I-win,

tails-you-lose variety. She offered to relax all restrictions
on Dutch imports to Japan if the N.E.I. would lift the
restrictions on Japanese trade to Dutch territories. In short,
the proposal was that the N.E.I. should allow an unrestricted flow of goods she did not want from Japan, in
exchange for the right to send raw materials which she
would much rather not sell to Japan, fearing that they would
help arm a potential enemy. Similarly the Nipponese proposed to grant free entrance to a few Netherlanders into
their country if the large number of Japanese who wished
to set up commercial enterprises in the Dutch colonies were
unimpeded by immigration restrictions.

The Dutch soon had reason to suspect the timing of these
arrogant proposals. While they were busy preparing their
reply, Holland was invaded by Germany on May 10, 1940.
Van Mook found it difficult to describe the shock of this
event — "the sudden and overwhelming nature of the assault
had, for the moment, a numbing effect on public opinion."
The Japanese were not slow to capitalize on this numbness.
Within four days of the German invasion, the N.E.I.
Government was reminded by a second note that Japan
expected not only unrestricted supplies of mineral oil, tin,
and rubber but added an imposing list of other raw materials,
including bauxite 200,000 tons, nickel ore 150,000 tons,
manganese 50,000 tons, scrap iron 100,000 tons. At the
same time she jumped the demand for mineral oil from one
million tons to two. Rubber and tin had formerly been obtained by Japan from Malaya. Storm signals were flying
a-plenty.

Van Mook emphasizes the fact that with the blitzkrieg
cutting furiously through France, Holland, and Belgium, it
behooved the Dutch to return the soft answer, which was
a masterpiece of polite evasion. They were careful to point
out that the amounts of scrap iron, manganese, and wolfram
demanded in Japan's note were more than the total N.E.I.
production. The note approved in general the principle of

freer trade but avoided making any specific promises. Thus the Battle on Paper was joined.

The Japs soon realized that in note-making the Dutch were too shrewd to be backed into a corner, and they decided to try some personal browbeating. An economic mission under Koboyashi, the Japanese cabinet minister for commerce and industry, arrived,[3] attended by a large staff of assistants who started sending long reports on all kinds of subjects to Japan, adding to Dutch uneasiness considerably. However, the aims of the Koboyashi mission proved to be political as well as economic. The N.E.I. was offered the "benevolent protection" of Japan and thus would become a part of the co-prosperity sphere. The Dutch, however, waved the political issues aside and in reply to a stepped-up demand for three million tons of crude oil the Batavia Government referred the matter to the oil companies for private negotiation. When one million tons were offered by the companies, Japan complained that the quantity of aviation fuel promised was as good as nil. "But," said Batavia, "this is all we can produce for export after satisfying our own needs."

"Very well," countered the Japanese, "if you cannot produce the oil, we can. We will explore and exploit all oil territories within our sphere of interest, amounting to 17½ million hectares, or about 67 million square miles, of territory in Borneo, Celebes, and Dutch New Guinea. We will even get the oil out ourselves and pay the N.E.I. royalties thereon." When the Dutch refused this generous offer, the mission left Batavia with stacks of studies, including, as the Dutch feared, valuable data for the use of landing expeditions, all conveyed to Japan under cover of diplomatic immunity.

By now the N.E.I. Government felt like the bird that the serpent seeks to hypnotize before striking the fatal blow.

3 Van Mook records: "The ship was hung with bunting, but the captain had forgotten to hoist the Netherlands colours in the appropriate place."

Matsuoka, minister for foreign affairs in the Japanese cabinet, went so far as to declare that the Dutch colonies were already in the co-prosperity sphere, under the leadership of Japan and that the two countries were economically inter-dependent due to their geographical proximity. In short, the future of the Netherlands East Indies, if any, lay in the Orient and not in Europe. At the same time the Japanese press launched a campaign of hot denunciation against the Dutch who, they said, were merely stalling for time.

Van Mook makes no bones about it — they were. A show of negotiating had to continue. The discussions about oil concessions had to go on even at the risk of suspicion that the Dutch were selling out to Japan. Conversations on the Netherlands side, he says, were conducted with "infinite patience and endless explanations and reiterations that seem unavoidable in cases of differences of opinion with the Japanese." The Dutch were doing a masterly job of explain-ing and reiterating. The paper battle was proceeding on favorable lines.

Even with Japan showing her hand so boldly, there were still many who hoped for peace. The sandheap of Japan's military preoccupation with China ("bogged down in China" was the popular comment on the Nipponese war machine) was still a refuge for optimistic ostriches. Another support at which people clutched, not knowing it was a straw, was now coming to be known as the ABCD [4] military and naval front. But according to Van Mook, those in high places knew this was merely bluff. He blames the ma-chinery of democracy for "the deplorable inadequacy of co-ordination in the military preparedness for the defense" of the Far East. The Dutch were probably the least prepared of any. They, of all nations, preferred butter and cheese to guns.

In the meantime, the heat was on in Japan. Following carefully the pattern for forthcoming aggression set by the

[4] American — British — Chinese — Dutch.

Nazis in Europe, the press burst out in a chorus of denunciation with "dire threats, accusations of insincerity and
malingering, doubts expressed about the integrity of intentions," with the result that "the long-suffering Netherlands
minister" had to lodge a protest. Strict candor forces the
admission that for once the Japanese press was right. The
Dutch were fighting for delay, hoping that something would
occur to save them.

But the time came when boldness seemed the only course.
Winning the paper war was not really helping, and so the
Batavia Government scaled down the Japanese demands.
Instead of the 20,000 tons of rubber originally demanded,
they offered 15,000, the 200,000 tons of bauxite were reduced to 20,000, and the 50,000 tons of manganese to 5,000.
As a gesture no doubt of generosity, the Dutch were willing
to increase the original Japanese request for 4,000 tons of
castor oil seed to 6,000 tons — but mineral oil exports were
still to be arranged through the oil companies.

Strangely enough, there was no immediate reaction to this
inadequate offer to turn over the contents of one pocket
only to the highwayman. The Yoshizawa mission, which
had succeeded the Koboyashi delegation in Batavia, departed
for home and the farewell addresses seemed conciliatory.
The Dutch sought for comfort in their reading of Japanese
psychology. "History has taught us," says Van Mook, "that
Japan can retreat from almost any situation, provided the
secret is guarded and she does not openly lose face."

So as late as the middle of 1941, Van Mook records "a
wave of relief swept over the country. . . . It certainly
looked like peace with honour." The paper battle had been
won.

On June 12th the Germans invaded Russia and from that
point on, the Dutch in the East Indies, though they were
still loath to recognize it, came closer every day to the
ultimate catastrophe. After that event we still see Van
Mook casting a regretful glance backward at the sandheap,

so long occupied that it must have seemed like the old ostriches' home.

"It was everybody's failure," he writes, "to a greater or less degree, to perceive the inevitable consequences of Japanese aggression, but it seemed nobody's fault in particular; the democracies simply could not adapt the old rules to the new game. . . . In the Far East there might be reasons to mistrust Japanese expansionism, but it was still a far cry to outright southward aggression. . . . There seemed to be so many obstacles in her path to southern conquest that the chances of a move in that direction appeared remote."

These words could well have been taken from a Pearl Harbor report. But considering that Batavia lies two thousand miles nearer Japan and right in the path of the destroyer, the faith that these words express seems almost incredible. Every move that the Japanese had made for more than two years of negotiations had been a prelude to further aggression. There was travel between the two countries, and the Dutch, though they accused the Japanese of "linguistic incapacity," did not suffer from this failing. Had they possessed the urge to obtain intelligence with regard to Japanese war status and plans, they could undoubtedly so have informed themselves. Instead they trusted in their own "insularity of character" which seemed much better insulated than that of their enemies.

We may now turn to examine the state of alertness on another island much larger, much less fertile, and much farther from Japan than Java — the island continent of Australia. The Australian viewpoint in and around 1935 is ably represented by J. W. Eggleston who had been prominent in state politics there and had been chairman of three Australian delegations to Institute of Pacific Relations conferences. In *Who's Who in Australia* he lists his recreations as "none" and for such a serious-minded man he took a surprisingly cheerful view of the prospects for peaceful relations of his country with the Orient. Or at least, if war

came, he did not believe matters would be too serious for
Australia. To say that the next great struggle for power
would take place in the Pacific had merely, in his view,
"become a habit." He took sharp issue with British naval
experts such as Admiral Richmond and Captain Bywater
for their failure to consider properly the conditions that
would govern such a conflict in Pacific waters. As for lesser
experts, his opinion of their perspicacity was not high.
"Most of them," he said, "write of the Pacific as if it were
a continent." [5]

To this Pacific observer, conflict between any two naval
powers in that ocean would be a species of shadow-boxing,
in which raids on each other's commerce would be the most
serious acts of war. "It is generally true," he says, "that the
nations are so far apart, that they cannot strike effectively at
each other." Furthermore, "it used to be disputed, but is
now admitted, that the American and Japanese fleets cannot
fight each other conclusively — neither can be transferred
to the strategic area of the other without being so weakened
that it must be defeated."

Here again is the same old sandheap of impossible logistics
transported to Australia, a country of sandhills. Australia
did not need a fleet for defense, but an atlas. Hence "pil-
ing up armaments in the Pacific is a folly which must be
stopped."

With that forthright independence of judgment so characteristic of Australians, Eggleston continues to decry the
experts. Sir Herbert Richmond was, in his view, "the most
accomplished admiral who ever held binoculars in one hand
and a pen in the other." That would certainly be a confusing situation and the admiral might be excused if in time
of stress he stuck the wrong instrument in his eye. As to
Captain Bywater, Eggleston offers the gentle suggestion that
his impractical views on naval strategy in the Pacific might

[5] Eggleston, J. W. "Sea Power and Peace in the Pacific." *Pacific Affairs*,
September, 1935.

be due to defects common to professional education. Naval officers, according to the I.P.R. strategist, "go aboard ship at a tender age, and practically never emerge from their floating cloisters." Even if this writer's recreations are nil, his sense of humor is unimpeded. Warships as "floating cloisters" is a journalistic gem.

Three years later "informed opinion" in Australia as reported by Donald Cowie, was changing. According to this well-known writer, faith in the League of Nations had suffered a shock through its failure to restrain Japan and Italy in their policies of aggression. He reports a "Japanese scare" envisaging a possible invasion of Northern Australia and the setting up of a 36-million-pound armament policy for defense. But he discounts the scare by saying that both politicians and military experts seem to believe that no matter what the outcome of a major war, Australia and New Zealand would be unlikely to be invaded. "It would be too costly, dangerous, and impracticable for the enemy. Japan could scarcely land 200,000 men with the shipping it now has." [6] Incidentally, it should be noted that the Australian Labor Party wanted "a gigantic air force, instead of military and naval defense of the coast."

The experts can claim, of course, that they were right. Japan did *not* invade Australia, but could the experts have foreseen how close she came to doing so, they would have been scared clear out of their editorial sanctums and into the nearest foxholes.

The British view was fairly realistic as to the prospects of war but distinctly too optimistic as to what might happen. "For reasons too numerous to detail here," wrote Bywater in *Pacific Affairs* in 1935, "it is in the last degree improbable that Japan would undertake any large offensive against the American mainland or even Hawaii. . . . To do so would be to dissipate its forces and play right into American hands.

---

[6] Cowie, Donald. "The Arming of Australia and New Zealand." *Pacific Affairs*, September, 1938.

With all the advantages of a position ideal for waging an offensive-defensive campaign in its own waters, Japan would be mad to attempt any big stroke across the Pacific." Yet in a few years' time Japan staged two such strokes, one of which was successful beyond her own admirals' dreams, and the other was so nearly successful that it came within an ace of changing the whole character of the war.

Bywater, however, did not overlook the possibility of Japan's madness, and in the imaginary war foresaw our fleet being based on Hawaii to guard against "the improbable contingency" of an attack. On the other hand, he thought that American carriers could launch a surprise air assault on Japanese cities from their base at Dutch Harbor. Conversely, the Japs might attack in the same way but the goal would be Dutch Harbor, not Hawaii.

Here were the British borrowing our sandheap and using it quite freely. Japan, said Bywater, feared the American carriers more than our whole fleet. "But," says he, "it is unwise to attach too great an importance to air power in the campaign we are considering." He recommends a study of the logistics involved as a common-sense corrective. It would result in "fewer fantastic forecasts of a war between the United States and Japan, and consequently less 'war talk.'"[7] His motto was evidently "Trust in geography and keep your powder damp — there'll be less fear of an explosion."

Roosevelt, of course, was a keen student of naval opinions; and there are some who suggest that he adopted in his planning the principle that "whom the gods seek to destroy, they first make mad." Accordingly, they hint, he based the fleet in Hawaii with the faint hope that the Japanese might be foolish enough to attempt the mad stroke the experts discounted. For this suggestion there is no proof, but if it was Roosevelt's idea to bait the trap, he must have been horror-stricken with the results.

[7] Bywater, Hector C. Loc. cit.

Opinion in British Indian circles was more pessimistic, but naturally being nearer the scene of action they could not be as well informed as the experts in London. In October 1938, Geoffrey Rawson, a former British naval commander, wrote a letter to *Pacific Affairs* in which he described the British naval strength in Eastern waters as "quite inadequate for serious resistance to the Japanese Navy." Attack on Australia, he believed, could take the form of invasion or blockade, sea raids on commerce, or bombardment of ports. He did concede, however, that large-scale invasion was improbable on account of the vast naval transport and forces that would be required.

For this pusillanimous spirit, the editor, signing himself "O. L." [8] took the Commander to task, especially for his use of the "scare of defenselessness." "Commander Rawson," says the editorial comment, "does not even discuss the point that a navy can make no conquests without an army. Japan could not possibly send an army to Australia while entangled in the present hopeless attempt to conquer China. This is not simply a question of manpower. Even if Japan had the men to spare, it is not industrially equipped to arm and maintain them." Here again is the Japanese-involvement-in-China sandhill offered as a screen for the British.

Incidentally, though the I.P.R. had foresworn official policies, the editor by this comment shows his official leanings. When a leaning ceases to be a leaning and becomes a policy is hard to determine, but the tone of the magazine's reviews and articles indicates that the sandhill of Japanese exhaustion in China had, as its permanent tenant, the I.P.R.

Miss Frieda Uttley was one contributor who was not only granted space for her articles but had her books lengthily reviewed. These were said to be "heavily documented from I.P.R. sources." Her thesis was that Japan was "putting up a big bluff," was vulnerable because of economic and social weaknesses — a colossus, truly, but with feet of clay. By

8 Owen Lattimore was at that time editor of *Pacific Affairs*.

1936 a social revolution was already imminent — it only required the huff and the puff of economic sanctions to blow Japan's house down. It was so rickety a structure that it could never stand the strain of a real war. But war was not necessary — the bubble of her military aggressiveness would burst in the face of a few pinpricks in the shape of economic embargoes. While the experts sailed so boldly the uncharted seas of speculation, Japan went on with her plans. She became cut off from all trade relations with Great Britain, Australia, and America, and yet was able to carry on a widespread and for a time highly successful war against those nations.

Those experts who interpreted the German view indicated a similar distrust of Japan's war-making potential. A German writer, under the pen name of Asiaticus, wrote an article published in March 1938, entitled, "China's Advance from Defeat to Strength," which emphasized Japan's growing weakness. Another commentator named Rossinger, "specialist in Far Eastern affairs," in December 1939, spoke of Germany's conviction of "the growing inadequacy of Japan as an instrument for the furtherance of German policy." He reports that the German army also "had a low opinion of Japan's military prowess" — a view which corresponded with his own observation that Japan's exhaustion was already in its first stages. The Russians, also, according to Harriet Moore, felt that every day of the war with China made the situation for the ruling group in Japan more dangerous. Thus internal revolution became another hiding place for the omniscient ostrich.

The Chinese of course could not be expected to think well of Japanese chances of success. Kurt Bloch, one-time economic adviser to China, declared that "no new military long-distance expedition is likely as long as the China campaign is on" and that Japan, in addition, was "rapidly losing its rank as a naval world power."

As late as March 1940, when even the Dutch were scared

stiff, Owen Lattimore was still foretelling disaster for the
Japanese who he foresaw would proceed from stalemate to
tactical defeat, and thence to visible disaster and strategic
disintegration. He wrote: "This collapse — an intricate
matter of combined military prostration, financial strain,
and industrial inadequacy — is the only Japanese collapse
which can be realistically expected." It would seem that
this one collapse would be quite enough. The pronouncement reads like Mark Twain's news item, "The soldier died
of his wounds, nine of which were fatal."

One thing is certain, the Far Eastern expert can suffer
terrible wounds to his reputation and still remain alive. The
above opinions were published within a very short time of
the over-running of Malaya, Burma, Java, and the habitable
parts of Borneo, Celebes, and New Guinea, to say nothing
of Guam, Wake, the Solomons, and New Britain. British,
Australian, Canadian, Dutch, Chinese, German, Russian,
and American Far Eastern experts showed a most remarkable unanimity of agreement. They agreed in being completely wrong. The naval experts also were dead wrong,
though some of them now are merely dead. The Japanese
took a terrible beating in all of this paper warfare. When
the test came, they showed that they had hoodwinked us
all. There is more than a suspicion that they built us some
very inviting sandhills, notably the one in China. Perhaps everybody was mistaken about Japan, the inexpert
as well, but some had the sense to keep their opinions to
themselves, thus avoiding the slight discredit of unfulfilled
prophecy.

Meanwhile, in the period covered by this Pacific paper
war, Hawaii had organized the Diversified Crops Committee
of the Hawaiian Sugar Planters Association, its object being
to provide food for these islands in the event of being cut
off by a naval blockade; the community was talking about
organizing itself against air attack or invasion by instituting
what was called, even then, the Major Disaster Council.

CHAPTER V

How Hot Was the Melting Pot?

IN A PREVIOUS chapter we have set forth the theory that a combination of happy circumstances in the climate and surroundings of Hawaii has had a relaxing effect on the character and behavior of its people. Whether peaceable and inoffensive trends are to be considered virtues or weaknesses in racial temperament depends on the philosophy of the observer.

The history of Hawaii's native people shows that they have been quite successful in smoothing out or disregarding differences that ordinarily occasion uncomfortable social relationships. In the early days of white contacts the natives avoided a conflict of ideas by pulling down their temples, or heiaus, and burning their gods, their own high priests sometimes taking the lead in these iconoclastic activities. Once converted, they took their Christianity too literally to suit the prudent New England missionaries. They obeyed too implicitly the injunction against taking thought for the morrow, especially if it involved any toilsome spinning or weaving or seeking for food. Then, too, the Hawaiian back-slider could not understand why he was not at once re-admitted into the fold of the church once he had expressed a becoming contrition for his sins. The missionary's notions about working out one's salvation did not appeal to the native convert in the least. Religion he accepted as the white man's gift. Christianity was, indeed, a light for his feet, but when he didn't want the torch he blew it out. Why couldn't it be lit again like his own candle-nut torches? Thus

61

the Hawaiian was a good Christian only according to his lights, which were fitful.

It is highly probable that some of this easygoing tolerance of faults, his own and those of other people, has been communicated to the haoles or strangers in Hawaii's midst. How long it takes for a frosty New England background to melt completely in the foreground of Hawaiian sunshine is hard to say. At first the missionary aperture on life was small, the shutter-speed of his camera speedy, and therefore adapted only to taking the distant other-worldly view. Now the film is less sensitive, the focus is more universal, the aperture wider so that shadows as well as highlights and some of the natural coloring are reproduced. But the present-day tolerance and lack of the crusading evangelical spirit in the missionary descendants must have set their tough-minded, stern-principled ancestors turning rapidly in their graves. In fact when Gabriel blows his horn, some of these old missionaries, newly resurrected, will be so giddy they will hardly know mauka from makai.[1]

All this leads us back to the original paradox. With every inclination, natural and acquired, towards being security-minded; with all other Pacific communities convinced that the only potential trouble-maker was economically exhausted, militarily bogged down, internally disrupted, and sick of the barren fruits of aggression; with time and space and Great Britain, Russia, France, the Netherlands, Canada, Australia, and New Zealand on our side — could we be really serious in preparing for war? Could this excess of foresight be true of a people who not only did not believe in crossing their bridges before they came to them, but hardly believed in bridges at all, being just as ready to swim or wade?

But a paradox is not a contradiction, only an apparent one. Like any other situation it is subject to cause and effect,

---

[1] To the people of these islands there are only two general directions: *mauka,* towards the mountains; and *makai.* towards the sea.

except that some of the causes, though hidden, operate powerfully just the same. Hawaii's alertness, though unexpected, had its reasons. It was not haphazard, due to chance. It should be of interest to try and uncover the motivation that influenced our reactions toward a wholesome fear of Japan.

In the first place, in spite of geography, there was a bridge between this country and the Orient. We had pursued an entirely different immigration policy from that set up by Australia and New Zealand. While these countries had rigidly excluded Orientals, this country up to 1907, the date of the so-called Gentlemen's Agreement,[2] had invited wholesale immigration with the result that our population were in large proportion Japanese. Contrary to popular opinion, however, this proportion did not constitute a majority of the total, nor did it ever seem likely to do so. For twenty years, subject largely to immigration of other nationals, the percentage of Japanese had fluctuated somewhere between 30 and 40 per cent. Moreover, what has been called the "immigration from heaven" had tended to diminish through a decline in the Japanese birth rate. Perhaps the fact that there are no storks in Hawaii, and if there were, no chimneys down which to drop their bundles, accounted for this decline; at any rate, "come seven, come eleven" was no longer the Japanese family slogan, the dice of reproduction being apparently loaded in the direction of more modest threes and fours than towards the higher brackets.

However, nonetheless and notwithstanding, there were Japanese enough and to spare. Moreover, a great number of those resident here were aliens and kept up their connections with their homeland. All the children born in Hawaii and therefore American citizens were also registered as Japanese citizens at their consulate, and only by taking the positive

[2] This was like the Holy Roman Empire, which was neither holy nor Roman. One of the parties to the Gentlemen's Agreement was hardly a gentleman and the other hardly agreed.

action of renouncing their allegiance were they freed from dual citizenship. Only about 50 per cent took this course. The remainder were considered by their home government as Japanese citizens, and were required to obtain special exemptions each year to be freed from the obligation of military service. If any males of military age who had not obtained exemption journeyed to Japan, they could be inducted into the armed forces.

There were many other voluntary links with the home-land. Visits to Japan were undertaken for a variety of reasons. Those who had prospered in business or bootleg-ging naturally wished to display their substance to admiring relatives or former friends. Not infrequently a sick wife or child would be taken back for medical treatment; indeed, faith in their own doctors was so pronounced that occasion-ally incurable conditions such as feeble-mindedness required confirmatory diagnosis in Japan. Other aliens deplored the weakening of the home ties so much that they sometimes sent a favorite child to be educated in Japan.

For those who could not afford such expensive under-takings, there were the local language schools, established to inculcate Japanese ideals of conduct, and improve the facility of the children in the parents' mother tongue. In competition with English their speech was rapidly degener-ating into pidgin Japanese. In many families the speech of the elders was barely intelligible to the children, whose Japanese was so defective that they spoke it as little as possible. The Okinawans, who spoke poor Japanese at best, avoided the stigma of additional language handicaps among their classmates by not attempting to speak it at all, being thoroughly ashamed of their inadequacy. It was better to be silent than to manifest ignorance.

Many of the reactions of the Japanese which are misun-derstood by the whites really arise from pride, which has always been somewhat inordinate among them. Captain Cook was the first to contrast the Hawaiians with the

Japanese in this respect. "On all occasions," he wrote of the former, "they seem to be deeply impressed with a consciousness of their own inferiority, being alike strangers to the preposterous pride of the more polished Japanese, and of the ruder Greenlanders." [3]

Driven by this pride the older Japanese resisted strongly what is called Americanization, but which in their case would have been better called de-Japanization. They were aided in their conservative aims in various ways. Buddhist and Shinto temples were to be seen commonly in rural and country districts. Both priests and teachers for language schools were imported and brought an intensely nationalistic attitude with them. Discipline within the family was generally quite rigidly maintained. Females were kept in subservience and early took family responsibilities, if not on their shoulders, at least on their backs. It was not uncommon to see an eleven- or twelve-year-old girl playing hopscotch with a fat and stolid baby brother strapped behind. The eldest boy occupied the position of honor in the family, though the youngest was usually quite spoiled. Hence the second son was jocularly called "Master Cold Rice" in reference to the habit of serving him his food after his older and younger brothers. But boys were always welcome, and Boy's Day was celebrated by flying huge paper carp suspended from a bamboo pole, signifying the birth of a son into the family. The fish flew bravely, all fat and swollen by the wind, the symbols of good luck and fertility. Reverence for the Emperor was carefully inculcated; Japanese maids did not mind working on haole holidays but the Emperor's birthday was a universal celebration.

Intermarriages of Japanese with other racial groups were frowned upon. Instead, all the customary protocols were adhered to, with a go-between making the proposals and both families giving the balance of social position most care-

[3] Cook, James, and King, James. A Voyage to the Pacific Ocean . . . for Making Discoveries in the Northern Hemisphere. Vol. II, p. 228.

ful consideration. As a consequence out-marriages were, for many years, extremely rare though occasionally part-Japanese children were met with. One such child gave its ancestry as "part-Japanese, part-soldier." Another story that went the rounds told of a Japanese woman who brought her red-haired baby to the doctor's office. "Hey, mama-san," said the doctor, "whatsa matter? This baby's poppa have red hair?"

"Me no know, doctor," was the reply. "He no take his hat off." It was from such irregular unions that these rather uncommon part-Japanese children eventuated.

This rigid family control had some extremely good effects. For many years the percentage of Japanese delinquency and mental defect was by far the lowest in the population, and illegitimacy was rare. It was only with the relaxation of controls that the incidence of these among the Japanese began to assume the rates common among other racial groups in the population. They are still in a favorable position as regards respect for law. In this they make an excellent showing in comparison with the part-Hawaiian.

In spite of the fact that these circumstances kept us constantly aware of Japan, they were not of such a nature as to instill any alarm. Hawaii faced the Occident, rather than the Orient, looking all the time to continental America for "tourist trade," markets for sugar and pineapple, automobiles, food, and vacation trips. Japan, on the other hand, was 3,400 miles away, eleven days by steamer, and so posed no apparent threat. Japanese bowing before the Emperor's picture, flying their huge paper fish on Boy's Day, their squalid outlandish temples and dirty rambling language schools, even the hosts of Japanese children were matters of amusement rather than deep concern. To visitors new to such surroundings, who expressed anxiety about the future political complexion of these islands, we proffered such correctives as Professor Adams' predictions that on account of an estimated loss of 25 per cent through emigration, our Japanese population would remain considerably less than 40 per cent of the total. Moreover, the tidal wave of children that threatened to swamp our public schools would decline to a steady two thousand a year by 1930. Adams was at least half-right. The Japanese population did drop but not because of emigration. As to the number of children, though the birth rate declined, the marriage rate increased so that in spite of the statistical experts, the children managed to be born.

School population increased so that a quarter of the whole population was in school. The Japanese attended language schools after public schools closed for the day. In 1937 eighty-three per cent of them were in both school systems.

Whatever the political slant, there was considerable faith that it would never be slant-eyed. Sociologists, by means of some rather weird statistics, proved to their own satisfaction that the Japanese did not vote "en bloc." Why it was so necessary to prove that they did not so vote seems difficult to understand, since in the case of an Oriental and a white man both running for the same office, the haoles' vote would be solidly behind the man of their own color. Of course these voters would declare that they were voting for the better man, regardless of racial prejudices, but since in their opinion the haole would naturally always be superior, the motivation was unimportant.

Still others of the sociological persuasion proved, by carefully collected life histories, that those who could verbalize their conflicts were striving mightily to break away from their Japanese ties and become denationalized. All of this was very comforting. There was no Japanese threat of any kind. Their loyalty was unquestionable, for every school debate or essay contest brought out the passionate enthusiasm of the Japanese for the ideals for which their forefathers fought in 1776 or thereabouts. Many a Susie Suzuki thought she ought to belong, if only by adoption, to the D.A.R.

All this gave much satisfaction to the school men, as witnessing to the power of education in changing the Ethiopian's skin. Had not their efforts, in half a generation, changed all the sociological and psychological currents and set them flowing in the opposite direction, even though to the eye of experience it was uphill? It was a magnificent demonstration of the power of Christianity and the blackboard. It became both unpopular and undemocratic to doubt a full hundred per cent American conversion. Yet in the late thirties there were sundry happenings that caused some stirrings of skepticism. One was the pronounced surge of loyalty to the homeland and approval of Japanese foreign policies that became apparent during the Sino-Japanese War.

On November 6, 1938, a Mr. Shirai, the assistant manager of the Yokohama Specie Bank of Honolulu, attended a meeting in Hilo, chief town of the island of Hawaii, to discuss financial contributions to Japan. It was attended by several hundred representative Japanese from all over the Big Island and was duly reported by the *Nippu Jiji*, Japanese-language newspaper in Honolulu. According to its account, the men showed "a keen desire and loyalty to help the Fatherland." In fact the professions of loyalty were so numerous that it took all day from 9:30 in the morning until 4:30 in the afternoon to get them adequately expressed. The association took the name of Doshi Kai (Patriotic Bonds Subscription Society) and was sponsored by the Hilo Japanese Association. The goal set was the subscription of a million yen ($250,000 to $300,000) by regular purchases of Japanese emergency bonds. It began to look a little as if the Hawaiian melting pot was not so hot.

A network of *kumais*, Japanese community clubs, already covered the island, and these took the matter of raising the money in hand. According to information supplied by a former army intelligence officer, the head of each family was assessed one dollar per month, plus another dollar for each working male in the family group. In six weeks' time 60,000 yen had been contributed — a hundred per cent response.

Mr. Shirai, when interviewed in Honolulu, declared his visit to Hilo was purely a pleasure trip and had nothing to do with bond buying.

Then the Federal Security and Exchange Commission took a hand in the proceedings. The bonds, not being registered with the S.E.C., were being illegally sold. In order to avoid local repercussions the Federal Government asked Judge Neterer of California, on a convenient pleasure trip to Hawaii, to try the case. Injunctions against 87 Japanese defendants were granted, and the money ordered returned to the bond buyers. But there was no law against individuals making patriotic gifts. Much money went to the Japanese Red Cross, a thoroughly laudable object, nor could there be any objection against a drive for funds to equip a hospital ship; but somewhere along the line the latter plan developed into buying a bomber which was to be named "Hawaii." Through their press the local Japanese protested against Federal discrimination on the grounds that some Chinese War Bonds had been previously offered for sale. This particular transaction, however, was prior to the granting of an injunction against the sale of Japanese bonds in California. The Californian prohibition was known, so it was said, to the Japanese in Hawaii before they started the local scheme to help finance the "China Incident."

How much pressure was exerted by the *kumais* to obtain contributions is not known; but the individual receipts were carefully recorded, so that after Dec. 7th the F.B.I. had available to them a whole roomful of these and other records, from which they obtained evidence used in internment proceedings.

The loyal interest of the Japanese in their own land was further evinced on the occasion of a visit of two battleships and a supply ship to these islands in October 1939. Admiral Sawamoto, who was in command, had been naval attache in London and had made a couple of previous visits to Hawaiian waters. He was noted throughout Japanese naval circles for his extraordinarily keen memory. No doubt his reports were interesting from the standpoint of Japanese naval intelligence. Under the Admiral's command were 124 officers, 335 midshipmen and 1,531 enlisted men. In a speech in Hilo, Sawamoto declared the trip had a dual purpose, to train the midshipmen and "to build more cordial relations with the U.S.A."

The methods of attaining the latter goal were a little peculiar. Alongside the sentry guarding the gangplank were notices in Japanese, warning visitors of their own nationality to come on board suitably dressed and cleaned up for the occasion. Then in English appeared another notice which simply said: "Salute the sentry." Roughly printed on a piece of wrapping paper, this notice bore all the signs of being what the police would call "a local job."

The Hilo haoles, however, decided to do their share towards building cordial relations. The *Hilo-Tribune Herald*, in an editorial of welcome, exhorted the whole community "to help in extending true Hawaiian hospitality" to the ships' personnel. Accordingly an inspector of customs, Henry S. Wilson, proceeded to board the battleship "Yakamo" in order to offer the courtesies of the port of Hilo to the ships' officers and men. The sentry barred the way.

"Who you?" the sentry demanded.

"Customs officer," replied Wilson.

"You bow to sentry," was the command. When Wilson refused to do so, the customs man had to return to the pier from where he called for the officer of the deck who came off the ship to receive the courtesy letter. The chief clerk of the water works on his way to deliver a bill similarly refused to salute, but the matter was diplomatically handled by the chairman of the Japanese entertainment committee, who arranged for the bill to be presented "without incident."

Life magazine on November 13, 1939, published a full-page picture of the sentry, flanked by the notice requiring the salute. The picture bore the legend, "A Japanese sentry demands a salute from Americans on American soil." The incident thus received considerable attention and had a curious sequel. Wilson became a major in the Army and was captured and recognized on Wake Island. He was at once threatened with death for stirring up racial animosity.

"You are responsible for the war between Nippon and the United States," he was told. "For that you will be decapitated." However, this threat was for some reason not carried out.

In the report of this occurrence after Wilson's release in 1945, the *Hilo-Tribune Herald* gave a queer face-saving version of the story. The account, as printed on November 15th, described Wilson as drawing his pistol and backing the sentry right up the gangplank so that he could deliver his letter in proper style. Why it was necessary to save white prestige in such manner is hard to understand, but it shows how reports can be distorted. By 1945 it was *infra dig* to report that any redblooded American could be stood up and outfaced by any Japanese sentry. Hilo evidently felt that the occurrence as previously reported reflected on its martial spirit.

The incident made a very small ripple in Hilo, which offered the other cheek in fine style. The Inter-Island Co. delayed the sailing of one of their freighters from Honolulu so that the "Yakamo" could remain at the pier. The Rotary Club entertained the officers at a luncheon "as an aloha and token of good will between Japan and America." Some of the Rotarians two years later heard the scream and whistle of shells passing over their clubhouse in the bombardment of Hilo by submarines.

The Hawaii Japanese, of course, outdid themselves in the heartiness of their aloha. Traffic along the boulevard was blocked while "baskets of flowers, crates of canned goods and fresh fruit" were carried on board as gifts. The girls got out their best kimonos for a round of visits; public and private entertainment were tendered to the men of the fleet. The coming of the battleship may or may not have cemented goodwill; it probably cemented something.

In Honolulu, as late as March 1941, fifty tons of "comfort bags" were shipped to Japan by the local Japanese Chamber of Commerce. These bags contained blankets, shoes, sugar, candy, and other things likely to gladden the hearts of the soldier recipients. Fifteen hundred tons of scrap metal, collected in Hawaii, also went by the same ship.

It was early in 1940 that Tetsuo Oi, manager of the Japanese Chamber of Commerce, gave a very frank exposition of his feelings toward Japan at a meeting sponsored by Central Union Church in Honolulu. He spoke mainly on the Sino-Japanese War, but began by saying that, though he had been born in Hawaii and educated at Stanford University and in Japan, he favored his own government above all others. He admitted that the struggle with China was no "holy war," but one born of Japan's necessity to expand her trade and her opportunities to get raw materials. He complained bitterly that Japan was not financially able to purchase these materials in competition with Britain, France, and America. Therefore she had to take them by force. The occupation of Manchuria was disappointing, for Japan had to spend more money there than what she could take out. The Manchurians had been too backward in developing their own resources. North China, however, offered a much more lucrative job of highway robbery, though Mr. Oi did not of course call it that. He earnestly declared that Chiang Kai-shek's anti-Japanese policy would be corrected, even if Japanese lives were sacrificed in correcting it. He did not mention any Chinese lives in this connection.

But this was talking too much like Hitler to suit peace-loving Honolulu, even the Japanophiles. One of the most influential of these — essentially a man of good will and a very wealthy haole — called on the editor of one of Honolulu's newspapers and suggested that he suppress the report of the meeting. He felt that it might occasion ill will against the Japanese, especially coming on the heels of a published statement in Tokyo by Kuichi Gunji, former consul-general in Hawaii, which declared that "all Japanese are loyal to the mother country." When Eguchi, a former Japanese member of our legislature, challenged this as a ridiculous statement, he was taken severely to task by the *Nippu Jiji* for "insulting Honorable Gunji."

Most of this commotion had to do with the war with China and the local Japanese could hardly be blamed for some partisan spirit. But an article in the monthly magazine *Jitsujyo-no-Hawaii* of August 26, 1936, praised the appointment to the Japanese cabinet of Admiral Suetsuju who had advocated "driving the white race out of Asia"; it also deprecated the haste which Foreign Minister Hirota showed in apologizing for the attack on the U.S. "Panay." "To respect someone," said the article, "is because you are weak, and to apologize is because you have erred. It is the spirit of the Americans to look down upon a weak and evil person."

Even the *Hawaii Hochi*, usually a very moderate newspaper, discussed the matter of treaties in the following terms: "No nation can be expected to keep its word one moment longer than it is to its advantage to do so. In a sense a nation is 'beyond good and evil.'" Here was a frankly Hitlerian view published only in Japanese; but in another article in English the paper expressed its sincere hope "that the appeal for Red Cross funds to assist suffering Chinese victims of the war will be liberally supported."

The *Nippu Jiji* could be more blatantly two-faced. Speaking of a Chinese drive for flood relief funds, it said, "We wish them a great success. It is a splendid drive. But Chinese ought to remember that they alone are to be blamed for causing untold sufferings and hardships on the poor Chinese people around the Yellow River. Chiang Kai-shek did not care what became of his people in his insane attempt to check the advance of Japanese forces. Some day Chiang Kai-shek will be punished for his inhuman deeds." This statement was plain hypocrisy or imbecility, or both.

These extracts are taken from an I.P.R.-sponsored study by Edwin G. Burrows, who included in his survey news-papers, radio, moving pictures, and language schools as media for propaganda. The author points out the careful avoidance of conflict between the Chinese and Japanese in Hawaii. "On the whole, the behavior of the Hawaiian-born of either stock can be held up as model to neutrals. Even the immigrants, though not neutrals, have been careful to keep the peace."[4]

For those who returned to Japan from Hawaii for their education, the case stood differently. Five hundred Nisei, according to the Tokyo correspondent of the *Hawaii Hochi*, were graciously permitted to attend the 2,600th anniversary of some historic Japanese event. Among the organizations represented at this convention were the Japan-America-Hawaii society (with America, be it noted, in the middle), the McKinley Alumni of the Keizen Girl's School, and the Todo Gakuen of the North American Buloku Kai which claimed 7,000 members in Hawaii. Lieutenant General Hamada addressed the gathering and reminded the students that "the color of their skins will not change even if it comes to the period of the third, fourth, and fifth generation." However, the General wept copiously when a Canadian-born student told how cease-lessly he and his comrades worked and starved so as to make themselves more fit to return to Canada and Hawaii

[4] Burrows, Edwin G. *Chinese and Japanese in Hawaii during the Sino-Japanese Conflict.* Hawaii Group, American Council, Institute of Pacific Relations, 1939.

and "repay their debt to Japan." This was in October of 1940, just six months before Hawaii was having its first civilian-directed practice blackout and wondering in what kind of currency that debt would be paid.

As a final illustration of what the Japanese language school teachers and priests were accomplishing in Hawaii in filling their pupils' minds with gratitude to the soldier for nobly upholding Japan's prestige on the battlefields of China, we shall quote from a student's composition which appeared in one of the five Japanese language school papers published in the Territory during 1937.

THANKING THE JAPANESE SOLDIERS

I do not know how to thank the Japanese soldiers who are sacrificing their lives for their country either by fighting with the outrageous Chinese soldiers or by guarding the Japan-Soviet Border.

They endure the extremely cold winter, so cold that even the moonbeams seem frozen and the hot torrid summer when the water appears boiling.

We, in Hawaii, who are living hundreds and thousands of miles away from the actual scene of the battle, owe our comforts and peace to the Japanese soldiers who have taken up arms for the sake of justice in the Far East.

Last night my mother packed a comfort bag with gum, chocolate candy, cigarettes, etc., for a soldier fighting in China. I included a letter of thanks to the soldier.

I went to the Sheridan Theater last week and saw the Japanese soldiers at the front. The scenes of brave soldiers fighting in a "shower" of bullets and nursing their steeds after severe battles moved me deeply.

The soldiers can hardly sleep at night, for they do not know when the enemy will attack them. A bitter fight all day long and hardly any sleep at night! We are happy indeed to be able to study peacefully and sleep in safety at night.

At the front the soldiers eat only cold rice and cold side dish. For side dish, they can have only such things as canned food and pickled plums. When we think of their hardship we should not complain of our meals.

The heavily burdened soldiers walk continuously for fifty or sixty kilometers in snow storms or in pouring rain without uttering a word of resentment while we complain of being tired and our feet aching when we have walked but a short distance.

I cannot read those impressive war stories in the *Shonen Club* and the *Shojo Club* (children's magazines) without tears. When we think of the difficulties the soldiers must go through, we students cannot neglect our study. Moreover, we must work just as hard as the soldiers at the front, and strive to become good American citizens of Japanese ancestry.

In considering all the foregoing, one thing should be kept firmly in mind — it was, after all, just what could be expected. Patriotism, much more than justice, should be depicted as blind. Had it been possible for the situation to be reversed, so that Americans occupied the position of the Japanese in Hawaii, and vice-versa, the same things would have happened, or at least we hope they might. The faith that so many Americans hold, that everything about America is so vastly superior, and that being American is so obviously better than being anything else, does their patriotism credit, but still is mainly faith. Such people cannot understand other nationalities' pride of birth or possessions. Moreover, it is incomprehensible to them why Americanization, once it is possible, is not instantaneous and complete. That anyone should value things or viewpoints that are unamerican is almost beyond belief: it would seem to be proof of the crassest kind of stupidity.

But people who live in other lands, especially the democracies, believe that their lives are just as unimpeded, the four near-freedoms are just as close to realization in their homelands as in America. They refuse to grant her any monopoly of beauty, wisdom, art, music, opportunity, high principles, or of any of the things men live by and for — even though admittedly she has everything, including other things not so admirable, in abundance. Nor is loyalty tied up with being a citizen of a huge and powerful nation, the richest and therefore the most disinterested in the world. Patriotism can flame just as ardently in a little country such as Switzerland, perhaps more hotly than in one of huge extent.

In the Japanese empire it is not surprising to find a strongly national spirit, one which would be readily transplanted to other lands in which the Japanese found themselves. Consequently, for those living in Hawaii, loyalty to their mother country, unquestioned in the case of the older Japanese, divided at best among the second generation Nisei, was exactly what might have been foreseen.

A feeling of deep affection for one's native land, especially when the associations are those of youth and childhood, and identified with those pleasures and adventures in living that we all look back on with such heightened emotion — this is an important part of the basis of loyalty. No soldier has yet given a satisfactory and full explanation of what he is fighting for. He rarely knows, but these memories, even though subconscious, are perhaps the background of his motivation.

If a man changes his habitat so that he comes under a different flag, if he finds his security increased so that the fear of oppression or poverty or social indifference or degradation is materially lessened, then loyalty for the new land begins to grow. He probably first acquires a cosmopolitan viewpoint, the idea that all men are similar in their basic humanity with all its faults and foibles, and so it seems to him that one citizenship is about as good as another. But the growth of even this neutral attitude is a slow process, and it would be rare indeed to find such a person completely denationalized.

To bare the facts does not necessarily mean to condemn, and fact-finding is mainly what we are concerned with. The alien Japanese in Hawaii behaved on the whole better than could be expected; the second generation, considering their home influence, quite immeasurably so. But this does not mean that there were no pro-Nipponese leanings among our population. [5] Again it is worth restating the thesis that both mental and physical changes in the young Japanese may be ascribed to Hawaii's peculiar environment with its stimulating or humanizing effects. Some of the changes in viewpoint and behavior were due to education, but in Hawaii educational efforts swam with the current and not against it, as is so often the case.

Ridiculous as may seem the identification of the Hawaiian-born Japanese with American traditions, it was a long step towards political assimilation. This identification sought to emphasize spiritual relationships, or commonalty of principles which would eventually transcend blood ties. It was not long before America's adopted children felt that a country which had fought long and successfully for independence, and had bitterly defended its unity in another great war of principle, a nation that had produced a Washington and a Lincoln, certainly had claims to respect and loyalty.

Then too, that sense of security that is associated with a family life spent in familiar and enjoyable surroundings is at the root of the happiness of youth. Should we change to an environment where we find these things in increased measure, we are at once "at home." This idea of belongingness, of being at home, is essential to the building of the patriotic complex.

In the case of the alien adult, even though by migration he has escaped certain social handicaps and has prospered in his new community above his friends and neighbors in his former home, the idea of changing allegiance is slow in developing. Against it is arrayed all the nostalgia of the past, its harsh experiences mellowed by time. It is, therefore, a long time before the alien begins to verbalize this situation in terms of other loyalties. Increased prosperity and security

[5] The graves of four Japanese aviators, killed in the attack on Pearl Harbor, and buried at Wahiawa, are kept green with fresh flowers and surrounded with ceremonial offerings of cakes.

in the new land may develop a kindly neutrality, but little
more.

For the Japanese, with their extreme national pride, and
their affection for the natural beauty of their own land,
coupled with considerable faith in the stability of its insti-
tutions, the switch in allegiance was particularly difficult,
especially when there were such evident physical bars to
assimilation. General Hamada's words were echoed in many
a Japanese home. "You are descendants of the Yamato
people. Your skins will not change."

These things being so, and seeing that any worth-while
loyalty does not veer like a vane in the wind, the pattern
of Japanese behavior in Hawaii was quite normal. They are
not inconstant, vacillating people. On the other hand,
stability, determination, and strength of purpose appeal to
them. They could not be neutral at heart, much less support
the foes of their country. Only the purblind, their incau-
tious, over-enthusiastic friends, could believe otherwise. In
my opinion the older Japanese would have lost rather than
gained in moral stature had they changed so easily. It was
the younger Japanese who were caught, and are still held,
between the upper and the nether millstones. Their conflicts were tragic. Compelled to repudiate their parents'
ideas, they found themselves rejected by those with whom
they tried to align themselves. It was for them a most
unhappy time.

CHAPTER VI

Parasites in Paradise

IN 1939 and early 1940, the first six months
of war, the world was in an extremely disturbed and nervous state. But the conflict in Europe and
North Africa had not yet developed into World War II.
Every major disturbance set up a ripple in the Pacific but
it soon subsided. For each alarming feature in the news there
was something reassuring, often in the next column of the
same newspaper.

There had, however, been occasional disquieting items.
After the sinking of the "Royal Oak" in Scapa Flow by
submarine action, Churchill had been moved to utter a
serious warning. "In this new war, with its many novel
complications, nothing must be taken for granted." He gave
the clue to the reason for the disaster by implying that it
was a sense of false confidence in the immunity of the naval
base from attack, which "had led to a too easy valuation of
the dangers which were present." This should have been
a warning to us not to trust our own inviolability, but was
hardly taken as such. We were not yet at war and if the
British could rely so heavily on their navy and twenty or
thirty miles of sea-channel to preserve them from German
invasion, surely we could depend on naval power and over
3,000 miles of ocean to shield us from the Japanese.

Thus it was that for every one who cried "Wolf" there
were many who were ready to allay our alarm with the cold
compress of facts. If on February 27, 1940, Major Evans

arlson[1] could issue a stern warning that neglect to stop
pan in China soon would lead her to attempt world ag-
ression, we could brush aside the cautionary finger with
e thought that it was Carlson's unique experiences with
e brave Chinese 8th Route Army that made him so des-
erately anxious to bring them speedy help. At the same
me Carlson also decried the strength of Japan. He thought
n American embargo on exports would bring her to her
nees in six months. China, he declared, had a better than
ven chance to win the war.

Again, while the Japanese Finance Minister was reassuring
he Diet by pointing out that Japan was eight million yen
cher in annual income than at the beginning of the Chinese
var, Sir Victor Sassoon, British capitalist, straight from
hanghai, reported in New York that the Japanese people
vere sickening of the army's attempt to conquer China and
hat "their internal economy was crumbling."

Most comforting of all was Roosevelt's profession of faith
hat peace was possible for us. "The simple fact," he said,
s quoted in an A.P. press report to Honolulu newspapers,
"without any bogey in it, without any appeals to prejudice,
s that the United States is neutral, and does not intend to
become involved in war." He went on to denounce as
groundless any fears that Americans might again die on
Europe's battlefields. This pronouncement was judiciously
imed to coincide with the repeal of the U.S. embargo on
elling munitions of war to the Allies. The statement was
good politics; whether it was good from the standpoint of
he truth as Roosevelt saw it was another matter. If at that
time the President did not foresee war, he was not very
smart; and if he was smart, he was not very truthful.

Here, in Hawaii, our faith in the persuasive power of the
aloha spirit was undimmed. Had not the strife in the Orient,
bitter as it was, been unproductive of incident in this Territory except for a fist-fight at, of all places, the Chinese Old

[1] Later to achieve fame as leader of Marine Raiders.

Men's Home. In the eyes of many people we were still the shining example of what Christian tolerance could do even to Buddhists and Shintoists. We suspected that the alien Japanese was too ignorant to change, but his son, the Nisei, was a horse of a different color, at least internally. Even these second-generation Japanese seemed to differ among themselves as to the question of the influence of such things as language schools on loyalty to America. In a public debate on the subject, Robert Murakami, a Honolulu attorney, declared that "those in charge of language schools would not tolerate any subversive teaching or fifth-column activity." But Stanley Miyamoto, a Territorial public school principal, was not so confident. He said that many of the language school teachers came from Japan, and were "thoroughly Japanized."

Whatever portents there were did not thrust themselves prominently forward, and such as were present soon faded from public view. The sentry incident in Hilo was just Nipponese obtuseness rather than arrogance, while scrap metal shipments, rubber and tin foil drives conducted by Japanese children, and collections of comfort bags and belts of a thousand stitches, forwarded to Japan by local associations, were regarded as emotional releases of a harmless, insignificant nature. The newspapers evidently felt that to give prominence to any of these activities would be to introduce a sour note into the cloying sweetness of "Aloha Oe," the sentiment of which flowed so smoothly over all international boundaries. The attitude of one of Honolulu's dailies can be described as less favorable to the Japanese, and it consistently adopted a watchful attitude. For example, on one occasion it pointed out that in the three years from 1937 to 1939, 57 per cent of Japan's key war materials were imported from the U.S.A. as against only 24 per cent from the British, French, Dutch, and American possessions in the East combined. The caption of this article, published on October 9, 1940, was "We Helped Japan Arm." Some

people deprecated the tone of this publication as contrary
to the "no pilikia" spirit, so characteristic of Hawaii.

But by April of 1941 the outlook in Europe had suddenly
become bleak. Churchill, in a serious mood, announced that
a million Germans were poised on the frontiers of Luxem-
bourg, Holland, and Belgium. "At any moment these
neutral countries," he said, "may be subjected to an avalanche of steel and fire." But the blow fell not there, but
in Norway. And then followed May and June, the two
blackest months of the war and probably in world history.
It was then that Hawaii shook itself and came at least partially awake. We were still thousands of miles from the
center of the disturbance. It was not, as far as any one
could see, heading our way, but men eyed each other with
a new seriousness, listened to the radio in groups, and broke
silently away, shaking their heads in dismay. When they
gathered again or scanned the newspaper headlines it was
with an air of "What new catastrophe now?" But we had
progressed little beyond the head-shaking stage.

Possibly the fact that so many of the people of the islands
were of British blood or descent was one reason for part
of our concern. For a long time contributions of money and
effort had gone from Hawaii to the British Red Cross, and
the Bundles for Britain movement received active and increasing support. On at least one plantation even Japanese
women under the plantation manager's wife were busily
sewing for the British. "All the same, men fight, women
and children hungry; we help," was the way they expressed
their sympathy and their loyalty to the local first lady.

Perhaps the exposed situation of these islands may have
contributed somewhat to our global view. We needed no
reminder that this was one world, and that what happened
on French and Belgian battlefields had at least some repercussions here. By painful experience we knew that some
great submarine subsidence as far away as Alaska, Japan, or
the coast of South America could set the ocean surface

pulsating in great waves or swellings of water that could travel 400 miles an hour and finally work destruction on these shores.

One might be tempted to relate our extraordinary acuity to danger to the fact that living on volcanic islands meant living dangerously, and that this fact gave us keener sensitivity to the approach of peril. True, we do have volcanic outbursts of remarkable violence, but these are so spectacular that we run to instead of away from them. On May 16, 1939, one of our local papers came out with these gloomy headlines, "Hopes for Volcanic Activity Subsiding." And in sober fact, we take our convulsions of Nature quite calmly. Immediately after the last disastrous tidal wave struck our shores, killing a hundred and fifty people, a prediction was made that a second wave would reach Hawaii in the early afternoon of the same day. Instead of panic seizing the population and driving it hurriedly to higher land, throngs of people lined the shores to see the show. This of course was not bravery, but damn foolishness, well expressed in the old Hawaiian saying: *"Pela no i Hawaii nei"* — that is how it is in Hawaii.

So then we come as a last resort to the most striking paradox about life in these islands. In spite of all the soothing effects of our equable climate and most satisfying natural beauty; in spite of all the tolerance and good humor that we gain from easy circumstances or which we caught from the Hawaiians; in spite of our apparent easy-going, nothing-caring, "no pilikia," philosophy; in spite of the complacency which was apparent in other communities much nearer the brink of war's catastrophe than ourselves; yes, in spite of all these invitations to push trouble away and take our ease, we were alert, because in a most important sense alertness to danger had become our normal state.

Just a brief glance at our economic condition and history will show that the whole commercial system in Hawaii has for a long time hung by a single thread. Not only the pros-

)erity we have achieved but our very existence as a whole
:ommunity has been dependent upon the success of our
najor industry, the growing and marketing of sugar. Any-
hing that threatens the cane, threatens all the people of
hese islands. Without it our internal economy would have
:ollapsed like a house of cards, just as it threatened to col-
apse with the decline of the whaling industry. We should
1ave had a handful of population, mainly Hawaiians and
)art-whites, a beachcomber economy. How many of us
:here would be is problematical. From 300,000 in Cook's
day (1778), the native population had fallen to less than
50,000 in 1865 with probably 2,500 whites; hence the
extinction of the native race was well on its way. By this
time the Hawaiians as a people would have been as doomed
as the Marquesans. Without the sugar plantations there
would have been no incentive for Chinese, Japanese, Portuguese, and Filipino immigration to these islands. Except for
a few tourists, whites also would have avoided the place.
Hawaii would have been of no more importance than Tahiti;
our political state would probably have been a native de-
pendency like the Virgin Islands, and if annexed by America,
we would have been then truly what so many of the Army
and Navy personnel call us — a military outpost, with nothing but what the Army and Navy brought with them and
established here. Now, after a hundred years of agricultural
development, the sugar industry is still our backbone. The
establishment of the pineapple industry also required
money, ships, railways, and population, all of which were
here because of sugar.

For many years the plantations operated with a very
moderate margin of profit, but as those operations were
extended by the utilization of all available land, by the building of mills and ocean landings, by wholesale mechanization
and the importation of labor, sugar became big business.
Large immigration schemes were put through, and banking,
insurance, and manifold related enterprises sprang up. The

industry operating on the world's markets and affected by financial and other crises, it soon became apparent that only by a closely-knit system of co-operation would it be possible for it to survive. So the sugar men set up what was called the Hawaiian Sugar Planters' Association (H.S.P.A.), through which was to come about a pooling of ideas with regard to the problems of the industry. These included methods of cultivation, irrigation, and harvesting, together with the selection and breeding of better varieties of cane. The scientists of the Hawaii Experiment Station became one of the most important groups in the H.S.P.A.

At the beginning of the present century, it appeared as if the major trials of the sugar industry were over, its profitable future secured. After 65 years of struggle, the planters could feel that the business was on a firm financial and agricultural basis. The mills were built, the irrigation ditches were flowing, annexation had assured a mainland market, labor had become available from the Orient and shareholders could take their ease. From a few stalks of wild cane grown by the Hawaiians at the time of Cook's visit, sugar had grown into an industry worth many millions of dollars. But just as achievement seemed stabilized, an unlooked-for disaster occurred.

It came in the form of a small insect called a leaf hopper. Entomologists knew the breed but did not fear it greatly. Leaf hoppers were familiar insects on the cane in Hawaii but this was a new specimen that entomologist Perkins saw flying around his lamp at Waialua in 1902. It had probably migrated with cane specimens from Queensland, and like all newcomers found Hawaiian hospitality entirely to its liking and so made itself at home. But this was no chance visitor, but a deadly scourge, a wholesale invader, so destructive that it was called *saccharicida*, literally, the cane killer.

The damage was done in this wise. The females laid their eggs on the midribs of the cane leaves, which developed red spots as the results of fermentation set up around the little

holes where the eggs were inserted. When the young hoppers hatched, their excretions of honeydew were conducive
to a growth of black mould that blighted and wilted the
green of the cane.

By the end of 1902, the enemy had thoroughly infiltrated
the islands of Oahu and Kauai. Next year it invaded Maui
and Hawaii, the Experiment Station helping to distribute
the pest along with infected cane for experimental plots.
Some idea of the scale of attack may be obtained from Vandercook's [2] description: "The hum of their devouring presence," he wrote, "could be heard at great distances. The
swarm of these incredible billions moved like a visible cloud
across the land."

The magnitude of the threatened disaster may be judged
from the fact that on Pahala in Hawaii, a plantation which
specialized in the hoppers' favorite cane, the Yellow Bamboo, the yield of sugar fell from 19,000 tons in 1903 to about
850 tons in 1906.

The planters were desperate. It was evident that if they
were not to be completely defeated, they must find some
allies. Entomologists went wherever hoppers lived to search
out and collect the natural enemies of the pest. Ohio had
a gang of leaf hoppers which were preyed upon by several
species of insects called dryinids, but when these were imported to Hawaii they speedily "lost fight," to use the pidgin
English phrase, and developed Hawaiian rheumatism. This
is not a painful though a common complaint in the Islands.
Its only symptom is that when you sit down you find it very
difficult to get up again. Great hopes were pinned on a
Javanese parasite which vigorously attacked the leaf hoppers
in the Dutch plantations. Unfortunately when this was
brought to these islands it also developed the aloha spirit
and lived on quite friendly terms with the cane killer.

Finally Perkins and Koebele discovered the home of the

[2] Vandercook, John W. *King Cane. The Story of Sugar in Hawaii.* Harper
Bros., New York, 1939.

pest in North Queensland where it was kept in check by its enemy, a bug called *Paranagrus*. But it was a trying problem to persuade *Paranagrus* to come to Hawaii to help the planters in their battle. Shipment after shipment died of pneumonia or sea-sickness, even though cane leaves on which were parasitized eggs were packed in the dampest moss and carried in the steamer's cooling chamber to Hono-lulu. Finally the scientists landed with eight friendly females, four of which were liberated in the cane, and four reserved for the breeding cages.

To anyone unfamiliar with the fecundity of Nature at the insect level, the idea of pitting such a corporal's guard against a vast host of enemies would have seemed most ridiculous. But the entomologists evidently knew their *Paranagruses*. The leaf hopper females laid their eggs in the cane and the *Paranagrus* Amazons followed them around, paralleling their activities by depositing their eggs inside those of the leaf hoppers. The parasite egg hatches first and finds just enough nutriment in its hostess egg to feed on until pupation is completed. Morever, *Paranagrus* has two broods to the leaf hopper's one and, with time and arith-metical progression on their side, the parasites eventually began to fight the enemy on more equal terms. Then too this species is what the entomologists call partheno-genetic, which means that she is a very independent sort of female. She appreciates the male's company but he is not essential to her sex activities. She has been observed to go on with the business of laying fertile eggs for eight months without the male *Paranagrus* having put in an appearance at all. *Perkinsellia saccharicida* didn't have a chance. Two years after the introduction of the original eight parasites, the leaf hopper menace was almost under control. However, it took 20 years of combat before peace was declared. The finishing stroke to the invader was the importation by Dr. Frederick Muir of the champion egg-sucker of North

Queensland, an insect called *Cyrtorhinus mundulus*. By 1923 the leaf hopper was no longer a burden.

The value of what might be called the intelligence de-partment of the H.S.P.A. was exemplified by the doings of Dr. Muir. The year 1906 found him working in South China, where cane has been raised since time immemorial. The Chinese called it the "sweet bamboo," and from there it spread to many countries. China may well have been the land referred to in Scripture. "To what purpose," asked Jehovah, in the words of Jeremiah, "cometh there to me frankincense from Sheba, and the sweet cane from a far country?"

The Chinese farmers looked with amazement on this little man in a khaki suit and a sun helmet who spent his time poking around the cane, or transplanting single stalks to grow in tubs on the balcony of his hotel in Macao. How much sugar, they asked, did the crazy foreign devil expect to get from these few tubfuls of cane! Truly the man was mad, certainly not worth the local bandits' time in taking him for ransom. Had these same bandits known it, this little man was worth millions of dollars to the Hawaiian sugar industry.

Muir's wanderings in search of parasites for the leaf hop-per extended over Japan, Formosa, Java, New Guinea, and the Philippines. *Paranagrus* had worked well for some years, but life in Hawaii was too easy with such an abundance of leaf hoppers on hand. She went soft and, so it was reported, formed the habit of sheltering from the frequent showers under an umbrella of cane leaves instead of going diligently about the planters' business of ovipositing. Only when *Cyrtorhinus*, the egg-sucker, had been discovered could Muir turn his attention to other enemies.

This is how the late director of the Experiment Station, Mr. H. P. Agee, summed up the results of these entomo-logical efforts. "The value of this work in economic ento-mology," he wrote, "cannot be measured in millions of dollars, regardless of how high we carry the count. It saved an industry that has been the mainstay of modern Hawaii — a Hawaii that brings about rich advances in Pacific better-ment; developments that are cultural, sociological, industrial, scientific in character."

Once this entomological crisis was past, the planters looked forward to a long period of peace and prosperity. But it was not to be. They were suddenly faced with evi-dence of sabotage of the most destructive and insidious kind. A borer beetle, one of the minor pests of sugar since 1865, went on the rampage. In the 'seventies when the total output of Island sugar was about 8,000 tons, the damage wrought by the borer seemed less significant, but when its operations began to cost a couple of million dollars annually, the planters were suitably alarmed. This large sum of money was not exactly hay, but it was certainly a vast amount of "frass," the polite entomological term for the cane fiber passing through the borer larvae as an excremental issue.

The beetle is often called the bill-bug because it has an elongated bill or beak, at the end of which are minute but very powerful jaws by which it champs its way through the outer rind and into the fiber of the cane. The only conces-sion the bill-bug made to the enervating effect of the Hawaiian climate was that it preferred to bore through the softer varieties of cane, which readily break down when weakened by this tunneling. Some fields lost half their crops by this form of boring from within. By careful observation the entomologists determined that a half-grown larva tun-neled two inches a day, which means that with an average life cycle of 81 days, each borer got through 13 feet 6 inches of cane stalk, depositing its frass behind it as it worked.

Koebele studied the sex and other habits of the borer until her life became an open book. Her generative life extended over six months, during which time she laid an average of 6 eggs a day, or roughly 1,000 in all. This meant such a reproductive multitude that the planters paid a bonus of 10 cents an ounce for beetles, 300 to the ounce. Bug fishing became a paying proposition, the bait being strips of fermented cane on which the beetles gathered overnight. One plantation paid for over one million bugs in a single year.

Like our other enemies, the borer came from the Far East. Its presence had been recorded in Queensland, Fiji, New Guinea, New Ireland, and Tahiti. It preferred sugar cane, but would also attack the coconut, royal and cabbage palms, and even the banana.

Apparently the entomologists were desperate, for their investigations took strange turns. They gravely announced that larvae survived 27 hours' complete immersion in water. The only person who could possibly have been interested in such a conclusion would have been Noah, since no one else could envisage a flood that would immerse the standing cane.

There seemed nothing else to do but to send scouts into the jungle highways and byways looking for the natural enemies of the bill-bugs, and Dr. Muir took up the search. It took him into strange places like the Federated Malay States, where the bug collector may himself be collected by a tiger, or gored by a gaur (a wild ox, also known as the seladang), or swallowed by a python. He lived in towns such as Pontianak in West Borneo, where the land was so flat that though it took nine hours' steam up a mangrove-lined river to reach there, yet the tide put a couple of feet of water around the stilts on which the houses were built.

But like a true entomologist, Muir had eyes only for insects, recording such things as the thousands of fireflies keeping time in their light pulsations so that clouds of them swept like comets across the mangroves. He mentions most casually the capture of a 15-foot python in his host's henhouse, but gets quite excited over the intestinal worms it contained. Entomologists are like that. On jungle journeys he wore pajamas and tennis shoes — it was easier to scrape off the leeches. His travels took him through Dyak villages, where the only road led up a notched tree trunk onto a long platform lined with houses, and down again into the jungle.

He did not feel that these head-hunting Dyaks attended to business very well. "The only heads they were keen on getting," he writes, "were Queen Wilhelmina's stamped on a silver coin." Probably the Dyaks, like the Chinese bandits, thought the head of such a crazy fool wasn't worth collecting.

Finally, the search narrowed down to the island of Amboina, 1,500 miles east of Java, but six weeks' search there failed to reveal any parasites. Six days' steam from Amboina was another promising island, and there, on Larat, Muir found the borers, both in the cane and in the sago palm. The steamy swamps and jungles almost made him complain. "Working in the sago," he said, "meant standing in ten inches of water. Mosquitoes used to often drive me away, even when I had my head covered with a net." But Muir went on splitting sago palms and infinitives impartially, finding thousands of borers but no parasites.

However, discovering the borer larvae in the sago palms provided a clue, and Muir hurried back to Amboina, in the sago swamps of which he found the borer grubs being parasitized by a tachinid fly. But attempt after attempt to get the flies alive to Honolulu failed. So Muir moved to Port Moresby in New Guinea and raised a generation of flies and borers there. The next stop was in North Queensland where the process was repeated. In the meantime, Muir came down with typhoid fever and the flies, left in charge of a man without proper experience, died. At last a third generation was raised in Fiji and though Muir was now suffering from malaria, he made the last trip to Honolulu, arriving with the flies and borers whose great-grandparents he had collected in Amboina. If there were any Victoria Cross awards in entomological warfare, then Muir richly deserved one. The ravages of the borers were soon checked, although the battle was not over. Other scientists such as Pemberton and Williams took up the task of finding parasites, though it was not until 1937 when Lyons' work

in developing cane varieties with harder rinds finally discouraged the borers. Perhaps they too were imbued with
the "no pilikia" spirit and gave up when boring became
difficult.

If this were the story of entomological science in Hawaii,
the tale could go on indefinitely. Perhaps mention should
be made of another Nipponese menace, the Japanese or
anomala beetle. To combat this, a tropical toad called *Bufo
marinus* was imported from the West Indies, proving that
the East and West can meet in Hawaii. The toads have taken
care of the centipedes as well as the beetles, though the
frog mortality due to traffic accidents has been very heavy.
The number squashed by automobiles on rainy nights was
at first prodigious.

Army worms, cutworms, Chinese grasshoppers, mealy
bugs, sugar aphis, are just a few of our invading enemies and
for each the pattern of defense is the same; careful scouting
of growing cane, identification of new pests and assessment
of damage all carried on through crop reconnaissance. Next
comes the work of G-2, an extensive search through all the
literature and records of museums, and the collection of
every scrap of information available as to the insect's life
habits, together with war maps of all the localities where it
has been reported, and if possible the locating of its original
habitat. The expedition then goes out to find a place where
the pest exists, but under biological control. Then comes
the search for the insect's "death factors" and the collection
of its natural enemies. But before any of these can be
enlisted as allies and imported to Hawaii, the entomological
F.B.I. goes to work to make sure that the present ally will
not turn into a potential enemy. Last comes the breeding
and multiplication of the assisted immigrants and their distribution to the front-line trenches. As we have seen, these
operations may take twenty years before a particular foe
is beaten.

The parallel between the H.S.P.A. and a military staff

command with its divisions of supply, operations, intelligence, etc., will not have escaped the reader. The chief difference between the civilian and military organizations is that while the Army's most intensive activities are for the duration of war, the H.S.P.A. is never at peace. For, of course, there are many more problems confronting them than scientific pest control. Manpower, equipment, finance, marketing, logistics, fertilizer supplies, irrigation, are a few of these problems, with public relations perhaps their greatest headache. The sugar industry is through with its growing pains but gall bladder trouble, appendicitis pains, and intestinal obstructions worry it quite a bit internally. The necessity too that the H.S.P.A. feels of keeping one ear to the ground in Hawaii and the other open in Washington would pose a difficult problem for any organization.

But these things trouble the scientific staff but little. Their concern is to keep a highly selected personnel ready to go to the ends of the earth at a moment's notice. Fortunately they have behind them the resources and good will of a scientific U.N.O. that knows no local bounds or restrictions. Everyone in the Islands gets his living directly or indirectly from agriculture, and that means that no one in Hawaii has need to be sold on entomological research.

The alert against invasion of these islands has continued so long, and is implemented in so many ways, that it is now easy to understand why a policy of preparedness against even the most remote danger was acceptable. Similarly, it was no part of H.S.P.A. policy to depend on other protectors, or to entrust its security to the watchfulness of other organizations, no matter how powerful they might be. Furthermore, it recognized fully our vulnerability, and that entirely new combinations of perils to industry in these islands may appear tomorrow. Thus the idea of community defense against hostile powers was by no means a new one in these islands. The sugar people had been in the business of defending the Territory against devastating insect in-

vaders and sabotage for forty years. Why should it not be
alert to danger from other enemies?

CHAPTER VII

Defend What Island?

IN A PREVIOUS chapter we had occasion
to cast our eyes to the Far East, to note
not only the thunder clouds visibly gathering there, but also
the reactions of those people, who, living much closer to the
danger point than we in Hawaii, watched the dark masses
grow, hoping that they would dissolve or pass by. We
dwelt on this situation in order to point the contrast with
our own preparedness, and to discover the factors that contributed to our readiness to be alerted against what seemed
to be a remote contingency. Now it is necessary, before we
attempt to describe the details of that civilian planning and
foresight, to turn in the other direction, and reconstruct, if
only in the barest outline, the sequence of events in Europe.

In early 1940, though this was still two worlds, having
not yet been fused into one by the fierce alchemy of war,
the barometers that were foretelling the universal storm
were rapidly falling. The great disturbance was still centered
over Western Europe. But those who looked at the glass,
eyed it bodingly. How could a strife so intensive, so all
inclusive in its tremendous human issues, be expected to
stay within its bounds! Midway in the year, the fatal events
of May and June indicated that the hurricane was working
itself up to a climax of fury, whose center must soon shift
from Europe to the Atlantic, and would then, almost in-
evitably extend into the already darkling Pacific. Would
another storm arise there and coalesce with the first, or
would the European conflict engulf the world? The answer

to this question was not of extreme importance. Whether the tempest hit us from East or West, we should be in it anyway.

For, suddenly, defeat and confusion had almost over- whelmed the Allied cause, culminating in Dunkirk, at once the most disastrous and the most glorious event in British military history. Churchill announced to the British parlia- ment losses amounting to thirty thousand killed, wounded, and missing, by no means as serious as in the Battle of the Somme in World War I, but because of the special circum- stances an almost crippling blow. "But," added Churchill, "our losses in material are enormous . . . all our transport, all the armored vehicles that were with the Army of the North," and, in addition, one thousand pieces of almost irreplaceable mobile artillery. In spite of the near-miracle of the extrication of the army from the German trap, the blow to British prestige was terribly heavy.

On June 10th, Italy declared war on France and Britain, and four days later the Germans occupied Paris. In America, *Life* magazine published a picture that even after these years of struggle and victory is etched unmistakably in memory — Hitler, like some vulture of evil, doing that stiff-legged fiendishly gleeful dance when the news of the fall of France reached him. Was it a dance of death to usher in the extinction of freedom in the world?

You will remember, too, that it was the same speech of Churchill's, announcing Dunkirk, that signified one of the most remarkable reversals of history. The year 1776 was the date of the American Declaration of Independence from England; 1940, only 164 years later, brought about the British Declaration of Dependence on America, preceded, however, by some of the most stirring words that were ever uttered by the leader of a great people in its darkest hour. "We shall defend our island," he cried, "whatever the cost may be. We shall fight on the beaches, we shall fight on the landing grounds, we shall fight in the fields and in the streets, we shall fight in the hills; we shall never surrender, and even if, which I do not for a moment believe, this Island or a large part of it were subjugated or starving, then our Empire beyond the seas, armed and guarded by the British fleet, would carry on the struggle until, in God's good time, the New World with all its power and might steps forth to the rescue and liberation of the Old." [1]

In the meantime, while Churchill's defiance was still ringing in the ears and hearts of all the friends of democracy, the clouds of invasion were threatening England. The battle of France was now over, the British leader declared, but the battle of Britain was just about to begin. At the same time, the Pacific horizon lightened somewhat. The British, sensible of their impending crisis at home, thought it necessary to placate the increasingly cocky and truculent Japanese. They agreed to close the Burma Road to all traffic in munitions to China for three months.

With all the crises happily behind us and the victory won, it is hard for us to realize the anxieties and misgivings of those 1940 days. The whole nation was in a state of mental conflict, trying to determine which was the more dangerous, to stay out or get into the war. For the first time the fatuousness of the "it can't happen here" faith was becoming somewhat apparent. Some stirrings of trepidation assailed us as we began to realize that if we fought at all in the Pacific, we must fight practically alone. Australia and New Zealand had sent many of their best troops to battle in Greece, Crete, and Africa; the French were a source of weakness rather than strength; Britain had her hands more than full; Dutch determination could be counted on, but their defensive dispositions in the N.E.I. were weak and their military strength was of little account. If any nation took upon itself to bar Japanese expansion southward it must be the American people. Our responsibility would be a grave and difficult one.

[1] Churchill, Winston. *Blood, Sweat, and Tears.*

To a few people in this happy-go-lucky, on *pilikia* clime, came the sick realization that it could be our islands that might be attacked, it might be on our beaches and in our hills where we must fight. Nothing was wholly dependable, not even defense by distance, nor the might of our armed forces. Reputedly the finest, the best professionally trained army in the world had been powerless to save France from destruction. It had stood just about five weeks of intensive assault. Poland, Norway, Holland, Belgium, Greece, Yugoslavia, France — the pattern of Nazi conquest had been the same in each case. Was Hitler the world's greatest military genius or were the new mechanisms of war, the tanks, the mobile artillery, so vastly superior that courage and manpower were outmoded? The civilian leaders of Hawaii looked about them questioningly. Perhaps it was unwise to depend so utterly on our professional defenders. Was not Hawaii in the position that it had found itself with regard to enemy insect invasions, forced to take matters into its own hands, and plan its own contributions to defense?

The military, in their thinking, had come to regard such a suggestion favorably. They too had been thunderstruck with the happenings on the battlefields of Europe. It was natural for them to accept very wholeheartedly the view so commonly advanced in news reports, namely, that these European countries were rotten at the core, that internal strife and doubtful loyalty behind the lines accounted for weakness and collapse. Sabotage became the great bugbear and fifth-column activities the military scapegoat for defeat. If these things could happen to France because of internal subversions, what would happen in Hawaii — where one-third of the total population was Japanese, including a very large number who, as dual citizens, at best divided their allegiance, at worst owed it to the country with which we might soon be at war. Thus again, in Hawaii, sabotage became the mouse under the bed, whose presence overshadowed all other dangers.

Civilian disquiet over the world situation found expression in a meeting called at the Mayor's office, which businessmen and community leaders attended and discussed the serious outlook. This meeting was called on July 8, 1940, three days after the Petain government had broken relations with Britain, thus emphasizing the gravity of the latter country's position. A major disaster affecting these islands though unlikely, was possible, and the advisability of preparing plans to meet it seemed to deserve some consideration. The nature of this disaster was set forth by a sub-committee that met on July 16th. The dangers envisaged in order of imminence or likelihood were, "sabotage during the period of strained relations; war with its attendant possibilities of partial blockade; blockade; bombardment; bombing; landing of parachute troops; landing of major boats or troops." In view of later developments, it is interesting to note that the declaration of martial law was even then anticipated. The military leaders, still obsessed with the threat of sabotage, thought of no other means of civilian control.

Then one of the strangest things in the history of the war happened. For some almost inexplicable reasons, alarm subsided. God knows there was no more ground for optimism at the end of 1940 than there had been six months previously. Because the blow did not fall at once, men were deluded into thinking that the sword no longer hung in air. Our Major Disaster Committee having set forth the dangers, and passed the appropriate resolutions, went home. It was not until nine months after the conception of the idea — the usual gestation period — that the Major Disaster Council was finally born, its birth certificate having been signed by the Honolulu Board of Supervisors on April 26, 1941. It was this Council that did all the preliminary planning and took matters in hand before the Office of Civilian Defense (O.C.D.) began functioning under the Territorial M-day law.

That no Caesarean operation was deemed necessary, and

that the scheme for local defense could afford to proceed beyond even the normal period of pregnancy, can be related to the strange public habit of not only clutching at straws but trusting to them as a life-raft. There is a queer community blindness that prevents a people even on the brink of destruction from believing the truth about its own condition. Just as panic can be communicated to a crowd, so also there is a false courage that resides in mere numbers, even though they be unarmed. In fact it is only when this faith in multitude fails that panic ensues. So long as the attacks of its enemies are confined to the fringes, the great school of fish or the herd of buffalo or the crowd of men go unconcernedly on their way. Only when fear strikes to the heart of the mass does flight or stampede follow. It is one of the strangest psychological phenomena observable that isolationism is a factor of gregariousness. In other terms, the most narrowly self-sufficient views are to be found at the geographical centers of population. It is explicable on the grounds that there are two kinds of partial blindness — one which cannot see the forest for the trees, and the other which cannot see the trees for the forest. Isolationists suffer from the first type of clouded vision. The most outstanding characteristic of any great aggregation of living creatures is its mass stupidity.

One straw at which we clutched hopefully in late 1940 was the unsuspected toughness of the British defense. England survived the intensive air assaults of August and September, and the spirit of her people was still unquenched despite the destruction in her cities. The great spokesman of this time was not slow to seize on this for verbal inspiration. In February 1941, Churchill was able to declare:

"We stood our ground and faced the two Dictators in the hour of what seemed their overwhelming triumph, and we have shown ourselves capable, so far, of standing up against them alone. . . . We have broken the back of winter. The daylight grows." And to America he optimistically said, "Give us the tools, and we will finish the job."

At this time, there seemed grounds for confidence. The Italian Army had been soundly drubbed in Libya and turned out of Abyssinia. The Greeks were putting up an heroic resistance and Churchill was already turning a strategical eye toward the soft under-belly of Europe, into which might be directed the spearhead of effective attack.

But by the end of this same February the barometer of public confidence fell quite alarmingly. Japanese truculence reached a new pitch. Their lower house was assured by its Government leaders that they had every confidence that her Nan-Yo, or southern expansionist policy, could be pushed without extreme national risk. Japan's navy had already decided on its counter-measures if either the United States or Britain, or both, stood in its way.

Moreover, America's decision to spend four million on the defenses of Guam was, according to Vice-Admiral Toyada, plain evidence of her intention to encircle Japan. Such pronouncements fitted exactly into the pattern that Nazi aggression had made so familiar in Europe — bluster and threats alternating with hysterical complaints of strangulation and encirclement. The parallel was complete when Japan, on behalf of poor little bullied and injured Thailand, sent an ultimatum to the French in Indo-China. The Japanese press excitedly reported movements of British and Chinese troops into Burma, another evidence of encirclement. Next the war of nerves was intensified by Tokyo's announcement that her naval forces were moving south, and that her nationals were beginning an evacuation from threatened points. The French, of course, were in no mood for bullying anybody, unless it were her former allies, and on March 1st ceded two provinces to Thailand, thus vindicating Japan's assumption of the role of the champion of the oppressed.

Then followed another familiar move — a conference of the aggressors. Matsuoka, the Foreign Minister, would go to Rome and Berlin, to confer with Hitler and Mussolini, confirming the immutability of the Tripartite Pact. Trouble was at the moment brewing for Yugoslavia, and the question of invoking the pact and transforming it into an active alliance was discussed, if either that country or the United States should enter the European war. The Japanese talked of naval and military intervention in Africa, if these things should happen. On April 2nd, the "Tatutu Maru" carried back 390 Japanese from America to Japan, and these were joined by 250 "tourists" from Honolulu. Eight hundred Japanese nationals were also evacuated from Panama because of restrictive conditions.

Here was the handwriting on the wall so plain that anyone could read, except Senators Wheeler and Nye and their extensive following in the safe, well-insulated, but least isolated areas of continental America. Suddenly there was a great flurry of "co-ordination of defenses" in the Far East. Brookes-Popham, British commander-in-chief, conferred with Admiral Hart in Manila, and later visited the Dutch possessions on a trip of inspection of what was beginning to be known as the A-B-C-D defense and which proved later to be about as alphabetical in its simplicity. In the opinion of the civic leaders of Hawaii the time had come to gird ourselves, and to marshal every resource in our own support. The fog of uncertainty as to what islands must be defended was visibly lessening. The major disaster was rapidly getting beyond the committee discussion stage. It was a dire threat to our whole people. By April 4th the Mayor of Honolulu decided that the Major Disaster Committee must be swiftly reconvened and set to work.

By the time the ordinance setting up the Council was approved on April 26th, everyone who had any thinking capacity was fully seized with the need for hurry. Germany had invaded Yugoslavia on April 6th and five days later, with characteristic Hitlerian bombast, had announced that the Yugoslav Army as an organized fighting force had ceased to exist. And, characteristically, Hitler was right.

But the most disturbing threat of all, from Hawaii's viewpoint, has not yet been mentioned. On April the thirteenth — unlucky day — Russia and Japan signed their five-year neutrality pact. The same month the head of the Agricultural Extension Service of the University left Hawaii for Washington to arrange for the purchase of 15,000 tons of rice, 6,000 tons of wheat and flour, 2,500 tons of canned milk, 1,500 tons of fats, all of which represented six months' supplies of staple foods for the population. About the same time, prompted by the army commander, General Herron, an H.S.P.A. committee urged all householders to make room on the shelves of warehouses and stores, by purchasing and storing large quantities of vital foodstuffs. The call was heeded, and many citizens hastened to stock cupboards and storerooms with canned goods. This committee was the Diversified Crops Committee of the H.S.P.A., which since 1935 had carried on a continuous and thorough-going evolution of plans and study for the relief of an if-and-when situation, the blockade partial or complete of these islands in the event of war with Japan. Supplying our population with food would then indeed be a crucial problem.

At first thought, the matter of making an agricultural community such as Hawaii self-sustaining would seem to be a simple one. It would be, anywhere else in the world, but this Territory is only agricultural under the most unique conditions. The success of the sugar and pineapple growers has effectually masked those conditions.

In the first place, it is an undeniable fact that Hawaii is not naturally suited for general agriculture and only the best scientific knowledge combined with efficient industry has made our sugar production profitable. The climate and rainfall vary so much within such narrow geographical limits that it is difficult to find any large area where optimal conditions prevail. It has been calculated that for every pound of sugar in the sugar bowl, four thousand pounds of water must be used on the plantation. Hence irrigation on a large scale is entirely necessary. On Oahu most of this water must be pumped from underground.

But the popular conception of our Hawaiian soil as being of tropical richness, waiting only for water to put forth a riot of growth, is widely astray. If not reinforced with abundant fertilizer, it is doubtful whether the sugar lands could keep more than a single plantation mill going on each island. Any old photograph of the original Hawaiian landscape will show why this is so. Here was no jungle vegetation, dropping its leaves for countless centuries to build a great depth of humus, but bare hills and treeless plains. Only above the levels where sugar can be profitably grown did the forest commence. As much as a ton and a half of fertilizer is needed on a single acre. Thus stimulated and enriched, this acre may produce 150 tons of cane, which in turn boils down to from 8 to 12 tons of sugar. Thus the Hawaiian sugar industry is both bottle and spoon fed.

Someone asked a famous English painter with what he mixed his paints. "With brains, sir," was the reply. So too the production of sugar requires a considerable admixture of the same rare and precious material. Engineers, busily planning labor-saving machinery or plotting water tunnels and irrigation pumps, soil physiologists and analysts, plant geneticists, plant pathologists, entomologists, chemists, together make up an army of technologists enlisted in this service, and no single group could drop out of the picture without disaster to the industry. The pineapple people are in the same boat. We have already seen what the contribution of the entomologists is and how vital their work. If it takes a man with a green thumb, as they say, to make a successful horticulturist, then it takes green brains to grow sugar.

If then the production of Hawaii's major crop is such

a complex process, what are the difficulties in the way of growing other food plants that supply the ordinary menu of people on the mainland. The matter was put in a nutshell by Dr. Lyon, head of the H.S.P.A. Experiment Station, in a letter dealing with the problem of supplying this community with home-grown food. "Hawaii," he wrote, "is tropical and its fields are not suitable to the cultivation of temperate zone crops." The proof of the cabbage is in the growing, and this is how Lyon sums up the situation: "Anyone undertaking the production of truck crops in Hawaii on a scale sufficient to satisfy the local demand for these crops is embarking on a course that will lead to financial disaster." After the emergency had passed, these truck gardeners could not compete with mainland growers. Up to the present it has always paid Hawaii to import most of its food, and any emergency production would require financial underwriting by the Federal Government, which prior to the war, showed no disposition to do any such thing.

But of course in the face of possible mass starvation through a total blockade, profits would be of little or no account. No matter how financially disastrous the setting up of an extensive food raising project might be, it would have to be undertaken with or without Federal support. The H.S.P.A. had no illusions about either the necessity or the difficulty of the task, for the matter had been previously considered in 1917, when a similar emergency threatened. The problem of planning to meet it had been turned over to the Experiment Station whose staff prepared a "Food Number" of the *Hawaiian Planters Record*. The gist of the matter was thus stated in June 1917. "There is no doubt but that Hawaii can feed herself. If compelled to do so, beans and sweet potatoes must be her 'staff of life.'" Fortunately that crisis passed, but emergency was again in sight and the H.S.P.A. again set up its Diversified Crops Committee to tackle the same old problem. But now, however, it was much more complicated. The civilian population of Hawaii had grown from 225,000 in 1917 to over 465,000 in 1941, of whom 310,500 were on the island of Oahu alone.

The "Food Number" sets forth the food products that were imported into the Territory in 1916 — over a million dollars' worth each of rice, meat products, flour, and animal feed. Six million eggs were also brought in, the total value of imported food amounting to over $8,500,000. The publication set forth the crops from which carbohydrates are obtained, those which are rich in proteins and the sources of fats. Data regarding the growing of cow peas, pigeon peas, peanuts, were also given, with a section on the combating of insect pests, use of fertilizers and long contributions on the nutritive values of foods, dietary standards, etc. In fact, the "Food Number" seemed to be long on what you should do with the food when you had it, but rather short on telling how and where it could be obtained. Any people who had starved in 1917 would at least have had the satisfaction of knowing in scientific detail how they got that way.[2]

[2] There are, however, several tidbits of knowledge in this publication that ought to be preserved. A clay soil, it seems, "may be changed to a friable clay loam by a little work and brains." "But," the article adds, "horse and cow manure give best results." If this is the case, it seems a pity to waste the brains. As to work, the writer of the contribution on market-garden crops seems to think little of it. "A piece of heavy clay on this Island," he says, "has produced fine crops of lettuce and other vegetables after having had sawdust thoroughly spaded in to the depth of about one foot." Rather than undertake such spade work, many no doubt would forego their lettuce.

I am also very much puzzled over the activities of the melon fly, which attacks the cucumbers. The entomologist tells us that "a sweetened poisoned bait has been used to spray on the vines for protection, the flies visiting the vines feeding on this and dying before laying their eggs." Apart from the rich participial content of this sentence, I consider this posthumous egg-laying by the melon fly quite clever, possibly a last convulsive effort. But most intriguing of all the volume's contents is a recipe for cow pea cookery that is called "Hopping John." Who John is, or why a mixture of cow peas, rice, and two tablespoonfuls of butter should make him hop is not explained. Any family that possesses a John might try it.

Having all this interesting information at their disposal, the 1935 Committee on Diversified Crops did not exactly start from scratch. They worked in close relationship with the Emergency Food Committee of the Pineapple Producers' Cooperative Association and with their thirteen subcommittees, plus three inter-island committees, performed a tremendous amount of study. They issued a mimeographed, legal sized, inches-thick report, covering every possible phase of the subject of food production. The whole effort was a splendid example of the kind of large-scale co-operation common in Hawaii. Not only were the Experiment Station scientists fully engaged but all members of the staff of the University Experiment Station were members of the various subcommittees in their particular spheres of knowledge or skill. The Army was also represented.

It is impossible to present anything but the scantiest review of these years of labor and thought. The committee's "basic plan" was predicated on a possible total blockade so that the whole civilian population must be fed, the principle as enunciated being, "If prepared for the worst, any lesser emergency can be easily handled," civilian thinking in this respect being somewhat ahead of military thought. One form of the plan envisaged the complete isolation of Oahu with its 310,500 people. In a letter to the Governor dated June 19, 1941, Dr. H. L. Lyon, chairman of the committee, sets forth the main features of the food production program.

As he points out, a life-sustaining diet requires proteins, but while our standards crops are notoriously rich in carbohydrates, they are very low in protein. Like other plants, sugar cane, pineapples, and bananas manufacture their own protein out of carbohydrates but make little of it available in their useable products. Beans, however, store protein in their seeds, and dry yeast is 50 per cent protein. Hence being unable to make our protein as the plants do, we should have to rely on beans and yeast. These might satisfy nutritional requirements but would certainly add to inflation. The best thing about yeast is that it can be grown in a weak sugar solution, and the H.S.P.A had already established a pilot plant.

But people who are used to varying their diet with meat, milk, and eggs would not be content with beans and yeast, which are hardly eaten with gusto. Hence we must grow forage crops for cattle, root crops for hogs, and seed crops for poultry. The emergency diet worked out by the nutritionists and animal husbanders allowed for one egg every five days, to be included in the average daily allowance of 2,600 calories.

But as we have seen, these essential crops will not grow overnight and each requires excessive coddling. It would take six months before they could reach full production. So in the meantime, food for humans and feed for livestock would have to be purchased and stored to take us over the interim. This would require an outlay of $2,500,000, and no one seemed to have any ideas as to where this money was to come from, in addition to the other $2,500,000 it would take to implement the Basic Plan. The amount of fertilizer that would be required was truly tremendous — about $800,000 worth. As for seeds, that too was a load of staggering proportions. The Maui Emergency Food Committee themselves seemed to be impressed with the magnitude of the task, for as they remark, "The total imported seed required comes to 25,072 tons. This is a large order, and when added to the requirements of the other islands becomes enormous."[3] So enormous is this amount, that in my ignorance I thought — why bother planting; let the Maui people eat the seed. There are only 52,000 of them and surely half a ton of seed each should last them for the duration, especially if all the livestock were killed off.

The report itself provides an irrefutable proof that the

[3] *Emergency Production Plan for Islands and Territory.* Appendix, Sect. V-A (2), Page 2.

matter of getting down to earth is apparently one of the most complicated processes known to man. I would not recommend the report for week-end reading. I have perused it conscientiously, becoming more astounded at every page, not only at the number of words agriculturists know, but, seriously speaking, at the evidence of well-coordinated effort, which is truly amazing. I am sure that there was never a plan more thorough and detailed in conception nor supported with more conscientious and painstaking studies.

The net outcome of all this work was practically nothing, and the disappointment felt by the Committee is modestly veiled in a letter from the Committee's chairman to the H.S.P.A. On August 11, 1941, Dr. Lyon, after summarizing the Territory's needs in the way of seed, fertilizers, pest control supplies, food for livestock and fuel oil to pump the water needed, wrote as follows: "The Diversified Crops Committee has repeatedly pointed out the absolute necessity of obtaining these essentials prior to the emergency, but no steps are being taken to provide them. Lacking these essentials, the Committee's plans cannot be executed so it will have but wasted time in making them."

As it happened no food emergency arose. Except for the first few weeks of war, we were not blockaded either partially or completely. The Army and Navy were able to bring down great stocks of food. It would be ungrateful to say that we fed like Lazarus on the crumbs from the generals' table. We can, however, cheerfully admit that the civilian population not only lived, but lived well, for the duration. The military very wisely handed over the problem of provisioning Oahu to a very efficient civilian committee under the chairmanship of Mr. H. A. Walker.

But this, it should be noted, amounted to no more than a policy of muddling through, such as we accuse the British of pursuing in their national crises. The Battle of Midway *might* have gone the other way. If so the fleet base would have been withdrawn to San Francisco, and we should have been left to our own devices. Had this happened we should have been happy indeed to have had the Emergency Food Plan in operation, for of food there would soon have been little or none. Perhaps it was fool's luck which saved us.

CHAPTER VIII

Island Alert

WE HAVE already noted the wave of fear that touched these shores in July 1940, and its subsequent subsidence until the events of the following April roused us again to the imminence of war. Apparently the whole world was engrossed in the struggle for Britain, so engrossed that to many it seemed that nothing was worth doing or planning until that contest had been decided. It was much more than sympathy for the British, genuine as that may have been; it was the realization that if Britain fell, the United States would stand alone, facing two great aggressor nations on a dual front. Self preservation was dominant in our thoughts.

While the battle of Britain was at its height and things looked blackest for Britain, the U.S. took a long step nearer war when it transferred 50 over-age destroyers to help in the battle of the Atlantic. The date of the change of flags for this fleet was September 3rd, and it was in this same fateful month that Japan joined with the Germans and Italians in the Tripartite Pact. But the months passed and still we were not at war. In February, Churchill could speak confidently of the heavy defeats of the German air force; of the victories in Libya and Egypt; of the vast flow of munitions from across the Atlantic and of the lessening of the danger of invasion of England, unless it came as a last desperate stroke. "But," he said, "I must drop one word of caution; for, next to cowardice and treachery, over-confidence, leading to neglect or slothfulness, is the worst of martial crimes." Would that these words had been heeded here!

It is only fair to point out that the letdown that affected this community in the six months between October 1940 and April 1941 was by no means universal nor complete. The plans which had been so hastily discussed in July of the former year took root in at least one important instance. The Oahu Sugar Plantation Managers met with the police and military authorities and decided to set up a Home Guard, to be known as the Provisional Police. Realizing that it must be a concerted plantation effort, the managers appointed one of their number, Mr. T. G. S. Walker, as co-ordinator. He was to work up plans to meet any emergency, such as "sudden and unpredicted overt acts by disloyal inhabitants, whether accompanied or not by hostile 'blitz-krieg' from air or sea." A memo from the co-ordinator to the managers warned that this planning should be re-garded as purely precautionary and "does not necessarily denote a belief that such an emergency is near or even bound to come." But the managers were taking no chances, and on August 6th at a meeting held at the H.S.P.A. rooms, the Provisional Police Plan was approved. The burden thus shouldered was by no means a light one and General Herron hastened to convey his thanks for what he termed "splendid co-operation."

Though not attempting in any way to detract from the sugar men's foresight, we might point out, first of all, that it was the plantations' own property which was of military importance and therefore should be guarded; secondly it was immeasurably easier to organize plantation personnel for war service than the general population. The set-up of a plantation resembles a pyramid with the manager at the apex. Some have seen in its structure a resemblance to a fascist regime, but it is no more so than the organization of any large industrial concern, except that its base in terms of unskilled labor is very broad. It is, however, semi-military, with an officer corps under a field commander directing large bodies of rank and file. Such an organization, when a crisis approaches, is not likely to be content with passing resolutions; they get things done. It is not surprising there-fore that the plans for the Provisional Police were soon set in order, with the whole of rural Oahu divided into five dis-tricts, each of these being again subdivided into a number of "beats," covering all essential installations or locations where sabotage might be successful. In order to make clear to the reader's mind what was to be defended, some descrip-tion of the island's topography is necessary.

Oahu, on which Honolulu is situated, was in its first development two islands, formed by submarine eruptions along a ridge extending northwest by southeast underneath the sea. The older island had as its backbone the Waianae Range, culminating at Mount Kaala, its highest point. The second island arose along a crack about 20 miles to the east of the first line of eruption, and paralleling it, with its ends overlapping the first island both to the north and the south. After the first crack stopped erupting the second continued, sending down to the southwest successive lava flows which finally filled up the strait and ponded against the eastern slopes of Kaala and the Waianaes, thus forming one island out of two. A deep gulch, called Kaukonahua near Waialua, follows in part the line of junction between the two land masses.

The map of Oahu looks like the head of a game cock with its beak at Kaena Point, its comb at Kahuku, and its wattles at Barber's Point. The southwest slope of the Waianae backbone is to leeward and the mountains send down several sharp spines to the sea, each of them a red or terra-cotta ridge with sharply fractured edges where one-time torrents have cut deep valleys. The sides of these valleys, dry and rough with prickly pear, are arid and grim in the noonday heat, but beautiful when the sunset colors are imprisoned there. In an elbow of the range, the streams have made a fertile fill large enough to accommodate the small plantation and village of Waianae. Here, in one of the deepest valleys, the military made haste to put most of their oil and ammunition underground. Erosion of the mountain chain has also created a pass, called Kole Kole, meaning the red earth mountain. Through this, if the sentries will allow it, you may drive down to Schofield, the great military post.

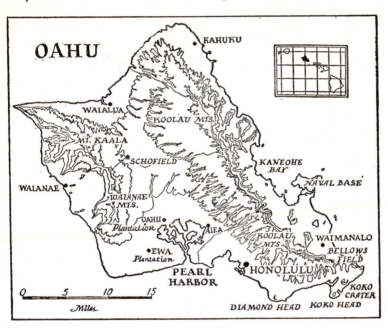

Farther to the southeast the Waianae Range, showing no longer the broken edges of lava flows, is represented by a bare ridge, here deserving of the title of "red earth." Indeed Kole Kole is a better name for the mountains than Waianae, which means good mullet water and applies to the region off shore. This terminal ridge falls short of the sea by a mile or two and marks the western boundary of the coastal plain.

Into this plain is set the fretsaw outline of Pearl Harbor with its long narrow neck and the irregular indenting of the east and west lochs. Because the Waianae mountain barrier

fails to join the sea is the reason why the long beaches
stretching past Nanakuli down to Barber's Point are militarily important. An enemy force, landed and established
there, could move in on the left flank of Pearl Harbor's defenses. So the big guns of Fort Weaver have been placed
in position to command the approaches to these beaches.
In the early days of Oahu's war games, before we en-
countered the real thing, this stretch of coast was the scene
of many a simulated invasion. This was before the days of
"ducks" and similar amphibious landing craft.

The western extension of the coastal plain is occupied
by Ewa Plantation, minus those areas that have been taken
up by huge landing fields, gun positions, forts, and sprawl-
ing military cantonments, now nearly empty. What was
originally a bare and dusty plain is now covered with the
bright green of sugar cane, overlaid in places with a light
mask of silver grey where fields are in tassel. This transfor-
mation has been wrought by millions of gallons of water
pumped daily from the artesian basin underground. The
land owes its richness to the fact that this whole coastal plain
lies in the wash between the Waianaes and the Koolaus,
receiving the silt from both ranges at a time when rainfall
in the islands must have been much heavier than now. The
Koolau Mountains, though they are only from two to three
thousand feet in elevation, stand squarely athwart the northeast trades; hence the precipitation in the wettest areas is
three to four hundred inches annually. The Koolaus shade
the lower end of the Waianae Range so that Schofield is
comparatively dry and Ewa with only 20 inches is decidedly
so. Kaala Mountain, being the highest land in the Waianaes,
catches more of the trade wind precipitation, and has a two-
to three-hundred-inch rainfall.

From Pearl Harbor at the southern end of the slot between the two heights of land, the ground rises gradually
until it reaches a thousand-foot elevation near Schofield and
Wahiawa. Oahu and Honolulu plantations both abut on

Pearl Harbor, but the more level lands of the Schofield plateau are given over to pineapples.

The picture looking up from Pearl Harbor to Schofield
is not of a plateau but of an almost level plain, filled from
side to side with a light green wash of sugar cane; but the
plain is an optical illusion. Aviators who have tried to lift
heavy-laden planes from Hickam to fly them straight across
to Schofield soon know that there is a 900-foot rise in their
way.

If its sides dropped down to the sea, this height of land
would be apparent; but cupped between the gaps and eminences of the Waianae Mountains on one side and the
gradual slope to the distant cloudhung bank of the Koolaus
on the other, the elevation disappears. To swoop down in
the opposite direction from Schofield over Hickam and
Pearl Harbor is easy, as the Japanese found on December 7th.

The smoothness of contour looking to the eastern rim of
the apparent plain is also illusion, for traveling over this area
you will find it deeply cut into by a succession of gulches —
Kipapa, Waikakaloa, Wahiawa — the products of a thousand centuries of stream erosion. Only when the Koolaus
bend to face the south and the sea, do the deeply scored
valleys, often shrouded in grey drifts of rain, give the on-
looker the impression of a rough, barely accessible mountain
mass. But God pity the hapless hiker who tries to traverse
these ranges without benefit of carefully-graded trails.

Waialua Plantation occupies the seaward slopes at the
northern end of the slot and devotes part of its land to pineapple culture. The main island highway dips down off the
plateau to the village of Haleiwa and then trends north-
westerly, following the coast till it reaches the cock's comb
at Kahuku. There it rounds the northern end of the Koolaus
which retreat inland sufficiently far to leave a belt of sugar
land that is finally pinched out a few miles from Punaluu.
This coastline is an exposed stretch without sheltered water

until Kahana Bay is reached. At Kahuku there is a large landing field and a wireless station nearby.

The Oahu Railway line, which skirts the coastline all the way from Honolulu and edges its way past Kaena Point, ends some miles beyond Kahuku but some distance short of Kahana Bay. Another air-strip was constructed about half-way down this northeastern stretch of coast, not because there was much flat land hereabouts, but because the success of the first Japanese attack scared the Army into putting its aircraft under cover. Here the nearness of a steep mountain-face to the sea made the task of hiding the planes in revetments and tunnels much easier. When no further attacks came, parking the planes in the open seemed much less risky, and this air-strip was almost deserted. Now frigate birds, on watch for fish-fed boobies returning to their rookeries, soar around the grey lichen covered cliffs, undisturbed by the hum of motors or the drone of incoming planes.

Only one more plantation remains and that is a small one, grown still smaller from military encroachments. Waimanalo's sugar lands are tucked into a bend of the Koolaus, which here present sheer precipices furrowed with parallel fissures, each groove in the rock face debouching onto a fan-shaped delta of scoured-out boulders with other detritus at its base. Over the rim of this half-bowl the clouds collect to give the plantation a forty- to sixty-inch rainfall, lessening considerably the need for irrigation. Bellows Field, the Army outpost, and other military installations have cut heavily into Waimanalo's holdings.

The only other military establishment on this side of the island is the Naval Air Base at Kaneohe Bay. Between this bay and Kailua Beach is the Mokapu Peninsula, named after the crater that marks an easterly extension of the Koolau volcanic system. Here, at the side of the bay the Navy has built its hangars and has cleared the waters of coral rock so as to provide a seaway for their P.B.Y.'s and other amphibian aircraft. Incidentally, they have pre-empted one of the loveliest views of the island.

Kaneohe Bay itself provides a foreground of quiet water. Behind the little palm-fringed Coconut Island, the foreshore, a green and gently-wrinkled expanse, lifts itself gradually to the foot of the mountains beyond. Over these the clouds are continually hanging. This view is best in the early morning, for then you see clearly, in between deeply-sculptured recesses, the sharp edges of the ascending ridges, line after line, each picked out for you by the slanting sun. At evening the mountain wall seems to recede into a purple background, which, if sun and clouds are right, may be cloven in two by a broad shaft of sunlight streaming through the Pali or the Kalihi gap. Those people who had their little cottages alongside the bay, before the Navy took them over, well remember the charm of the scene of which I speak.

But the mountains, beautiful as they may be, are too close for aviators' comfort. For a long time the building of the air base was delayed while careful studies of the tricky air currents were being made. But the nearness of war cut all the restrictions of uncertainty in such matters. A base on the windward side where the big flying boats could be sent up to guard the Molokai channel was necessary and by half-circling the bay and coming in across a low hilly promontory, the heavy craft could be set down safely with a cross wind. The take-off was also cross wind over the low neck of land that joins Mokapu to the mainland.

If one wishes to take the most direct land route to Honolulu, he must climb the Pali Road which zigzags to and fro across the face of the steep ascent. The gap itself marks the head of Nuuanu Valley and the road is continuous with one of Honolulu's streets, Nuuanu Avenue, five miles lower down. This road up the Pali was kept heavily mined and guarded and any successful enemy landing on the windward side would have been the signal for sending the road's vital abutments and supports hurtling down the green cliffs. On the city side of the Pali is a water reservoir from which the city's water supply could have been precariously augmented, if the main artesian pumping station had been bombed.

Continuing on the round-the-island highway, your route is up and over another gap — a very low one, alongside the hill on which Makapuu lighthouse is perched. The dry ravines and rugged coastline of Koko Head follow, an area more fully described in our first chapter. There is only one break in the cliffs, at Hanauma Bay, where small craft could shelter, but being overlooked on three sides by high land it would be most easily defended. Far more vulnerable is the bay on the Honolulu side of Koko Head Crater, but this beach would be under direct fire from a ridge three miles to the west which is thickly studded with gun emplacements. These hold artillery of sufficient caliber to land shells all the way from Waimanalo beaches on one side to Kapalama Basin on the other and at the same time dominate Diamond Head Crater. The Koko Head sands with the reef protecting them made an excellent training area for amphibious landings, and during the staging periods for the Pacific offensive, acres of "ducks" were lined up on the lower slopes of the crater. A small reservoir and a Naval Wireless Station were the only installations likely to be sabotaged on this side of the city itself.

Honolulu calls for no particular description at this point, except to locate some of the danger points or probable targets in case of bombing attack. Chief among these is the powerhouse of the Hawaiian Electric Company which supplies the city with electricity. It was conspicuously located with two smokestacks to mark the spot, very near to the waterfront. Even more vital to the city population is the waterworks pumping station just at the base of Punchbowl. With this station bombed, half the city would be uninhabitable. A quarter of a mile away in one direction is one of the large radio stations, while within a short half mile is Hono-

lulu's biggest general hospital. Of great importance to the
city's functioning and to the whole island are the docks and
piers thickly clustered around Honolulu's crowded harbor.
Most of these are within a one-and-a-half-mile circle with
its center at the City Hall, and the Pumping Station near
its circumference in a direction opposite to the piers. In
the middle are also grouped the Governor's residence, the
Telephone Building, the Capitol, the Law Courts, the Post
Office and Federal Buildings. Within the circle also are
to be found the two largest banks, the big commercial offices
of the so-called Big Five, and practically all the doctors' and
dentists' offices.

Thus because of this undue concentration, Honolulu is
one of the most vulnerable small cities on earth. A shower
of bombs, or a single atomic bomb dropped within this
circle would deal Honolulu a paralyzing blow from which
it could never recover for years. The city has grown that
way, partly because of lack of building space, but also on
account of our foolish sense of security. Even now, city
planning lags so far behind the atomic age that there is no
public discussion of dispersion and duplication of vital installations, nor of the necessity of getting as many public
facilities as possible underground. There seems to be little
recognition of the plain fact that cities of Honolulu's design
are as out-of-date as the dodo. The places that will survive
the next war will be those whose civic centers are hard to
find. Even in the year of grace 1942 a single well-directed
air-raid or bombardment could easily have reached satura-
tion proportions. Then Honolulu might have matched the
ruined cities of prophecy, over which was stretched "the
line of confusion and the plummet of emptiness." If the
Japanese had diverted twenty of their bombers for the destruction of Honolulu's nerve center, they might have sunk
one less battleship but would have come nearer winning
the war.

The city's design was of course well known to the Japanese, even though our military intelligence, in a lather of belated stable-locking, forbade the publication of any second-story photographs of the town, in case raiders might be able to identify their targets more exactly.

Consider, then, how potentially important were the various plantation facilities, the only decentralization that these islands possessed. If the city's large general hospital had been bombed, how invaluable would have been the small hospitals and laboratories which each of Oahu's seven plantations possessed. They would have been very inadequate, but vastly better than nothing. Again, the plantations' water pumping systems, though unable to feed into the city's supply, would have been able to serve the whole population, if evacuation from Honolulu had been necessary. Water and electric power from one plantation were in a couple of emergencies supplied to Pearl Harbor. The plantations having their own electricity and cold storage could have provided the refrigeration necessary for the preservation of blood plasma and vital serums. Their warehouses and stores could have tided the city's evacuees over an acute food shortage. The plantations were thus our last lines of civilian defense. Fortunately we did not need to fall back on those lines.

Then too it should be remembered that the highways and bridges having been built originally to connect the plantations with the harbor at Honolulu, those plantations were strategically well placed for the purpose of guarding them. Every road on Oahu after December 7th became of military importance, for in any scheme of effective island defense, rapid troop and artillery movements were essential. Thus if widespread sabotage had been seriously intended, these roads and bridges as well as all the other plantation facilities would have required a night and day watch. Two items used extensively in plantation operations would also have been invaluable to saboteurs. These were dynamite and arsenic, the former used for tunnneling irrigation systems, the latter for wholesale weed eradication. Both were guarded jealously.

To arrange for military personnel to guard all these danger points would have called for a very large force of men. Their housing, feeding, supervision, and relief would have occupied the full time of a considerable garrison which could never have been withdrawn for other duties without inviting trouble. For the plantations, the problem was so much simpler. The men could live nearby in their own camps and villages, plantation trucks could provide transport for their relief at change of shifts, and supervision would be easy. Probably three times as many soldiers would have been needed to do the job. Then too, the civilians knew not only the country but the local population, so that the presence of any stranger would have been at once detected and suspicion directed towards him. Local residents if sabotage-minded would have been loath to attempt such attacks because of the danger of recognition. For all these reasons the Provisional Police Plan, including through its co-ordinator the personnel and resources of all the islands' plantations, was quite eagerly endorsed by the military authorities. They foresaw that in the event of war, a very heavy responsibility would be lifted from their shoulders.

As the island was divided under the plan, District No. 1 included the Telephone Center, five railroad bridges, the water supply installations, and the two radio stations, requiring 144 men as guards. District No. 2 covered the Waialua and Schofield areas, with a force of 221 men. District No. 3 took in Ewa and areas near Pearl Harbor, and required 299 men. District No. 4 extended from Kahuku to Waimanalo Plantation, employing a force of 172 men. To keep up a 24-hour watch, three shifts were needed, trebling the total number of guards. All important military and civilian installations were to be kept under constant surveillance, housing, food, and transportation being the plantations' responsibility; the weapons, mainly riot guns, were to be supplied by the Army.

As to training, that was provided by officers of the regular police, who gave weekly instruction to the men at each plantation, stressing particularly methods of guard duty and how to make arrests. By the time the Major Disaster Council was fully established in April 1941, the Chief of Police was able to report a force of from 2,000 to 2,500 men available for service. In May 1941, 582 men who had undergone training were scheduled to take part with the army in 24hour maneuvers, taking their allotted posts in three shifts. Backed by the American Legion, and encouraged by army authorities, the plan was adopted enthusiastically on each of the outside islands, so that very shortly the Provisional Police organization was Territorywide in scope.

From a strictly military standpoint, the project was of somewhat doubtful legitimacy. Possibly the arming of citizens with riot guns and setting them to guard installations of military importance might have run afoul of the Geneva Convention rules. For this, or some other reason, the Army was chary of claiming credit for this sensible scheme to forestall subversive tendencies. In a memorandum addressed to the Oahu Plantation Managers Association on July 30, 1940, the army liaison officer wrote: "It is requested that this work be kept as confidential as possible, and the Police be mentioned as the instigators rather than the Army." Such modesty in disclaiming the paternity of a good idea was unusual. Such a fine brain wave was excellent proof that the professional military mind did not operate in a dead calm.

Another civilian emergency organization that got off to a flying start, thus beating the guns of Pearl Harbor, was the Preparedness Committee of the Honolulu Medical Society. Since the members of this profession would be the first called upon in the event of disaster, the state of the world in July 1940 concerned them greatly. As a result of the doctors' alarm, they went so far as to appoint Dr. Fronk as their representative on the National Committee on

Medical Preparedness. They also set up a committee of four doctors to arrange a local emergency plan. Then in common with the rest of the population the doctors, reassured that nothing untoward could happen here, relaxed their vigilance. In a report on this matter, Dr. H. L. Arnold says that the committee "made plans and endeavored to interest the profession, but, in general, their efforts did not meet with much success." [1]

But, as we have seen, April 1941 brought a rude awakening from lethargy and "no pilikia" assurance. The complexion of things changed rapidly for the worse. The only uncertainty now about war was how, when, and where we should be first engulfed in conflict. The medical profession, once again alerted for action, set up a new Preparedness Committee of seven doctors (Larsen, Judd, Strode, Pinkerton, Withington, Faus, and Arnold). It met on April 15th with, as Arnold says, "the conviction of every member of the committee that war was imminent and that it was urgently necessary for preparations to be made to care for a potentially large number of injured civilians." Dr. Faus was named as executive officer in charge of plans and training, and a close relationship was maintained with the Red Cross, the Nursing Association, and the City and County Medical Department under Dr. Mossman.

The efficiency of the medical plans was beyond question. Physicians were assigned to first-aid stations and local hospitals, while arrangements were made for a group of surgeons and their nurses to go directly to military hospitals to assist with the great influx of casualties that might be expected in the event of a serious attack. Others were assigned to civilian hospitals. Twenty first-aid stations were set up throughout the city at schools and other public buildings. Plans for extended training in first aid were at once put in motion by enrolling large classes of selected individuals for

[1] Arnold, H. L. *Medical Preparedness in the Territory of Hawaii Prior to December 7th, 1941.* Report to H.S.P.A., compiled by Colonel Moore.

advanced training. These people could then act as instructors, after being duly qualified by examination and given
diplomas by the Red Cross. Soon, by this means, three
thousand adults of all ages and nationalities were applying
fracture splints and discovering arterial pressure points and
learning the other rudiments of first aid.

The value of this program was to be amply demonstrated.
God knows there was enough confusion and bewilderment
on December 7th, without the panic that would have attended an unorganized medical and first-aid service, with a
large toll of unattended casualties making frantic calls for
attention. Credit is again due to the Army for efficient
backing, the surgeon-general of the Hawaiian Department
rendering all the assistance and encouragement his disposition would permit.

The education of the public in general as to the aims and
work of the Committee was also essential. The newspapers
joined in to give the movement constant publicity. Someone
has made an exact tally of the space allotted to notices, reports, etc., and finds that it amounted to 3,775 inches. Over
one hundred yards of newspaper space makes a considerable
amount of copy. Those whose knowledge is measured by
what they read in the papers must have been well informed
with regard to this program.

Initial financial backing was supplied by the Red Cross,
the Chamber of Commerce, and by many individual contributions. A full volunteer staff for each station was enrolled,
consisting of doctors, dentists, nurses, nurses' aides, ambulance drivers, clerical assistants, messengers, etc. After amal-
gamation of the Committee with the general Major Disaster
Council, $6,000 was allotted by the Board of Supervisors
and $5,000 was raised by a benefit football game. As the
outlook for peace darkened, the Red Cross hurried medical
supplies down to Honolulu from Washington, costing in
all $40,000. In June 1941, the City Board of Supervisors
voted another $60,000 for supplies and equipment, in addi-

tion to $7,500 for equipping ambulances and provisional police cars with two-way radios. Other contributions of the Red Cross are listed and fully described in their published reports.

It is most interesting to note that this program of first-aid training, provision of medical supplies, expansion of hospital facilities and ambulance service was strongly urged in a letter from General Short to Mr. Alfred Castle, head of the local chapter of the Red Cross. In this the general called the plan "the program of preparation for emergency relief for the civilian population, to become effective in event of disaster *particularly such as might eventuate from an enemy air attack on the city.*" Here was an instance of excellent long-distance vision in a man whose near vision on December 7th has been considered faulty. General Short urged that the program be put into effect "in the shortest practicable time," in order to meet any disaster or emergency situation. This statement, so remarkable for its foresight and prudence, is so incompatible with the Army's state of alertness when the emergency arrived that it provides a most interesting psychological puzzle. It is noteworthy, also, that it was the Army which loaned to the Red Cross the equipment for sixteen first-aid units for civilian use, thus giving evidence that it thought an attack possible.

One of the most obvious needs for community disaster aid was the provision of adequate ambulance service. Three ambulances were donated by the Liquor Dealers' Association, the Consolidated Amusement Company, and the Schumann Carriage Company respectively, but the equipment most relied upon consisted of 250 trucks offered by commercial firms in Honolulu for conversion and use as ambulances. Drivers from two of "The Big Five" — T. H. Davies and American Factors — took weekly courses in first aid from June 1941 until after the crisis had passed. This was merely typical of the community spirit at this time.

As is usual in such conditions, opposition developed from

those who felt outraged that their accepted and long-established routine had been suddenly disrupted for no good reason. The Federal Narcotics Bureau staff, for example, thought that their regulations for the control of morphine could not be brushed aside merely because some excitable people believed that a war was coming. Hence they strenuously objected to stocks being allotted to the care of the Red Cross. Red tape was only relaxed when the morphine was deposited in a safe deposit vault. Stocks of typhoid serum were also accumulated, since an epidemic was feared if the population had to be evacuated from the city into areas where the water supply might be easily contaminated.

Local chairmen were appointed to head medical committees on each of the islands and preparedness went on apace. Surveys of accommodations and resources of all hospitals were undertaken and plans instituted to evacuate ordinary cases of sickness when the stream of casualties came in; refrigeration facilities for storing drugs and serum were eyed critically; married or retired nurses were registered for emergency service, and every community was apprised of the possibility of disaster.

Blood plasma was another prime necessity, but it was very hard for the general public to envisage clearly a violent assault, with hundreds or thousands of casualties needing blood transfusions. Many people gave willingly of their time and money in furtherance of general precautions, but balked at this business of donating blood by the pint to be stored against a possible but unlikely contingency. That seemed to be playing the war game too realistically. Hence Dr. Pinkerton, director of the project, had a difficult task in securing sufficient donors, thus imperiling the success of what was to prove one of the most direct aids possible in disaster. But the Bank's sponsors took one smart step. Older people are an extremely difficult group to urge towards any extreme action; they have seen so many threats averted, so many bridges that did not need to be crossed, that complacency becomes one of the marked characteristics of middle age. Only the very old and the young view with alarm. Someone was shrewd enough to enlist the interest and support of the Junior Chamber of Commerce. They had both blood and enthusiasm to spare.

Pressure was then brought to bear on the senior Chamber of Commerce, and they were induced to vote $4,000 towards the expense of equipping laboratories and paying technicians. Eight hospitals, both city and rural, joined in the program, and in three months 77 flasks of plasma were obtained from 96 donors. In October 1941, when world relations seemed most chaotic, the number of donors doubled in five weeks and a revised goal of 200 flasks was attained. But with the let-down of November, interest in the Blood Bank lapsed. The Bank had been offered as a going concern to the Red Cross, but the Washington office did not approve and the offer was refused. Possibly the central organization felt that Hawaii had gone far enough in preparing for a crisis that somehow always fell short of actuality. The Chamber of Commerce also believed the demonstration had gone far enough to protect the community in case of war, and they withdrew their support. Pinkerton, in his report, notes that the stock of plasma accumulated by six months of effort lasted just six hours in the actual emergency. The Bank's directors, aware of its tiny capitalization, closed its doors just about three weeks before the attack.

In the meantime the Major Disaster Council with its 23 subcommittees covering communications, power and light, fire and gas protection, food production, evacuation, etc., was carrying on. Typical of the thorough and painstaking work of many branches was that achieved by the transportation subcommittee. It made a complete survey of the island, listing everything that could run on rails or roads, besides all means of water transport. It also listed machine-shop and service facilities in the island, recording 5,000 vehicles with the names of the individuals responsible for each, or in the case of business firms, the addresses or telephone numbers of key personnel who would be accessible if the attack occurred at night. Machine tools and repair equipment were also listed, together with all machine workers' training and experience. Separate lists were compiled for rural areas, in which the mechanical and personnel resources of each plantation were included. For a community with no experience of anything approaching disaster, this blueprint for emergency was complete. Its thoroughness can be taken as evidence that our population, though inclined naturally to complacency, was stirred by a most discomfiting sense of impending peril.

It would be idle to attempt to bestow special encomiums on any group or section of the people as regards foresight or state of readiness. It is much more important to emphasize that this effort was not confined to the business leaders, nor to the sugar plantation managers, nor to the doctors and scientists, but was a concerted effort of *all* the people, a community pull-together such as Hawaii had never experienced before. Regardless of the outcome in terms of actual dangers met and overcome, and despite the fact that no great strain was ever placed on our capacity for courage and endurance, the proof that we could be so organized and unified in purpose and effort is worth recording. In these days of confused counsels and chaotic ideas and purposes, the realization that we can stand together is a grateful and heartening memory.

The keynote for this community responsibility was struck by a joint statement of the Medical Preparedness Committee and the director of the local chapter of the Red Cross, issued April 25, 1941:

"While the United States is not at war and there is no reason for war hysteria, the international situation is so critical that the civilian population of Honolulu must realize that the time has come *now* — not tomorrow — for intelli-

gent, adequate civilian defense preparedness. No sane per'
son can think otherwise. The Army and Navy are not
here to protect the population of Honolulu; their duty is to
defend Hawaii as one of the most vital parts of the
American defense system. In case of emergency the civilian
population must be prepared to defend itself."

This note of self-reliance was of course applauded by
Army and Navy authorities, who thought it the sign of a
very healthy civilian spirit. In April it was quite true that
no sane person thought otherwise than that great dangers
threatened us. How strange then that this same population,
both civilian and military, without apparently losing its
sanity, was caught so plainly off base on December 7th.

CHAPTER IX

Climb Mount Niitaka

SO FAR the white heat of enthusiasm, the flurry of expectation, the bustle of planning, the final links of co-ordination, and one would like to be able to report the job well done and the ending fortunate. But now comes the pause of weariness, the almost inexplicable negligence, the relaxing of vigilance in that last critical hour of the watch, the hour before the dawn. No doubt we could find many excuses — that the crisis had been too long expected, that we had lived too familiarly with danger, that we had planned so well that we were afflicted with complacency, that seeing the sword hang by a thread for months persuaded us into thinking the silk thread was a steel filament. That perhaps is the essence of the war of nerves, the thrust repeated and withdrawn so often that we finally believe it will never be struck home. One cannot endure an agony of apprehension indefinitely; sooner or later we are at home with our fears; we stand carelessly for an instant on the brink of disaster, and in that fatal moment of relaxation, in that inexplicable let-down of vigilance, we slip and fall.

We have already noted that there were distinct tidal waves of apprehension that hit these shores, and each except the last was followed by a recession, an allaying of fears. After the almost-panic that we experienced in July 1940 came a period of reassurance, lasting from November of that year to the following March. Then in April 1941 came the second inundation followed by all the activities of preparation which the last chapter described. In November could be observed the final ebb, just before the tide of destruction was upon us. As we have seen, it was just about this time that the Honolulu Blood Bank closed its doors and on November 24th a reporter's survey, as printed in the *Honolulu Advertiser* of that date, showed that householders had dipped very heavily into those emergency food stores so hurriedly built up five months before; in fact many of the reserve shelves were empty of vital foodstuffs. Now people were more concerned with amplifying luxury items, such as whisky and gin. Some individuals gave as the reason for depleting their stocks or exchanging necessities for luxuries the fact that the emergency hadn't arrived as expected, but the price increases had.

As to the military, we know now that their guard was temporarily let down, their armor laid aside. To the people of America this was so inexplicable that inquiry after inquiry, involving dozens of witnesses and reams of expert and inexpert testimony, has been held without getting to the bottom of the matter. Perhaps there is no bottom. One theory is that just as there is no perfect crime, so too there is no perfect planning. There is always a thousand to one chance of failure, and sometimes the thousandth chance comes off. Admittedly this is a theory of coincidence, and the coincidence was by all odds a wild one. If we accept that theory, it would seem that we must agree that the Japanese stroke was the luckiest — if we reject it, that their planning was the most astute in naval history. The truth probably is that it was something between the two.

What makes the theory of luck scarcely tenable was the fact that the brief military somnolence synchronized so perfectly with momentary civilian lethargy. The whole camp as well as the sentries was asleep. Otherwise there would have been two thousand instead of two hundred flasks of blood plasma available; so many of the plantation executives would not have been in Honolulu to attend the

Shrine Benefit football game on December 6th and their meeting scheduled for two days later; the anti-aircraft guns would have been in station, their ammunition beside them; the radar stations would have been properly manned; defensive air patrols would have been out; the men on the battleships would have been at their gun positions. There had been other troughs between waves of dread anticipation. How did it come about that the Japanese struck at the lowest ebb of apprehension and readiness?

The writer's belief is that the chief reason is to be found in human nature itself, but to clarify this theory will require a short excursion into experimental psychology. The notion is based on the work of Pavlov, the Russian psychologist, who found that by repeatedly sounding a bell at the same time as food was presented to dogs, the flow of saliva, called the salivary reflex, could be evoked just as well by sounding the bell alone without giving the dogs the food. Thus was set up what was called a conditioned reflex.

But in further experiments involving a delayed reaction, e.g., withholding the food for 60 seconds instead of 10 seconds after the bell had sounded, Pavlov observed that in the interim even the greediest and hungriest dogs went to sleep. Moreover, when the conditioning stimulus was something most unpleasant, as for example a strong electric shock instead of the sound of the bell, the effect was the same — the waiting animals went to sleep.

The explanation which the writer has advanced[1] is that all other brain activity being suspended, and all other stimuli pushed off the stage of attention during this period of expectancy, this condition is the most favorable to either hypnosis or sleep. The dogs' somnolence bore all the earmarks of hypnotic sleep. The basis of hypnosis is just that — the concentration of attention on a single stimulus, usually as simple as listening to a metronome, gazing at a tiny light

[1] Porteus, S. D., and Wood-Jones, Frederick, The Matrix of the Mind. Arnold and Co., London, 1929, p. 390.

or mirror, or watching the slow, monotonous movements of the hypnotist's hands — under the spell of which the subject goes to sleep, accepting at the same time the suggestion that it is the hypnotist who has made him do so.

The situation in Hawaii had much that was akin to this process. The stimulus, in this case the threat of attack, appeared several times; there was tense expectancy, but nothing happened. Again the threat was repeated, with the same psychological let-down following the lack of culmination.

The stimulus appeared once more; holding the expectation of attack absorbed all our mental energy; the reaction was delayed and we went to sleep. The condition in which the military and civilian population found itself in November 1941 can best be described as one of suspended animation. We were self-hypnotized into a feeling of security that was entirely unfounded in fact. The only way in which Pavlov's animals could be prevented from sleeping was by interpolating some other stimuli or disturbances into the waiting interval. Perhaps that was where our generals and admirals went wrong. They should have made our fear stimulus stronger by doing all they could to increase the expectation of crisis or have set new goals in the way of training, maneuvers, etc., which would have spread attention in the interval of waiting.

In any case, a new psychological problem is posed as to the most effective way to carry on the war of nerves. Experiments could be instituted to discover what degrees of intensity of the stimulus, i.e., the threat of danger, are necessary and what intervals should intervene between the shocks to bring about most completely a state of attention so absorbed with the future that we become oblivious to current events. I do not think the Japanese were clever enough to have thought out all their plans beforehand. They too were at the mercy of chance in world events, but they came very near achieving a perfect demonstration of how to induce suspended animation. To that extent they were both lucky and astute.

Certainly there was nothing in the state of the world to induce reassurance. There was indeed little ground for optimism, though of course optimists as a class do not need much to stand on. The whole world had smoke in its eyes. Consequently November was a month of indecision of mind, with the strangest mixture possible of good news and bad and contrary interpretations of the situation appearing in adjacent columns of the same newspaper, often emanating from the same news source.

Judging by the date lines, we were tremendously inter-ested in what people were saying or thinking in Shanghai, Tokyo, Singapore, and Manila, and these people were apparently trying to make up our minds for us. Distance from Honolulu was one of the touchstones of credibility. If it was not Tokyo dispatchers, then it was Washington correspondents who had all the dope. Occasionally a British opinion was headlined. Most of the news was on the basis of "I know a man, who knows a man, who was told thus and so," — in short common reportorial gossip.

Looking back, the trends of policy and the inevitability of events seem clear. Japan was undoubtedly playing the game of nerves and undoubtedly playing it well. It may be taken for granted that in this kind of war the opponent who knows exactly his final intentions will win. The Japs played their cards well — alternately truculent and conciliatory, extreme and moderate. Their use of the smoke screen device was excellent. Perhaps we can spare a little time for a summary review.

The beginning of November found Japan's *Nichi Nichi* declaring editorially that the supply of oil was the vital issue, and that there were limits to Japanese patience. A spokesman for Tojo's Government declared that it had completed all preparations "proper to our immutable national policy." This was the signal for the vernacular press to burst into an excited chorus acclaiming the speech as earnest of Japan's determination to break through the bonds of hostile encirclement. America must make up its mind at once to withdraw all embargoes, or else. Soon it was time to begin the conciliatory cycle. On November 4th, Ishii, the Government spokesman, denied that any time limit had been set for the ending of negotiations, though of course these could not be continued indefinitely. In the midst of the turmoil the announcement was made that Kurusu, signer of the Tripartite Pact for Japan, would go to Washington to assist Nomura with the negotiations currently proceeding with Cordell Hull.

At once the news commentators began searching eagerly for signs or portents in the Kurusu appointment, chief among the discoveries being that his wife was either English or American, or at least spoke English, and therefore Kurusu's attitude was bound to be more friendly than Nomura's. A Honolulu newspaper declared that there was little concern on the mainland about Japan, which would not dare attempt an aggressive move. It quoted the opinion of a prominent member of the local chapter of the "Committee to Defend America by Assisting the Allies" that Honolulu was "probably the safest place on the globe, because we are so isolated and so heavily protected." But Germany was a different prospect and a shooting war with Hitler was predicted within sixty to ninety days.

At the same time, dispatches from Washington reflected a comfortable view of Kurusu's mission. Japan was unprepared for conflict; hence his arrival was calculated to prolong the discussion so that Japan after all her truculent declarations would not lose face if she had to back down. This view was echoed by a crowd of anonymous soothsayers, variously labeled as "diplomatic quarters," "informed observers," "authoritative sources," who announced that while China still resisted it would be impossible for Japan to make a major move. Here again we meet with the old sandhill in which the I.P.R. ostrich felt so much at home. These anonymous experts should have carried no more weight than opinions of unnamed doctors who, as the radio commercial declares, have found that somebody's face cream contains more Vitamin X than any rival preparation.

Then it was time for a more pessimistic note. The Japanese press united in taking a gloomy view of Kurusu's chances of reaching agreement with America, quoting odds of ten to one against a peaceful issue. Chinese newspapers were even more gloomy, and set November 15th as the deadline for the breakdown of diplomacy.

In America, one who had made viewing with alarm his particular profession predicted war with Japan within two or three weeks' time. But this opinion was not particularly disturbing, coming from someone who had cried "Wolf!" as often as Martin Dies. But the withdrawal of U.S. marines from Shanghai certainly did give the outlook a gloomier turn. On the other hand, the very next day a dispatch from Shanghai warranted the reassuring headlines, "Kurusu Bringing Milder Pacific Peace Program," but whether this was a fact or the headline writer merely indulging his taste for alliteration, no one could determine. The prospects looked rosier still when the special envoy, landing in Honolulu on his way to Washington, said that Japan and America had a common responsibility to maintain peace in the Pacific. Of course this was the most obvious truism, but those were the days when truisms were laid to our souls as comfort.

Peiping, relying on "informed persons including Japanese sources," seemed to know all about it, even to the details of the proposals Kurusu was carrying with him in his jealously guarded brief case. The program had five points. China was to recognize Manchukuo, Japan would then evacuate China, except for five cities, but would return economic control of five northern provinces. She would then renounce all aggressive expansion southwards and any hostile intentions towards Russia. There is little doubt but what

Japanese sources were concerned in this heartwarming dispatch, for it bore all the marks of a cleverly laid smoke screen. But hardly had hopes been raised before they were depressed by a resolution of the Japanese Diet, setting forth a bitter complaint that China's obduracy and continued resistance was wholly due to America's refusal to recognize the altruism of Japan's Greater East Asia Co-Prosperity scheme.

Perhaps Honolulu's decline in alertness may have been partially based on a flurry of contradictory reports from Shanghai, which Japan seemed to have selected as its chief communications channel. One dispatch gave substance to the headline "Japan Believed Ready to Quit Axis Partners." It interpreted the bellicose spirit manifested by the Diet as being merely a "stage show" to impress Roosevelt with Japan's unity. But the next column was headed "Japan Ready for Action if Kurusu Fails."

So in this inchoate fashion the world wagged on its wobbly course. November 26th was probably one of the important dates in world history, for that was the day when Hull issued his uncompromising statement of America's basic policies in the Far East. Up to this time many people in Japan hoped that in some way America could be bluffed or cajoled into compromise. Only the most moderate and liberal elements retained any further hope of peace, once Hull had made public America's stand. Tojo, on the other hand, saw his opportunity. "Here," he said to the Emperor, the Imperial Staff, and the Cabinet, "is America's ultimatum, which we must bow to or fight. Can anyone doubt that war or national humiliation are our only alternatives?"

It was on the day of Hull's statement that the Japanese fleet had assembled off Etorufu Island, 150 miles northeast of the main island of Hokkaido, ready to steam for Hawaii. Much has been made of Hull's declaration as precipitating the attack, but the best evidence available points to the fact that the fleet was already assembled when the note was delivered to Tokyo. But even if the two events almost exactly synchronized, we know that the assault on Pearl Harbor had been planned for several months and the orders to Admiral Nogura to assemble his fleet at the Japanese rendezvous must have been issued some days before the declaration of the American Secretary of State. Though Hull's note served to disillusion many in Japan who thought compromise was still possible, and on the other hand confirmed many waverers with regard to an aggressive policy against America, it was by no means the match to the trail of gunpowder that it has been represented. It was merely putting in writing what everyone in America and many people in Japan knew to be our only consistent course. We would not in any circumstances withdraw support from China; we would, just as definitely, not acquiesce in Japan's Nan-yo policy of further expansion to the South. The whole debate as to whether Hull's note arrived on the 28th or 27th of November, Japanese time, and whether the Japanese fleet sailed before or after its receipt, is characteristic of the confusion of thought in which the events of the time have plunged this nation. We are still bewildered, as we usually are, when we make our first attempts to rationalize attitudes or actions which turn out badly. We set up our brass serpents and then blame them for our own self-deception. As suggested previously, the roots of action go as deep as human nature itself, and that of all things we seem to know least about.

But in the meantime the chaos of uncertainty continued, and we looked around for counsel — and the further abroad, the better we thought the counsel. One of our newspapers published the extremely reassuring news that the betting in London was two to one against a Pacific war. London, like Shanghai, had the inside dope. The Kurusu proposal, according to unnamed but reliable sources, was for a three months' cooling-off period, at the end of which Japan would withdraw her troops from Indo-China, and America would partially lift the arms embargo. If wishes father thoughts, this was the high point of wishful reproduction. But the very next day Washington was predicting that appeasement of Japan in any form would be rejected.

But now what of the local scene? The Hawaiian legis-lature had met in October in special session, and had passed the M-day bill giving the Governor extended emergency powers, almost equivalent to martial law, and appropriating money for civilian defensive measures. This was passed in form somewhat different to the former Army-sponsored bill, which lay neglected on the clerk's table when in the previous April the Speaker of the House suddenly banged his gavel and declared the regular session ended. Some of the legislators approved the new bill because they thought sweeping powers allotted the Governor would make the declaration of martial law unnecessary. With the setting up of the new machinery, the Major Disaster Council becoming now the Office of Civilian Defense, a stirring appeal was made for volunteers for the city's organization of fire and air raid wardens. As grounds for quick action, the appeal stated that peace and war now were hanging in the balance.

From this point on into late November, the pace of events quickened. The shadows grew ever nearer. Peace was dying in the world, the lights were going out; and to some thou-sands of our sailors and a couple of score Japanese aviators, there remained, if they had only known it, one more week of life. Whether any of them had intimations of mortality there is no telling, but premonitions of tragedy were plenti-ful, if people had eyes to see them. Manila was reporting movements of Japanese troops and equipment down the China coast towards Indo-China, where rumor had it that there were already 100,000 Nipponese massed against Thai-land. Other dispatches foretold preparations to attack British Borneo, source of valuable oil supplies. Mr. Roosevelt hurried back from Warm Springs to consult with Cordell Hull in Washington.

Then events in Europe again occupied the spotlight. The Germans had been driven back from Rostov, great industrial center in south central Russia, but were concentrating immense forces for a final drive on Moscow. Suddenly, reports of localities of desperate fighting included the town of Tata, only 23 miles from the Russian capital. *Pravda* issued its gloomiest bulletin of the whole war — the situation was admitted to be critical. The world's press hastened to proclaim Moscow's fall was near; a typical headline — "Burn or Abandon Moscow, Russia's Choice."

Then as if to deepen the Stygian dark came bad news from North Africa. The great British offensive, spearheaded by American-built tanks, a movement ballyhooed as the encirclement of Rommel's army, not only was bogged down in the desert, but was itself being rolled back and important divisions of its own encircled. London blamed Cairo for its too-optimistic reports; Cairo said all the alleged victories had occurred in London. Was there ever such a time for despair?

Perhaps these dire happenings did divert our attention somewhat from our own peril. The Russian and British disasters were real. Ours was at present only the threat of danger, and, we thanked God, a distant one at that. Three thousand miles still seemed a long way to us. But on December 2nd the Japanese task force had almost reached the spot in mid-ocean which they had chosen for the last momentous pause, the crouch before the kill.

Now it was time for the offensive smoke screen. The Tokyo spokesman announced that the Washington talks would continue at least two weeks longer, and voiced his country's hope that a peace formula would be found. Nomura in Washington reiterated his confidence of a peaceful issue. Some of the people at least were fooled, for the Chungking spokesman — and who should know more of Japanese intentions — declared that, owing of course to China's heroic resistance, Japan was unready to invade Thai-

land or any other country. There would be no war in the
Pacific. Strangely enough, this optimism was shared by
British and American residents of Shanghai. Had not
Colonel Akayama, Japanese army spokesman, declared
through its newspaper as late as December 3rd: "Japan is
most hopeful that Washington negotiations will be successful and even if war comes, she will not take Shanghai." This
was straight from the horse's mouth, even though it was
only a Ming horse — so why bother evacuating? From
Bangkok another Japanese spokesman joined in the hymn
of hope and trust — Japan did not want war; the whole
question of peace lay with Washington. On December 3rd
the enemy task force reached its final rendezvous northwest
of Hawaii.

But on the other side of the picture these portents might
have been noted. On December 2nd Roosevelt had asked a
blunt diplomatic question. For what purpose is Japan moving troops into Indo-China far in excess of the numbers
agreed upon at Vichy? At once the Japanese army newspaper rushed into print with the accusation that this tactless
inquiry surely violated the spirit of the Washington conference by daring to question Japan's honorable intentions.
The shoe was on the other foot. Were not Britain and
America, to say nothing of the Dutch "aggressively eying"
poor little defenseless Thailand? Nevertheless, Japan, in
spite of such Rooseveltian insults, still was "hopeful of
rapprochement."

Lest all be dark, a ray of hope came out of Utah. Senator
Thomas, Utah expert on oriental affairs, asserted his belief
that Japan would not stick by the Axis when logically her
place was with the Allies. But this was followed in the news
by a statement from Under-Secretary of the Navy Bard,
which was quite British in its character of understatement.
Said he: "The Navy does not underestimate Japan's power,
but is thoroughly prepared to face the fact that in the re-
grettable event of trouble in the Pacific, that trouble will

not be a minor one." Bard was never more right, the trouble was not minor; but there were no long distance navy patrol planes out, and the Japanese were steaming for Hawaii.

The following three days, December 4th to 6th, were surely some of the most momentous in history. Perhaps the time of the attempted flight of the French king from Paris, as described by Carlyle in his "French Revolution," had equal dramatic qualities. But it would take his pen to convey to the reader that sense of intolerable suspense that hung over the world in those early December days. In Tokyo, stocky black-haired Japanese admirals and generals sat grimly at their desks, knowing that the first explosion must come at any time soon. Hundreds of their underlings hurried hither and yon, dragging the smoke pots to wherever the winds of publicity threatened to part the smoke screen or increase the visibility. For at 170 degrees east longitude and 42 degrees north, six carriers, two battleships, two heavy cruisers and nine destroyers of the Japanese task force stopped their propellers just about 1,000 miles from Hawaii, waiting for the zero hour.

One question in various forms possessed the mind of every man in that fleet — had the presence of the flotilla been discovered? Were American battleships getting ready to steam out of Pearl Harbor to cut them off? Were the crews of the heavy bombers lined up waiting for the word that the Japanese were within their striking range? Admiral Nogura had his orders. If the fleet were discovered before X-day minus two, it was to turn and hurry home, its mission announced as reconnaissance or maneuvers. If discovery came within the period of X-day minus one, the Admiral must use his own judgment as to his course. But if detected after midnight December 6th, then the die was cast. It would be too late then to disclaim hostile intentions; the attack must be pressed home at any cost.

The minutes, the hours of the Admiral's personal responsibility were rapidly passing. As yet there was no sign of detection. From the radio bearings given by the American search planes, they seemed to be concentrated in the sector southwest of Hawaii, the logical direction from which attack would come, and their operations seemed to accord with their ordinary routine. No message of warning came to the Admiral from the three fast submarines that cruised ahead of the fleet. No countermanding orders came from Tokyo. Either the Americans felt quite secure, or else the trap lay open, its teeth ready to close once the Japanese fleet came within its iron jaws. Who could tell the answer? But, in the meantime, would Saturday midnight never come?

But while every inkling of hostile intentions was guarded, and every Japanese wore his customary blank mask, yet in spite of all the smoke screens, the tension in the whole Pacific area unaccountably tightened. A dispatch from Washington on December 5th prompted the headline "Pacific Zero Hour Near: Japan Answers Today." Representative Taber said he would not be surprised if the West Coast, Hawaii, and the Philippines were to be suddenly attacked. The same day the Melbourne radio spoke of advices "seeming to indicate an immediate break in Japanese-American relations." Washington reported a delicate situation "generating mounting suspense despite a temporizing answer by Japan re troop movements in Indo-China."

For these movements the Nipponese disclaimed any hostile intent, and this action was interpreted by news purveyors as a desire on their part to keep the Pacific pot from boiling over. But it was suggested that this attitude might change for the worse if Russia lost Moscow, or the British Libya campaign went as badly as it promised. Thus again our preoccupation with Europe helped the Japanese.

The hourglass of peace was rapidly running out, and obviously it was time to pour fuel on the smudge pots, to feed into all the news agencies of the world those obvious items of misinformation which, if we had been fully awake, would have proclaimed our unmistakable danger. A Tokyo dispatch dated December 5th — her fleet had already been a day at its Pacific rendezvous — stated the obvious fallacy that Japan was desirous to continue negotiating, even though there was now nothing to negotiate. She acknowledged there were still many points of difference between the American and Japanese points of view, but hinted that some progress had been achieved. In the meantime, the talks would go forward "in the hope of finding a common formula for the solution of the crisis." Our Government, of course, knew that *no* progress had been made, and that no formula other than a backdown by Japan was acceptable. But this was no Government secret. Except for our temporary hypnosis, all of us should have known the same thing.

As part of the soothing hypnotic process, the word "peace" began to be slipped into every item of news from the Orient. The *Nichi Nichi* again accused America of seeking a Far Eastern hegemony, while all of Japan's aspirations were obviously towards peace. Ambassador Nomura said it would be several days before Tokyo could finish its study of Hull's declaration of American diplomatic principles. Bangkok reported that tension had lessened with the arrival in Thailand of Ishii, former Government spokesman in Tokyo, to initiate weekly conferences. Following this bromide, was the announcement from Batavia that, though a 10,000-ton liner would soon arrive to evacuate Japanese nationals from Java Consul-general Ishizawa would remain at his post. Dutch Commander-in-chief General Van Poorten tried his own little bluff: "The N.E.I. has complete confidence in its defenses."

Coincident with the news from Washington that two heavily-escorted convoys were steaming south towards the Gulf of Siam, came the belated announcement that President Roosevelt would send a personal appeal for peace to Emperor Hirohito. And the United Press began its War Review for the week with these words, "A critical week of war news was highlighted by heightening tension in the Pacific, *but no new developments towards war.*"

Despite this reassurance, which Honoluluans read after the bombs had fallen, the whole Pacific basin was seething with direful expectations. Even Singapore, the unready, felt the strain. All its army, navy, and air personnel were recalled to stations. The men of an Australian division — who had recently arrived, and with their traditional contempt for brass hats had lined the troopships' sides to throw pennies down to the generals and admirals waiting to receive them on the pier — felt that their chances of gaining distinction equal with that of their fellows fighting in Libya and Crete were getting rosier by the hour. The Government declared a state of emergency and ordered all volunteer defense personnel to be mobilized for instant service. H.M.S. "Prince of Wales" and "Repulse" — the former the pride of the British Navy, got ready to steam out of the harbor without air cover or destroyer escort, to try and beat the Americans to the glorious task of blasting the Japanese Navy from the seas.

But while Singapore, the unready, forsook its tea tables and stood to arms, how was it with Hawaii, the unreadier? With all the battleships, except one, of the Pacific fleet tied up to their convenient stations in Pearl Harbor, hundreds of officers and thousands of men were already going ashore for their liberty, looking forward to parties and dates and to whatever of wine, women, and song Honolulu had to distribute among thousands of the incoming fleet personnel. The lights of the city were ablaze and a stream of speeding cars, taxis, and buses jammed the Pearl Harbor highway, which like all the city's facilities for enjoyment was being sadly overworked.

The other sixty per cent of the ships' personnel, left behind to guard the great battle wagons against an improbable attack from an enemy navy supposedly three thousand miles away, went about their duties. Every man from Admiral Kimmel down credited the Japs with enough sense to stay in their own home waters where they had harbors and plane protection, rather than to come clear across the Pacific into our own front yard, looking for trouble. Most probably, the men thought, we shall have to smoke them out from their hideaways and bring them to battle. Yes, to men from the sea, Honolulu with its thousands of home lights sprinkling all the heights above the town — Aiea, Alewa, Pacific, St. Louis, Manulani — was really attractive, especially with the glow softly reflected on the curtain of clouds overhanging the mountains. And, near at hand, the dark foreshore of the Peninsula jutting out between the darkling waters of Pearl Harbor looked quiet and inviting, especially when the lazy trades brought to the senses the mixed floral odors of this languorous, semi-tropical land. Heigh-ho, thought many, we are the unlucky ones who have ships' duties on such a night; how unlucky they little knew. For this was the last time that the scents of the garden, the sweet savor of life itself, should be in their nostrils, forever and ever.

The die of their fate was already cast. All that afternoon the six great Japanese carriers with their attendant warships had been steaming east to a designated point 700 miles due north of the western tip of Lanai, which lies between Oahu and Maui. Now as Honolulu's street lights pricked the dusk along the city's foreshore, these many miles away, bells clanged, the course of the grey flotilla was suddenly changed to south. Smoke poured from the funnels for there was no longer need of concealment from scouting aviators. The speed was increased to 21 knots; the pilots gathered in the ready rooms, the bomb bays were filled, the mechanical crews gave their last look over the engines, and every man on every bridge of the speeding fleet faced tensely to the south. The great adventure had begun.

By 3:00 A.M., the town being somewhat somnolent and the entertainers overworked, the parties had dispersed and except for a few Waikiki roisterers whose drink had not yet died in them, the whole population was in bed. None knew of the message, "Niita kayama Nobore" that Admiral No-gura had been handed on the bridge of his battleship "Akago." "Climb Mount Niitaka" [2] the message read — attack Pearl Harbor was its meaning.

Since midnight the fast carriers, each with its low plume of smoke and a bone in its teeth, had been rushing south-wards. From the decks of the foremost ships, several fast planes were launched so as to be over Pearl Harbor at dawn, whence they could observe and report any movement of ships. At 3:00 A.M., 200 miles from Lanai, the carriers swung into position for launching their planes; and in two waves, half an hour apart, 81 fighters, 145 dive bombers, 104 horizontal attack planes and 40 torpedo bombers took off. They circled to get into formation, and leaving 39 of their fighters aloft to repel the expected counterattack, they set their course for Pearl Harbor. At 6:00 A.M. both ships and planes tuned in their radios to the wave lengths of the local stations KGU and KGMB. Both began their usual Sunday morning broadcasts without interruption or hint of the unusual. The navigators corrected their courses care-fully, the pilots settled more comfortably in their seats, the bombardiers took their positions. Honolulu was still asleep.

[2] Mount Niitaka, also known as Mount Niitakayama, is the highest mount-ain in Formosa, with an altitude of a little under 13,000 feet.

CHAPTER X

Plain People's War

FOR YEARS to come, possibly for hundreds of years, unless civilization is swallowed up in some more dreadful holocaust, December 7th will be one of the most famous, or infamous, dates in Pacific history. There is no need at all of the slogan, "Remember Pearl Harbor." Indeed, since slogans serve a temporary purpose, it will soon become as pointless as "Remember the Maine." On that day there was heroism in plenty, and not all on the one side. For America it was her day of greatest humiliation, signalizing one of the worst naval defeats in all history. For almost any other country it would have been decisive; for her, it was the incentive for a recovery that was nothing short of marvelous, a come-back in which thousands of shipyard workers, designers, engineers, machine shop workers as well as sailors shared. But there is no need to remember Pearl Harbor for its own story. We could not forget it if we would.

Of all the shots fired round the world, the first gun on that fatal morning surely reverberated loudest and longest. For days and weeks afterwards, the word Hawaii was on millions of tongues. The whole of the Orient buzzed with it; in the sands of Libya, on the Siberian steppes, in the streets and factories of a thousand cities, men spoke it in tones of exultation, shame, incredulity. Other places have been lit momentarily by the spotlight of notoriety; Pearl Harbor had its own enduring if shameful illumination. Only the tales of courage that came out of the catastrophe, the devotion of the men who served their guns while the ships were settling amid flames and explosions, salved the nation's pride. It cannot be forgotten; for generations no visitor to Hawaii can fail to be reminded of that Sunday morning of terror from on high, when death without warning fell from the sky on thousands.

A few minutes before, these people were going about the business of living, their ears concerned with inconsequential chatter, or casual everyday sounds, their eyes filled with the familiar appearances, the common surroundings of ships, homes, and barracks. Then came the drone of airplanes, so commonplace in Hawaii that not one in twenty would cast his eyes aloft to the skies. Suddenly there was the roaring crescendo of diving aircraft, the whistle and shriek of bombs, the rattle of machine guns. For an instant there was the paralysis of utter surprise; then shouts and screams and hysterical orders. At first from the ships there was but a splutter of machine guns, but soon there was a great continuous roar of gunfire, punctuated by louder shocks of great explosions; at first too there were mere swirls of smoke, but then billows of it, and beneath it all the spatter of blood and fragments of flesh. To hundreds, even thousands, came the sledge-hammer blow to consciousness, the searing flash that ushered in the eternal dark. Those were the lucky ones. Death came to others in a slowly creeping flame, or in gulps of choking oil, or in a suffocating dark, as the decks above them rolled under.

There is little need to amplify the tale of horror and heroism. It has been told and retold, and since that time death from the skies has become almost commonplace. Pearl Harbor's agony was hardly then, nor is it now, unique. But thousand-ton bombings and atomic blasts were unheard of in 1941, and Pearl Harbor served to usher in a new age of wholesale, unheralded destruction. What makes the cataclysm seem so impressive was its unexpectedness. Now what happened in the Hawaiian Islands may be placed in the category of ordinary anticipation in the wars of the future.

If we needed any reminder, there are those unforgettable pictures that the Navy, with commendable frankness, released for publication just a year after the event. Out of the midst of billows of smoke, looking almost solid in its inky blackness, protrude huge turrets, crazily awry, with cranes pointing skyward and big guns displaced, while on platforms and bridges and corridors high above the floods of blazing oil, men can still be seen standing, awaiting their doom. Hooks dangle like gibbets from the hoists, while the massive steel superstructures of the battleships appear to float in mid-air, their bases obliterated in a foul curtain of smoke. To one side of the dark screen of this greatest of man-made conflagrations faintly gleams the hull of the capsized "Oklahoma," floating belly up like a dead fish.

The camera has done all that can be expected of it, yet the picture is mercifully unreal. It brings immobilization to a maelstrom, fixity to a tornado, silence and stability to a mad confusion. Underneath is the unrecorded blood spreading in thick puddles, human flesh frizzling on red hot grills, men coughing their lungs away in agonies of suffocation. Perhaps in saddest state were those who, sealed in steel compartments, scrawled their last messages in chalk on the bulkheads or tapped out, hour after hour for days, their desperate appeals to other men who listened in sick despair and helplessness. When the "Oklahoma," steel coffin for hundreds, was finally righted and opened, its hull was such a charnel house that it can hardly be written of. Men, by this time toughened by tragedy and inured to the sight of death and the extremities of violence, turned away and vomited with horror.

Since this is not a military history we may turn aside from the happenings at Pearl Harbor to consider some civilian experiences on the seventh. It is a story of what befell plain people, who fortunately lived outside the vortex of the cataclysm, and who had no gallant role to play. It may be interesting to learn of the impact of war on those who were near enough to hear the sound of the guns, and to wonder what lay beneath the high plume of smoke which all that day stood so mysteriously above Pearl Harbor. For this too was a plain people's war. To this end we believe that one individual's account of the first forty-eight hours of war might be worth quoting in full.

At eight o'clock on that Sunday morning I had a little chore to do in the front garden, while Shamae, our Japanese maid who had been with us for eight years, was putting the breakfast on the table. A paint job on our house had left some blisters under the eaves and the workmen had scraped them off for repainting, leaving the white flakes untidily where they fell on lawn and garden. "Those Japanese are terrible — they leave things in such a mess," my wife had remarked, with no thought of prophecy.

Then, as I worked, from over the rim of Roundtop, the smooth mountain slope behind the shoulder of which lies Pearl Harbor, seven miles distant, I heard the rumble and boom of gunfire, a sound so common in those days that at first I paid it little attention. Presently it grew louder and swelled into a roar like drum fire. I looked up and saw white bursts of anti-aircraft shells interspersed by black balls of smoke that seemed to hang in the air against the background of drifting clouds. This was something unusual, for anti-aircraft fire was commonly directed out to sea, and this was noticeably over the land.

I went inside to speak to my son and to turn on the radio to one of my favorite Sunday morning broadcasts — the Salt Lake City Tabernacle choir. It was singing as its opening hymn "Come, Come Ye Saints" written, I believe, in one of the dark days of Mormon history, each verse ending with the cheerful assurance, "All is well, all is well."

The phone bell rang. "Yes," I answered, "the lieutenant is here." My son took the phone, listened for a second or two, gave a curt answer, then grabbed his service cap from the table where he had left it as he came off duty the night before. He was not in uniform but he was hurrying away.

"Anything the matter?" I called after him. "There seems to be a most unusual racket of gunfire going on."

"Just some more maneuvers, I suppose," he answered. "But if it isn't, I wish they would start their wars on Monday, and not on my Sunday off."

With that he clattered down the stairs to the garage and presently, with a hurried clash of gears and a roaring engine, my son went down the driveway — to come back almost exactly four years later freed from military duty, with a last assignment in Japan. Again I heard the choir, "All is well, all is well."

The noise of gunfire increased and brought my neighbor and me together on his front lawn. Presently we saw four or five silvery-looking planes, very high, and apparently circling slowly over Waikiki. My neighbor trained his binoculars on them.

"Those are not our planes," he exclaimed, "they seem to have red crosses under their wings." As he hurried in to answer a phone call, I watched these planes swing over towards Honolulu and a little while after five others came from behind the clouds and moved off in the same direction. They might have been up five thousand feet. I, too, went into the house, where the choir was still singing.

Suddenly, just as the next verse began, the music ceased and a strangely shaken voice broke in. "Listen, everybody," it said, "Oahu is under attack by the enemy. The island is being bombed by enemy aircraft. This is no practice alert — it's the real McCoy! We are being attacked! Keep your radio on!" Then he swung back to the musical transcription "All is well, all is well."

In a few moments there was another break and a crackle of disjointed instructions. "Honolulu is being bombed. Keep your car at home. Don't go out on the streets. Don't use your telephone. This is war! Keep calm!" But the last injunction was given between gasps, as if the announcer had run a mile. The choir came back, singing the last verse.

"If we should die before our journey's through
Happy day — all is well, all is well."

Thus war came to Hawaii. At first I believed the raid to be nothing more than a hit-and-run affair. We had been assured so often of the strength of our defenses and of the might of our navy, army, and air forces that I little doubted but what these raiders would suffer for their boldness. Our planes, I thought, would surely be in the air shooting them down, our fleet out scouring the seas for the carrier or carriers from which the hostile aircraft had come. But it seemed very strange that, look as I would, I could not see evidence of any air battles. I watched a single heavy bomber near Diamond Head, slowly lumbering along, quite low. It was headed for Pearl Harbor but presently I saw it coming slowly back as if uncertain where to go.

Then I heard the announcer again, his voice calmer but his

message grim. "Will this group of doctors proceed at once to the Fort Shafter hospital where they are urgently needed," he asked. Then followed the names of about twenty doctors, many of whom were known to me. A little while later, all truck drivers and mechanics were told to go to Pearl Harbor and warehouse managers were asked to open their stores and issue drills, shovels, and tools of every kind. When the next list of doctors was called I realized that it was no nuisance raid but, as the announcer had said, "the real McCoy." For the first time I began to suspect that all was not well with our fleet and air arm. I had seen not a single dog-fight. The skies seemed empty.

The Salt Lake choir music must have been a transcription for it came on again at intervals. Once they got through a whole verse without interruption.

"Why should we think to earn a great reward
If we now shun the fight.
Gird up your loins, fresh courage take;
Our God will never us forsake.
And soon we'll have this truth to tell
All is well, all is well."

I got the words afterwards from a Mormon friend — I'm afraid I did not follow them at the time except the refrain, "All is well, all is well." When they sang this hymn in Utah, the choir certainly could have had no idea that its accompaniment would be shells and bombs and machine-gun fire when it was heard in Hawaii.

As my wife and I sat by the radio, there seemed to come a renewed burst of gunfire and presently there was a tremendous crash that set the echoes rolling around the valley. My wife jumped from her chair, and then sat down again. Both of us thought — so this is it! We realized at once it was futile to run and hide — there was no place in which to shelter, nothing to do but to sit and take whatever came.

Then we remembered Shamae, our maid. I found her sitting under a tree in the garden, crying quietly. She had evidently heard the announcement that the raiders were Japanese.

"Don't worry, Shamae," I told her. "We know how you feel. You can't help this business. The attack has nothing to do with you. You're an American, and we are all in this thing together. No, I wouldn't try and go home. They said not to go out on the streets. I'm sure your mother will be safe. We'll phone her as soon as the trouble is over. It won't last long — it's only a raid. Perhaps it would be wise to pack a couple of bags with blankets and some food — but don't cry."

Just then my wife came out to remind me that our daughter-in-law, who lived up the hill from our place, would be left alone with her two small children, as our other son was a member of the special police who had been called to duty. "You had better go up there," said she. "Shamae and I will be all right here."

By clambering over my neighbor's wall and going across lots, I managed to keep off the streets except at one place where I met two Japanese girls, who seemed in a giggling, happy mood. I was suddenly very angry. "Where are you going?" I asked. "To the store," one of them replied with a silly laugh.

"No, you're not," I said sternly. "You're going as fast as you can run back to wherever you came from! Haven't you been told to keep off the streets. Now scram!" They turned and ran. My little outburst of temper seemed to relieve me, and I went, rather self-righteously, on to the house.

But no one was there except the Japanese maid, who was either sleeping, or pretending to be asleep in her room. As I came out, a door opened across the street and my daughter-in-law called, "We are all here." I found four young mothers in the living room, strangely undisturbed, their little children playing quietly around them, all the young men in the neighborhood having gone to their posts. One of the group produced a piece of shell that had fallen in the garden from the explosion on the side of the hill, half an hour before. It showed some rifling so I guessed it was a bit of our own anti-aircraft shells. But the young women were all perfectly calm and quite convinced it was only a nuisance raid, to be soon dispersed when our airplanes got back from attacking the carriers. That was a happy thought that one of the husbands had left with them.

Just about this time there was a lull, but no sooner had we returned to the house when a great commotion broke out again. I laid a mattress down beside the stone wall of the garage and made the mother and two children lie there. "Granddaddy," said the little four-year-old, "why did this have to be enemy Sunday?" Why indeed!

A storm culvert at the top of the street had already been discussed as a bomb shelter, so I went to investigate. There I found a couple of boys putting boxes in the tunnel for people to sit on. Presently two men arrived whom I did not know but they seemed very willing to accept my suggestions. We laid planks on the bottom of the conduit to keep people's feet out of the water, then pulled up a hedge and threw in the bushes to cover a six-foot drop at the tunnel's mouth. Now if anyone fell in his hurry to get to shelter, there would be no broken limbs. Soon we had a shelter that would accommodate 40 persons.

Just as we finished, a car, the first to appear in the neighborhood since the attack, drove into the street. Two officers, it seems, were evacuating a woman from Hickam Field. The roof of the coupe had a jagged hole over the driver's seat, another low down on its side and half a dozen bullet holes in the hood. One of the officers, with wings on his tunic, walked around the back of the car to examine another hole in the rumble seat. It was my chance to speak with him alone. He stood, dull and inert, looking rather stupidly at the jagged hole.

"How bad is it, lieutenant?" I asked him. He roused himself as though coming from a long distance. "Damned bad," he said, "our air force is gone — every goddamned plane. The bastards got 'em all. All we've got left to defend this place are our anti-aircraft guns and what's left of the fleet." His words were violent, but his speech was flat, as though all emotion had been drained out of it.

After ten o'clock, when there was a final burst of firing, everything simmered down. But with the quiet, the rumors grew. The water in the reservoirs was poisoned. Enemy parachute troops had landed on the other side of the Pali and had been seen at the head of Kalihi Valley. We were to watch out for men in blue suits with red arm bands. Our fleet had been destroyed and Kauai had been invaded and captured. No, that was not true. News had just come that our fleet had caught and sunk the three carriers from which the attack had been launched. The water was not poisoned but incendiary attacks were expected that night, so fill your tubs with water, get some sand in buckets — and a hose up on your roof!

Late in the afternoon a Japanese, wearing a special police badge, had arrived for Shamae, and from him I got the first news of damage in the city. A bomb had destroyed a couple of houses and killed a woman and her son just at the mouth of our valley, and in Nuuanu Valley there were scores of casualties. The hospitals were crowded, with the dead and wounded lying in rows in the corridors.

Our son dashed in to get his uniform and steel helmet. A bomb had dropped within a hundred yards of his car but everything else was O.K. It was only a raid and there were no paratroopers. Anything else he knew was a military secret, but, anyway, here was a .38 pistol, fully loaded, and a box of ammunition.

"Don't forget the safety catch is on, Dad," he warned. "Everything's under control, but don't open your door tonight until your visitor identifies himself."

"By the way," he added, "Bill (the elder son) was guarding the roof of the wireless station. Wish we could hear from him. But he'll be all right. The army has everything under control. So long, and keep cool."

And keep cool we did, remarkably so. We soon caught our breath, and confidence returned, although as we knew later, there was little or no basis for confidence. We were really not frightened enough. We surely could not be defeated. By this time help must be on the way. So too reasoned the men on Bataan and Corregidor, but to them no help came.

That night as we gathered in total darkness at our neighbor's house, there was another burst of gunfire and a great flare in the sky over Pearl Harbor. With the pistol cocked under my raincoat, safety catch off, and flashlight ready in case I was stopped, I set off for my son's house. I decided I would do the challenging if I met anyone. A car approached but when I stood bareheaded and shone the light for a moment in my own face to show I was not a Japanese, the car turned up a side-street and I went on.

With all lights out, the houses quiet, and the rain sluicing down, it was like a city of the dead. Yet I knew that everywhere people were sitting waiting, perhaps listening to my steps on the pavement. But that part didn't matter — no ill-disposed person would advertise his movements. At the house, my daughter-in-law seemed quite surprised that I should offer guardianship for the night. She had the boy in bed with his clothes on and a bag packed with dry clothes and food. If an attack came, she planned to take the baby in her arms and the boy by the hand, leave them in the tunnel with the neighbors and go back for the bag. With my coming things would, of course, be easier. My elder son had phoned her that he was all right. She thought she might as well go to bed, but would keep her clothes on.

Just before dawn I heard the sound of planes crossing and re-crossing high up above the valley. I wondered if that was our own dawn patrol, or the first wave of enemy attackers waiting for daylight to begin dropping their bombs. As I stood by the open window that faced towards Pearl Harbor listening for gunfire, I had the strange thought that this must be like the old Indian days

— the women and children asleep in the cabin, the men standing
at the cabin windows listening for the war cry and the first volley
of shots — only this time it's Jap planes we watch for and not
naked Indians.

On Monday morning the rush on the grocery stores began. When
I arrived at the shop where we usually went, it was full of people
grabbing cans off the shelves and putting them in baskets without
even looking at the labels. One fat man in the line before the
cashier's desk had a box in front of him almost as heavy as himself.
A well-known dowager from one of the best families had her
Japanese chauffeur with her, loading up her Packard car. When
she found she had forgotten canned milk, she came back, gathered
a basket full and swept majestically toward the top of the line, but
found herself blocked by the fat man.

"Get back to the bottom of the line, where you belong," he
growled, "and if you send that slant-eyed chauffeur of yours back
here again, I'll drop this goddamned box on his toes."

Nevertheless, an obviously pregnant woman was passed along to
the head of the line, while the fat man, noticing a girl with a baby
struggling with a heavy box, took it and placed it on top of his
own. Then he wheezed and sweated his painful way to the cashier's
window. Chivalry, I thought, is not quite dead in Honolulu.

"Attention, all!" A naval officer with a gob in attendance stood
at the door. "This place is under martial law," he announced. "You
can buy your ordinary amounts of goods, but no more!" With
that he was gone, but the hard-bitten sailor with a couple of stripes
on his sleeve pushed through the crowd, swinging his club, and
talking out of the side of his mouth.

"What the hell do you goddamned civilians think this is," he
demanded, "a Fourth of July picnic?"

All very well for him to damn the civilians, I thought, but the
navy aren't doing so well themselves. Perhaps I should have told
him the Japs were giving the picnic. But I was glad I kept quiet,
for just then his eye fell on the plutocratic dowager with her basket
of canned milk.

"Hey, you!" he yelled. "Who the hell do you think you are?
Put half of that goddamned milk back on the shelves where you
found it, then get to the bottom of the line." The fat man chortled
with joy. "That's the second time in her life that dame's been
told off, bub," he said, "and both times on the same morning."

The gob grinned and turned to the checking clerk.

"Listen," he said, "scale every damn customer down to five buck apiece, an' don't you play no favorites."

It took a war, thought I, to make democracy work as it ought to

We believe the foregoing account is fairly typical of wha happened to us, the plain people of Honolulu, in the firs forty-eight hours of war. It was a time of fears and anxieties justified and otherwise; of precautions, both foolish and necessary; of altruism and selfishness; of sudden bursts o irritation and flashes of wry humor. Jitters were not ap parent, but the underlying strain showed itself at odd mo ments and in unlooked-for ways.

Though it may have been the valor of ignorance, civiliar spirit stayed high. But, without doubt, rumor took a firm hold of the armed forces. There must have been treachery somewhere, thought they, or this horrible thing couldn't have happened. Many of the utterly false statements then current on the mainland could only have had their origin here — such, for example, that men at Hickam Field were mowed down in their tracks by machine guns concealed in a milk wagon that drove onto the air field at the height of the attack. Another canard was that warning of the at tack could not be flashed from Kaneohe to Honolulu because the telephone wires had all been cut. Still another was that many homes were invaded by Japanese evacuees from the city, forcing the white women to go elsewhere. Arrows also had been cut in the canefields to direct the Japanese aviators to Pearl Harbor, although one wondered why directions would be necessary, since the Harbor couldn't be missed. These, of course, were not rumors but downright lies. For their dissemination many of the women evacuated to the mainland were responsible.

By nightfall on the seventh a number of our brave de fenders, particularly some of the newly enlisted Territorial Guards, were trigger-jumpy. They shot at lights in buildings, they shot at automobiles and trucks, they shot at the moon reflected in windows, or they merely shot. Fortunately their marksmanship was atrocious and hardly anyone was hit.

For the next few days the Governor's office was besieged by hundreds who felt that there must surely be some work they could do, short of digging trenches or stringing barbed wire, though many would have been glad to do either if they had been asked. The situation was eased, however, by the order that every man must have his own bomb shelter. There was little to do at the office so everyone hurried home, donned old clothes, and started to burrow in clay or volcanic ash, or to chip his way through layers of blue lava. The work was fine as mental hygiene and helped to cement neighborly relations. It was a poor citizen who could not point with pride at something special or ingenious about his particular dug-out. Occasionally, there was domestic trouble. It was wearing on a man's patience to spend hours in unaccustomed toil to protect his family, only to have his wife declare she would rather be blown to bits than be buried alive in a flimsy earth-covered shelter. There were also trivial complaints about muddy leaks and standing water, mosquitoes, centipedes and general unsightliness of the structures. But planting the top as a rock garden was found to be effective both as camouflage against marauding Japs or unrealistic women.

The blackout was, by all odds, the most telling consequence of the war, as far as the civilian population was concerned. How many families it cemented, how many it disrupted, there is no telling; but a fair sociological summary would say that families which were already somewhat divided became more so, and those that were well knit became more closely integrated than before. But in many Honolulu homes the arguments were endless — which room to black out, how best to do it, who left the door open, who mislaid the flashlight, and so far into the night or at least as late as ten o'clock when all Honolulu and his wife (but not his dog) went to bed. By military order, dogs were put to bed at dark.

On the whole, the debit and credit sides of the ledger balanced fairly well. For some with tired hearts, the labor and continued strain were bad; for others the exercise was healthful. But it was noticeable that those who suffered the greatest anxiety — those who had a son or sons at the front — talked least about it.

The one topic of all blackout discussions was — where is the fleet? One of the neighbors supplied the answer: it was at the bottom of Pearl Harbor or beached along its shores. From the heights at Aiea, he said he counted sixteen disabled or sunken ships. The Knox report came in for scornful criticism, as did also the naval fiction that a ship was not sunk as long as any of her superstructure showed above water. The Pearl Harbor ship casualties were as far down as they could go. These optimistic reports included Roosevelt's face-saving statement, which reduced our losses so much that they were practically invisible. All this did not make us happy. We were of course not to know of the miracles of repair and reconditioning that were to be accomplished in Pearl Harbor and the rest of the nation's shipyards.

Life remained quite interesting for the rest of the war. We watched for convoys and listened for the air-raid sirens. A sense of humor eventually returned and the spy mania died down. Perhaps the prize complaint came from Black Point, which sticks out to sea a little beyond Diamond Head. A lady complained that a family there had taught their dog to bark in code — long and short barks serving for dots and dashes. But the armed forces also had the jitters at times, as for example when they shelled a large school of fish off Barber's Point, claiming that it was a submarine. Moreover, they reported that it had returned the fire and that one of the enemy shells had blown up the railway line at one point nearby. After being vigorously bombarded, the enemy disappeared, but not until lumps of seaweed knocked off the reef had been reported as survivors swimming ashore. Investigation showed that it was one of our own shells that fell short and wrecked the railway line. Another time, two enemy battleships were excitedly reported to be steaming round Kaena Point, but a check before giving permission to open fire proved that they were two of our own mine-sweepers.

On one occasion, planes flew round and round an incoming convoy, dropping depth charges to get some hypothetical submarines supposed to be trying to sneak into Pearl Harbor with the ships. The explosions shook one of the University Buildings where a first aid class was being held. The shocks were so severe that everyone rushed to the balcony, leaving a volunteer patient so trussed up in splints that he couldn't move. He nearly became a real casualty with rage.

Then too there was the story of the professor who was spending Sunday morning at Waikiki with his newly-acquired Scotch wife. "See, my dear," he said proudly, when the commotion was at its height over Pearl Harbor, "that is the way we carry out maneuvers in America. Look at that smoke screen. See those anti-aircraft shells and the planes darting in and out. I'll guarantee you saw nothing as realistic as that in the European war all the time you were in Scotland." She agreed she hadn't.

But of all eye-witness accounts, that given by Tai Sing Loo (Charlie), the Chinese photographer, deserves first place. It is printed separately as an addition to this chapter, not because of its merits of direct narration, nor because it reminds one so vividly of the prose of Gertrude Stein, but because it reveals so clearly the simple courage of a man who had no special call to be in the fray, but who worked calmly in the middle of it, giving whatever service that humanity called for or which came to his hand. A salute to the spirit of Tai Sing Loo, who fought all day long, and then quietly went home to his wife and children (four) with no thought at all in his mind of being a hero!

For the rest of us, the illusion of pioneer days persisted,

with houses closely barred and all lights hidden, though flashes on the horizon and the houses shaking with the distant detonations reminded us that this was modern warfare. Occasionally we had the excitement of flares dropped off Waikiki to expose any lurking submarines.

Later came the sick days of June 1942, when tension grew without even rumor to account for it. Then we inspected our bomb shelters and listened eagerly to the news. Soon there came reports of army bombers limping back and discharging their bloody cargoes of wounded and dead. We felt invasion might come and usher in our hour of supreme trial. Then the glad news of victory was announced and some of its glorious details. The men at the Pearl Harbor disaster had fought bitterly with the courage of despair, but if any of our men deserved a monument to their memory, it was those who gave their lives unquestioningly in the attack on the Japanese carriers off Midway. Once again the many owed so much to the few.

REPORT ON EXPERIENCES DURING JAPANESE
SURPRISE ATTACK ON PEARL HARBOR,
SUNDAY, DECEMBER 7, 1941

By Tai Sing Loo, Photographer

How happen I were at Pearl Harbor, on the morning of Sunday, 7th of Dec., 1941. On the 6th of December Saturday afternoon I had arrangement with the Tech Sergeant Christenot to have all his guard be at the Main Gate between 8:30 to 9:00 o'clock Sunday morning to have a group of picture taken in front of the new concrete entrance as a setting with the Pearl Harbor for Christmas Card, to sent home to their family. Sunday morning I left my home for Pearl Harbor after 7 o'clock. I was waiting for my bus at corner of Wilder Ave. and Metcalf St. saw the sky full of anti aircraft gun firing up in the air. I call of friend to look up in air explain them, how the Navy used their anti-Aircraft Gun firing in Practising, at that time I didn't realize we were in actual war. Our bus stop at Bishop & King St. We heard the alarm ringing from the third story building of the Lewers and Cooke Ltd. saw the window shattered. I walk up to Young Hotel corner and cross the street stop for a cup of coffee at Swanky Franky suddenly all excitement arouse the Honolulu Fire Engine rush down Bishop St. and all directions Taxi full load of Sailors and Marines dashing toward Pearl Harbor. I'm very much surprised whats all this excitement. I wave the taxi to stop & get on it to go back to Pearl Harbor when I approach to Pearl Harbor surprise with great shock thought one of our oil tanks caught in fire, showing Black Velum of thick smoke in the air. I got off at the main gate of Pearl Harbor, met all the guards with arms and machine gun in placed. I was great shock with surprise the war are on, watching many Japanese warplanes attacked Pearl Harbor dropping Bombs right and left on Dry Docks and Ford Island suddenly terrific explosion broke out. I was very calm and waiting for the opportunity to get a ride to the studio and get my camera. I was at the Main Gate stand by with Marines in action. A word of praised and thumb up for those Marine Guards at the Main Gates were bravery and cool headed to keep the bystanding away for safety and clear traffic. They were the young Fighting Marines. We were under fire. The Japanese plane painted in aluminum, Red ball under each wing, flew very low toward the Main Gate. I wish my graflex with me I would had a wonderful close up shot of the Japese. Again the Japese flew around the Navy Housing Area and turn back toward Hickam Field very low to drop a bomb to the hangers with terrific explosion set fire the buildings. More planes flew direct the dry docks. Suddenly I saw one plane had a hit. It flew direct toward West Lock stream of Smoke Screen. Now this my opportunity to get the yard, one of the leading men of Machine shop drove in his automobile I hop in, he take me to the Studio and pick up my Graflex camera to take some picture, second thought I change my mine, reason is because first place I didn't Had no order, the second place I didn't had my famous Trade-Mark Helmet on, I had a new English Helmet from Singapore given by admiral Murphin year ago, so I'm afraid some one will make a mistake me as a Jap and shot me down.

I went up to the Administration Building everything OK. I met Mr. Wm. McIlhenny and Mr. W. C. Bohley at the stairway, we talk and both went toward the Dry Dock. I went to the supply Dept. and saw many boy had a steel helmet on, so I went to see Lt. Comdr. Supply Officer for permission to get one the size are too large and heavy for me so I select one smaller size, painted green and white stripe. I went directly to the Dry Dock to help put out the fire on a ship that had the depth charges on her stern. I knew it was very dangerous it may explosed. We put our hoses directed on the depth charges keeping. An Officer came by said keep up the good work we had our hoses right at it all the time, and I turn around and saw an officer order all men stand back some thing may happen, So I obey his order and ran back sudden really happen the terrific explosion came from the destroyer. People were hurt and some fell down. I notice some large pieces of steel plates blew over the Dry Dock when I turn around and look, afterwards I notice two extra hoses without nozzles, so I went to the fire station and bought back two nozzles to service up and gave it to 2 volunteers pointed direct the depth charges, I call for more volunteers to help me clear and straighten up the hose around the First Street to clear for traffics. For the same purpose to gave the fire fighter a chance to extended the hose across over the bow of the vessel to fight the fire at the starboard side. Here come another Fire Engine from Submarine Base. I direct them to place their engine and connect this hydrant No. 151 and direct them to the depth charges, so everything are well done and successfully accomplishment their service. A few words of my appreciation and vote of thanks and successful Credit to Spear in charge with his gallant spirit to keep his staff and Volunteers calm right at the job to see the Depth charges were wet and keep away from the fires. The Marines of the fire Dept. of the Navy Yard, are the Heroic of Day of Dec. 7, 1941, that saved three ships.

I saw the crew throw out empty 5″ shell on the deck, I gather up in piles with some sailors so I met Chief Le Tendre to help me order some hose from Supply Dept. to place in this hydrant Cor. Ave. D, and First St. I also request Foster to order me some more hose, within half an hour the Chief brought back to new hoses and other load for Foster and other Chief which I have about 12 lengths of hose to stand by. Why I order this hose for? The answer for emergency something may happen I will be there with readiness, reason why the magazines were taken out from the ship and many Casing & empty shell, at the same time we were under fire the Jap Air planes flew over head where up in the Cloud. Anti Air Craft crews were in full action, I wasn't excited and very calm about my work directly placing two large planks across the 1st St. to protected the 2 new hoses. I were little worry because I have no nails & lumbers to nail between the two planks separates while the heavy Traffic goin by with Emergency Cases to the Naval Hospital without crushing the hoses. I met Swain passing by I had his permission to have the carpenter of the Boat Shop to help me nail this planks together. He went to telephone within few minutes four men marching down with nails and Lumbers I were very happy. Here comes the Carpenters ready to started nailing, suddenly the Roaring Anti Air Craft Guns in action, I call my men to dodging for safety, after the Enemy planes disappear, we all returns to our duty, the four men didn't come back at all left the hammers, nails & lumber so I was very fortunely for two of our local boys passing by and helping me to finish the job, it were very thankful to their service to stand by with me during the Emergency. I had two men standing by the Hydrant No. 119 locate Corner Ave. E and First Street near the head of Dry Dock No. 1, four men guarding the two hoses in emergency for readiness in case of fire broke out from the Magazine Casing.

I was self volunteer to be traffic Police and directing the Traffic during the rushing hours of emergency, I got a big piece of Maroon cloth to signaling the Ambulance to look at those planks, easily passing over, to save my hose and other word to give the wounded rest from rough crossing the heavy planks. I directed all four hours to keep the First Street clear of right away to the Naval Hospital. Many heavy trucks passing by with all Defenders & Emergency Call Employee to report to the shop for standby. I direct all this Group of Trucks turn up Ave E. and unloaded the Employees. Every things were successfully executing. I enjoyed my duty and a word of appreciation to my volunteers friends of their Bravery and Courageous to their service, during the emergency and Under Fired. Everythings were under control and we all secure and roll up the hoses and returns to the supply Dept. We were hungry no lunch so I bought each one a Box Ice Cream for lunch and we all dismissed about 3:30 P.M.

One of the Marine Patrol approaching toward me, If I will do the boys a great service of the Marine Guards & Sailors, which they have no lunch & some without breakfast, So I went to the garage to take my Red Put-Put to the 3rd Defense Fleet Ball Mess Hall to see my friend Tech. Sergt. Newland for help, I told my story regards the post guard have been neglected to relieve for lunch. Tech. Sergt. Newland were very kind and his cook to prepare some Sandwiches ham & chicken Fruit all i can delivery to the Post. You should hear what their saying. Charles you are our life saver. I have been riding round and round the Dry Dock until every one had a Sandwich on every Post except the Fuel O. 1 Farms. I sent 50 Chicken and Ham Sandwiches, Apples, & Oranges and Buns and Ham, After I return the Mess Sergant report no breads be served & water being posined. I serving some civilians and the Post on

guard Hot Tacks,[1] Apples & Oranges. The Water is poison. At
the Dry Dock all workman have no lunch and are hungry, working
on certain Ships. I ran short of everythings about 6 P.M. I told
the men go to the Mess Hall of the 3rd Defense to have their meal
without charges and drink tomatoe juice & fruit. About 7 P.M.
I went to the garage to have them take me to the Main Gate. At
the last thought, I have the driver take me to the Mess Hall. The
Mess Sergt. gave me 3 gals Can Iced Cold Tomatoe Juice and 3
dozen Oranges and bag full of Hot Tacks I left Navy Yard 7:30
P.M. at Main Gates. I was very fortinately an Automobile pass by
Lady invite me to take me back to town, she just off the Ferry Boat
from the Ford Island. She left off the Hawaiian Electric Co. It was
a black out night, I walk across to Army & Navy Y.M.C.A. to the
Beretania St. to walk directly to Thomas Square and stopping for
a rest. I ask the soldier guard on patrol with appreciated very kindly
if he will halt an automobile to take me home if convenience on
his way. I told him I am back from Pearl Harbor I'm Chinese he
shake my hand and glad to be of service to the Chinese friend. As
automobile approach and stop the soldier request the owner if he
will help to take me home to the University. Happening the
Driver knew me very well he heard my voice, so he invited me
in his car and drove me to my home, at the front door, I extend
my appreciation & thanks him very kindly to see safely home.
My wife and My children (four) were happy and thankful I were
safely home.

[1] Probably "hard tack" biscuits.

CHAPTER XI

Hawaii's Hour

AS REGARDS Honolulu itself, the most acute problem was, as anticipated, the medical one. Fortunately the careful planning of months forestalled panic and brought confusion to a minimum. The headquarters of the Emergency Medical and Ambulance Committee had been set up at Kaahumanu School which is a couple of miles from the center of the city, on the side opposite Pearl Harbor. Twenty-five minutes after the attack opened, the office was manned and sending out orders, and receiving emergency requests. Less than fifteen minutes later, T. H. Davies & Co. and American Factors had been contacted to send all their trucks to the Armory to pick up their casualty frames for ambulance service. Other firms were alerted very shortly afterwards. Then came the first military call for help. At 9:10 A.M. Colonel King, surgeon general, asked that as many trucks as possible be sent to Hickam Field to carry the wounded to the Military Hospital at Tripler. In ten more minutes 45 of the trucks, with drivers trained for first aid, were on their way to Hickam.

But the rush was far too great for the doctors at Tripler to handle. An urgent request for medical assistance was relayed to Queen's Hospital, where most of the doctors were attending a post-graduate lecture by Dr. Moorhead, a visiting surgeon, on wound surgery. His presence in Honolulu was one of the lucky breaks of the war. Twenty-six doctors and 20 nurses were at once on their way to Tripler Hospital. By 9:15 eight first aid stations, all within the danger area, were reported fully manned and ready for action, and by mid-morning all 20 units were in operation. The record shows that at these stations 2,344 persons were treated on December 7th for injuries or illness. One station at Lunalilo School was struck by either bomb or shell, set on fire, and its personnel compelled to evacuate to an adjacent building. Ten ambulance-trucks were dispatched to each first aid station.

By ten o'clock it was quite apparent that all regular hospital facilities would be greatly overtaxed and Farrington School, a mile from Tripler, was requested for hospital conversion. And so the morning went by with calls for men to act as stretcher bearers at Pearl Harbor, for extra doctors for the City Emergency Hospital, for flasks of blood plasma, for Palama station to stand by to receive a large number of casualties. The Red Cross set up arrangements to feed personnel of first aid and ambulance stations, a scheme in which the Honolulu school department, through its cafeteria service, joined.

Typical of the first entries in the official telephone log of the Emergency Headquarters are the following

12:05 P.M. Two trucks dispatched to Schofield Barracks for stretchers.

12:20 P.M. Twelve trucks to Territorial Hospital (where wounded from Kaneohe Naval Base were being treated).

12:35 P.M. Commandant notified Headquarters through the Red Cross not to send any more trucks to Pearl Harbor, as they are only in the way. (Attacks there had ceased at 10:00 A.M.)

12:50 P.M. Palama station reporting 3 dead; 2 near dead.

1:50 P.M. Kamehameha school reported satisfactory for hospital use by Army.

5:20 P.M.   Check made of all aid stations. All have more than enough volunteers.

6:45 P.M.   Most doctors back from Tripler. Five surgeons now available for calls.

9:00 P.M.   City and County Emergency Hospital reports 37 dead; 90 injured. These were all civilian casualties.

2:47 A.M.   (December 8th). Request 2 crews of twenty men each for Fort Armstrong.

5.05 A.M.   Wheeler Field being bombed, planes 8,500 feet over Oahu. (Report was inaccurate; probably it was the shooting down of some of our own incoming planes from the mainland.) All stations alerted.

7:20 A.M.   Radio address by Roosevelt. America declares war. Guam, Midway, Wake being bombed.

8:45 A.M.   Palama reports 4 dead, 14 casualties. Question of food for the Unit.

12:20 P.M. (December 9th) Request for 6 doctors to go to Tripler to do surgical dressings.

The above are but a few of the numerous calls received. The fact that requests of all kinds, for laborers, passes, car stickers, for blue cellophane paper to cover flashlights, for all kinds of medical supplies and equipment, could be at once acceded to is proof of smooth functioning following efficient planning. For a place that had never suffered a disaster causing twenty casualties at a time, Honolulu did very well.

Blood plasma was of course in instant demand. But when the director had delivered 75 flasks to Tripler for the military, 45 to the Pearl Harbor Naval Hospital, and 80 flasks to Queen's Hospital for civilian use, there was nothing left from six months' accumulation. Yet when the call went over the radio for donors, the response was overwhelming. Men and women of all types and ages — some lied about their years to bring themselves within the accepted limits —

actually stood hours in line to give their blood. War workers, dock workers, sugar and pineapple laborers did their
day's work then came to the Blood Bank. Dr. Pinkerton[1]
reported "a schedule of 50 donors per hour, 10 hours a day,
7 days a week was maintained for two weeks, with the labo-
ratory staff on 24-hour duty in three eight-hour shifts." In
short, while before the war it took six months to line up less
than 300 donors, in one week after the war 3,500 were
available. How many men otherwise marked for death were
saved by these transfusions there is no telling, but they were
certainly numbered by the thousands. As mentioned previously, the O.C.D. (Office of Civilian Defense) then took
over the Bank's financial support.[2]

In any appraisal of the part played by the medical profession on Oahu on December 7th, it should be remembered
that in common with a condition affecting the whole of
Honolulu, rapid growth of the civilian population had caused
medical resources, including the number of doctors, nurses,
clinics, and hospitals, to lag behind to such an extent that
even before the war the shortage was becoming acute. In
these respects, this community was ill-prepared to meet a
grave emergency. It was only by overworking these resources to the limit and using the most careful advanced
preparation that the crisis was met. That the record might
be a matter for some pride, may be gathered from an address
given on January 26, 1945, by Major General Norman Kirk,
Surgeon General for the U.S. Army. He said: "I want to
express the thanks of the Army to the civilian physicians of
Honolulu for the magnificent job they did on December 7th,

[1] Pinkerton, F. J. *Preparedness of the Honolulu Blood Plasma Bank Prior
to December 7th, 1941.* In the War Record of Civilian and Industrial Hawaii.
H.S.P.A. Report. Compiled by Col. E. C. Moore.

[2] A year after Pearl Harbor over 8,000 doses of plasma had been collected
and stored in 29 different hospitals, ice-houses, etc., throughout the city. Trucks
and trailers with electric refrigerators were also donated privately and these
traveled through rural districts collecting blood.

when they were ready for it and we weren't." [3] That was a magnanimous and frank admission.

Turning to the work of other committees of the O.C.D., we find it a most difficult task to invest a summary account of patient day-after-day effort with any qualities of vivid description. Figures are such stultifying things. For example, when speaking of the gas defense division, it is easy to say that 400,000 adult masks were distributed, plus 70,000 masks for children and 32,000 "bunny masks" for infants, the last all made locally. But those 400,000 adults stood somewhere in line, were handed their masks, signed for them, and then received individual demonstrations of how to put them on and wear them. If you think it was an easy job to work hour after hour fitting masks to people of all nationalities, and all degrees of emotional control, putting the instructions into all types of pidgin English, and helping mothers with scared and almost hysterical children, then you should unmask your own imagination. The people who did this received no commendation or ribbons of honor. All of them knew, however, that if the job were done in a perfunctory manner, hundreds of lives might be lost.

Then, too, consider the magnitude of the task of immunizing all residents against typhoid and smallpox and issuing certificates to every person; or the labor of finger-printing and issuing registration cards (made in duplicate) for those same 400,000 individuals, a task assumed by a corps of teachers who cheerfully shouldered the burden. What boots it to repeat that the various O.C.D. divisions employed 4,000 volunteers, and that 1,000 served "communications" by automobile, motorcycle, bicycle, scooter, or ordinary leg power. Only if you have a proper conception of the small size of Honolulu as a city, will you have any appreciation of what it means to say that the Army took over 818 units from the schools, including classrooms, storerooms, auditoriums, lavatories for military use — and only

[3] Quoted by Dr. H. L. Arnold, loc. cit.

if you have been a teacher will you realize the handicaps
of conducting classes in basements, garages, etc., of private
houses scattered all over the city. In addition the private
schools, Punahou, St. Louis, and Kamehameha, were at once
commandeered by the military for hospitals or the U.S.E.D.,
the school authorities evacuating most cheerfully. The
teachers richly deserved the military citation which the Department of Public Instruction received on their behalf, a
most unusual, if not unique distinction.

The personnel of the air raid wardens constituted a small
army of 6,500 men, who each took a minimum of 40 hours
work in training for these jobs and patrolled every block of
the city every night, watching for black-out infractions and
readying themselves for a possible attack. One thousand
of them were specially trained for fire control duty, using
hose and trailer pumps which were located at 50 per cent of
the 67 precinct headquarters.

Evacuation of residents from dangerous sections provided
another problem of organization, involving the enrollment
of 2,200 volunteer supervisors, the setting up of 35 evacuation centers, the storing of food supplies and spare clothing
by the Red Cross, and the issuing of the proper instructions
to cover the 65,000 persons to be evacuated.

In the meantime, there was the constant problem of feed-
ing the civilian defense volunteers plus 467 members of the
Territorial Guard who took the place of the men of the
National Guard taken directly into military service. Three
hundred thousand meals were provided by the Emergency
Feeding section in a single year.

Of measures related more directly to the military situation,
mention should be made of the building of splinter-proof
bomb shelters to seat 75,000 people, also gas decontami-
nation units. The latter are now all being torn down, though
a suggestion has been made that at least one chamber should
be retained for the benefit of some of our local politicians.
There were also mortuary and burial sections set up, and

some functioned very actively in identifying the dead after the attack and collecting their personal belongings. The co-ordinator, Mr. Walker, states that they did a splendid job under most distressing conditions and incidentally "ate an amazing quantity of aspirin" while carrying out their un-pleasant duties; they undoubtedly needed it. Two hundred seventeen volunteers served at these stations.

The civilian hospital accommodations were soon expanded by a thousand beds, one of the largest emergency units being set up at Sacred Hearts Convent, with 400 beds.[4] The am-bulance service was also increased to 52 units, 33 on Oahu. These were in addition to the 250 volunteer ambulances already mentioned that played a major role on the fatal seventh.

The B.M.T.C., or Business Men's Training Corps, was extremely active in training programs, though how some of its corpulent members carried on infiltration maneuvers in heavy brush is beyond understanding. Some of them remind-ed one of the cartoon depicting a line of London militia being dressed in line by a regular sergeant. "Back a little, Number Five," was the order when they were dressed from the front, and "Up a little, Number Five," when the sergeant looked at the line from the rear. But fat or lean, there were soon 900 of them enrolled and they provided squads for the guarding of some facilities, and turned out on regular alerts with the Army. A similar organization of city business men was the Hawaii Defense Volunteers, which was also under the con-trol of the Provost-Marshal.

Food, in the event of a real emergency, was our major anxiety. It has been mentioned elsewhere that Mr. Howry Warner had been sent to Washington in April 1941 to try to buy $2\frac{1}{2}$ million dollars' worth of emergency food sup-lies. This request was promptly denied by the Bureau of the Budget in Washington. Accountants look with a very

---

[4] The influx of defense workers by the thousands put a still heavier strain on our already overworked medical facilities.

jaundiced eye on any program for emergencies. They operate on the principle that emergencies rarely happen and and so it is more economical not to prepare for the unlikely. With the blissful ignorance as to conditions in the Territory that Washington bureaus usually display, these people thought it a very simple matter to convert our agricultural system to food raising. In December 1941, we had in Hawaii sufficient food to last the civilian population six weeks. Fortunately the Japanese attempts at submarine blockade were ineffective. A year later we had accumulated 111 days' supply. What would have happened if the Battle of Midway had been lost in June is too distressing to contemplate. The 15,000 home gardens and hundreds of acres devoted to the production of vegetable foods by the sugar and pineapple plantations would have helped, had we been able to live while the crops were growing. As we have seen, the Diversified Crops Committee's work came to be of little account, partly because of lack of funds and proper official backing, but mainly because the threat of blockade was withdrawn enabling the civilian committee in charge of the situation to ship adequate supplies to Hawaii.

Under governmental urging, the sugar and pineapple industries continued their production at a high level throughout the years of war. Both were considered essential crops. The military and lend-lease authorities together took between 20 and 30 per cent of the Territory's pineapple production of over 22 million cases of fruit and juice. The men in combat zones hailed enthusiastically this addition to their camp and service menus.

Sugar plantations did their share towards the nation's subsistence, exporting during 1942 between eight and nine hundred thousand tons of sugar. Yet the plantations lost over 7 per cent of their most valuable sugar producing land which was taken over by the military, contributed labor for making airports to the tune of 400,000 man days, loaned most of their heavy equipment and drivers to the U.S. en-

gineers, and at the same time saw their precious man-power
drained away into the Army and to take jobs on defense
projects. From 30,646 adult male unskilled laborers in 1941
the total fell to 26,371 in 1942, relatively the greatest loss
in any annual period. To keep sugar production to its high
level meant increased, all-round effort.

The goal set could not have been attained except for
student help. Public and private school authorities decided
that cultivating sugar was as important for the nonce as
cultivating the mind; hence for all high schools the school
week was reduced from five to four days so that the student
could volunteer for field work. Nearly all schools partici-
pated except, it is reported, the one religious section. They
had conscientious objections to war, but not apparently to
eating. The student contribution was gratefully acknowledged by the industry.

What should be made a matter of record in the contribution of Hawaiian industry to national defense is most
difficult to decide. Naturally the burden fell heaviest on
those plantations which were contiguous with Pearl Harbor
or Schofield, the military post. Ewa Plantation decided to list
its strictly military services and required over thirty closely-
typed pages to name merely the most important. How
these contributions interfered with plantation activities may
be gauged from the fact that Oahu, the next plantation to
Ewa, had its output of sugar reduced from 62,000 to 13,500
tons annually. Unlike many industries in mainland America,
plantations could not convert to gainful munitions or arms
production, so that reducing operations by more than 75
per cent represented a sacrifice that few business concerns,
except those in war-ravaged countries, had to suffer. Sugar
was a national necessity, and someone had to grow it. Sugar
men ask no special credit for those sacrifices; what they
would like to avoid are foolish and lying accusations that
they made large profits during the war.

Take the case, for example, of the plantation nearest Pearl

Harbor. Prior to the war, Honolulu Plantation's crop was 27,500 tons and among other improvements it had built the only important refinery in the Islands. It held, either by lease or in fee simple, about 6,000 acres of good sugar-cane land — good, that is, if each acre could have about 3⅓ million gallons of water pumped onto it each year, enough to cover the land to a depth of 10 feet 4 inches. When Poland was invaded in 1939, the military decided they must have room for Hickam Field and other installa-tions, and so they expropriated about 50 per cent of the total area, with of course no consideration of the location of the wells and ditches vital to the plantation's needs. Because of existing leases on other lands which had 20 years to run, pension liabilities amounting to over half a million dollars, plus a sense of obligation to the 3,000 people de-pendent upon it for employment, the company could not cease operations even though they entailed a loss.

When war came, the entire personnel was mobilized for civilian defense, the manager, Stafford Austin, being also the defense director for rural Oahu. Before the attacks actually ceased, plantation trucks, tractors, etc., were rolling down to Pearl Harbor, and gangs of skilled workmen were at work helping clean up the mess. Seventy-five wounded were taken into the plantation hospital on the first after-noon, and seventy volunteer nurses' aides, trained for such an emergency, took up their duties in day and night shifts.

These were full days, unimaginable in content to people in those happy eventless years before the war. Plantation folk must have often pinched themselves to prove they were not dreaming these strange happenings — the offices blacked out as defense headquarters; the call for carpenters to plug the bullet holes in the house roofs; the request for 25,000 jute bags as a single day's contribution to the task of build-ing sandbag screens for machine gun posts; one of the Pearl Harbor barrage balloons dragging its moorings across the power line, necessitating pumping half a million gallons into the naval water supply; the military police refusing to take charge of an unexploded mortar shell with its cap off and the manager loading it into his car and jouncing it down to divisional headquarters; the U.S. Treasury local officials bringing four million dollars in greenbacks to be burned in the mill furnace in fear of invasion — such events became a part of the avalanche of improbabilities that descended upon the little plantation village at Aiea.

These and many other dramatic happenings are concealed in the simple entry of 41,164 man days and 2,675 machine days lost to the plantation but won for national defense. The only way in which to get some conception of what these figures mean is to imagine this great army of men and machines working all together on a single day. There would be enough to build completely the great pyramids of Egypt. While all this was going on, the plantation went on making sugar, not by any means on a business-as-usual basis, but with the mill blacked out and unventilated, and temperatures well over 100 degrees, while the men in the fields listened all the time for the sirens that might herald another attack.

From the vantage ground of present security, uneasy though it may be, the incredibility of those early 1942 days may be easily overlooked and forgotten. Not the least remarkable in a catalogue of strange happenings was a gathering at the University of 150 Japanese students, many of whom had had reserve officers' training, but were forbidden to don an American uniform and go out to fight.

"If we cannot prove our loyalty by giving our lives," they said, "do not refuse the labor of our hands. We, too, have only blood, sweat, and tears to offer to the common cause. If you will not have the blood, then take the rest. If you cannot trust us with rifles, then give us picks and shovels. Put us to work." The offer was accepted. Later on, these young men became the nucleus of the A.J.A.'s, and gave their blood also in full measure with the other young men of America. The pledge offered in Hawaii was redeemed

on the battlefields of Europe. But that, of course, is a military story.

There is so much of civilian effort of which there is no
room to write, much, for example like the Air Force Morale
program,[5] which would require a chapter to itself. The Red
Cross and the U.S.O. did outstanding jobs, but have published their own reports, any condensation of which would
detract from their importance. There is, however, one supreme lesson to be gained from their perusal. They prove
that no one refused responsibility or stood aside in this
crisis. For rich or poor, leaders or led, there was only the
same number of hours in the day for work, the same limits
to which human endurance could be pushed, and each one
felt that his best was barely enough. No one looked for
credit or acclaim. The burden was too common, the prospects of defeat too grim. Perhaps the finest thing about the
Hawaiian community in crisis was this anonymity of service.
We could publish lists of names of leaders and cite their
decorations, but those who did not work for recognition in
the common peril will not seek it now.

As could be expected the women of the Territory did
their full share in defense work. Not only did thousands
of them participate by taking jobs in the O.C.D. or volun-
teering for finger-print registration and serving in countless ways, but they rallied around as volunteers for first aid
stations, nurses' aides, hospital visitors, U.S.O. activities, etc.
In addition, a small army of housewives gathered daily at
various centers to make surgical bandages and dressings for
Army and Navy use and for civilian hospitals. How many
woman-days went into this great task has not been calculated but it must have amounted to a staggering total. They
hurried away from their household duties for whatever
hours, half-days or full days, they could spare. Many made

[5] This was initiated in 1941, under a general chairman, Col. Harold Kay,
and a chairman on each island. Hospitality during rest periods was offered fliers
of the 7th Air Force at ranches, plantations, and private homes.

it a point of honor not to miss a day. All their minor and many of the major ailments were disregarded, for this was not an effort of the hale and hearty so much as of the old and middle-aged. It was a common saying —if the grand-mothers can hold out, we will win the war. And when, anticipating the stream of wounded coming back here after those bloody naval battles of the South Seas, the Navy called for a fuller stock of dressings, the women stayed overtime and worked like slaves. These services never received suffi-cient commendation, perhaps because it was women's work and therefore unspectacular.

Some scores of women also worked in canteens for military personnel. Others enrolled as Grey Ladies giving help to wounded men convalescing in the hospitals. Altogether the women of Hawaii did a grand service, much of it in ways that did not come readily to public recognition. Even the Japanese women attended Red Cross centers, though the haole women were naturally to the fore since they required no organizing. But scarcely a woman in the Territory did not assume heavier burdens during the war. There were few, if any, slackers. The worst that could be said of some was that they felt they had a sufficient burden to carry with-out taking on war work. But neutrally-minded women were rare; there was very little nonsense talked about keeping the home fires burning in Hawaii. Most women did their day's work and then found time to assume a great many other duties. All felt the need to do the extraordinary, the uncalled-for in the line of duty. Tired eyes, aching limbs, sore backs, weary feet were all in the day's work for thou-sands during a year of preparation and four years of war. It was by no means easy for those who were able to take paid defense jobs when they worked all day and came home to do their housework at night. The younger women who boarded the buses at six in the morning and worked all day at Pearl Harbor or Hickam Field certainly did their share.

I would be loath indeed to appear to be blowing up

Hawaii's civilian war contribution to heroic proportions. As a city, Honolulu did not suffer on any comparable scale with London, Liverpool, Coventry, and scores of other cities in Britain and on the continent of Europe. The civilian casualties on our single day of attack numbered 170, which is hardly measurable against London's thousands a week for week after week. We did not undergo the trials of the people of Hong Kong, Manila, Singapore, Batavia, for they were not spared the horrors of invasion. Apart from several ineffectual submarine shellings of the outer islands, we heard no guns except our own, from the second to the last day of the war. The only direct enemy action was when, a couple of months after December 7th, a lone Japanese plane dropped four bombs in the bushes near Tantalus above the town. This being at our low point of confidence in the Army and Navy, some people were unkind enough to suggest that this incident was due to some aviator returning from an unsuc-cessful mission and deciding to lighten his load for a safer landing. The naval theory was, I believe, that the plane was launched from French Frigate Shoals or from the deck of a very large Japanese submarine and that the pilot mis-took Tantalus for the Aiea heights overlooking Pearl Harbor.

Taking all things into consideration, civilian Oahu fought a very inconvenient but privationless war, and, after the first fatal day, a bloodless one. Compared with the island of Malta, the Hawaiian Islands were safe and sound, and we lived a decidedly humdrum existence. We thought we lived dangerously, because of the constant threat, but as we know now that threat was more apparent than real. Naturally, human nature being as it is, it was difficult for us to take a very broad comparative view. We were so much worse off than the rest of the people in America that it was hard for us not to exaggerate our plight.

In an excellent factual summary written by the secretary of the Hawaii Equal Rights Commission in January 1943, for mainland consumption, there is some sympathy-hunting apparent. He speaks of the infamous "sneak attack" that shattered Honolulu's Sabbath calm and transformed it "instantaneously into the center of the active combat zone it has become ever since." If this was the center of combat, then it must have been deadly calm around the fringes at Guadalcanal and other such places. The report goes on to state that Honolulu still bears the scars of that dread assault and affirms our people's firm determination "to stand steadfastly and unflinchingly in the face of the enemy's dropping bombs and their constant threat of repetition." The writer also prays God the rest of America may be spared our harrowing experience of a year of war, and solemnly pledges our faith to them that their fellow citizens in Hawaii will carry on the American way of life, "unswervingly in the face and under the threat of the enemy."

This, it must be admitted, was a little highfalutin'. We did make our refrigerators, electric stoves, automobiles, and the other things essential to the American way of life last for the duration. We had no choice. Similarly, we didn't swerve under the hail of bombs; there was no place to swerve to, and after the seventh there were no bombs. As for flinching, we did our share of that, when our own artillery cracked our ear-drums by practice shelling from positions, seemingly, on our back lawns. No one would wish to make light of our civilian casualties, but Honolulu's scars consisted of a couple of buildings destroyed, a few others partially destroyed, some spattered with blast fragments, and a few inconsequential craters on the road sides. War casualties were mainly from shell splinters from our own anti-aircraft fire, and very few in the city were victims of Japanese bombs.

Incidentally, I would like to advance the suggestion, even if it is unwelcome, that we cease being self-righteous about the "infamous sneak attack." The formalities of a declaration of war do not make the practices of modern war more humane nor honorable. Present-day conflicts do not resemble gentlemen's duels in the least. The people of Nagasaki and Hiroshima died just as unexpectedly as the people of Honolulu. We justify atomic bombings — if we care to justify them — on the theory that a terrific blow delivered without warning is the shortest and most merciful way of winning a war, even though many innocent bystanders are killed in its delivering. The Japanese had this theory too, but their infamy lies in the fact that they applied it first. Fortunately, the violence of the Japanese — and their mercy — did not match ours. With the pattern set by the Nazis in Europe, the blow at Pearl Harbor should have been fully expected and well guarded against. The sneakiness of the attack lay in the fact, not that the blow was given when we should have been looking, and weren't, but in its unqualified success. But the ethics of the whole matter I would gladly leave to the clergy in whose province such discussions seem to lie, even though some of them appear to favor fox-holes as a defense against atheism.

Returning to our war effort, we should cheerfully admit that there was nothing heroic in going about our business of raising sugar and pineapples. We did not of course give these essential foods to the nation — we sold them. Nor was there anything superpatriotic about our "victory gardens" — we all appreciated fresh lettuce, tomatoes, and string beans on our dinner tables, especially when we had not even the stale varieties on hand. It is not necessary, also, to make a brave, brave story out of the number of servicemen we entertained either privately or through the local U.S.O. I believe it is sufficient to say that we did what we could.

As much, that is to say, as could be done by thirty thousand middle-class haoles — plus a few thousand of others who had leisure and money to help with the entertaining — upon whom had suddenly descended a couple of million other haoles, all, no doubt, intent on spending their lives, but finding that for many months all they could spend was time and money in Honolulu. In the intervals of jungle and desk training, setting the watch or just setting, hundreds of thousands of men from all over the Union scrambled eagerly for that much publicized charm and relaxation that tired millionaires enjoyed so much in Honolulu before the war. It wasn't to be found, or there wasn't enough to go around, and there were bitter complaints.

We did our best to carry on the American way of life, not in the face of the enemy, which we never saw, but against the demands of our defenders. We seek no credit for civilian sacrifices and heroism, but we would like to avoid some of the criticism that is so unthinking as to be almost moronic. We certainly would have liked to have expanded Waikiki beach, which is normally crowded with 300 tourists, so as to accommodate 30,000, but it just couldn't be done. When thousands of soldiers and sailors had a couple of days' liberty, it was rather sad that Honolulu only had five or six reasonably sized hotels to give them lodging, especially considering that one of the two largest hotels was at once taken over for military use.

As to other more specific entertainment that was rather commonly expected, we might say that if every girl in the Islands had taken a service man to bed with her each night, there would not have been nearly enough nights and certainly not half enough beds to go around. Again, we did what we could, but not enough to dispense with the long lines of men standing before the houses of the prostitutes who came from the mainland to help those local girls who felt their patriotic duty inclined that way. In between times, the service men demanded honky-tonk amusement and honky-tonks sprang up overnight to supply it.

The rest of us picked up the soldiers and sailors in our cars and took them as far as our limited gasoline rations would allow. We brought a few of them home, where our wives — whose maids had gone to be photographer's models or cashiers in the aforementioned honky-tonks — cooked and served all the meals they could prepare in time spared from canteen or Red Cross service. We also exercised our racial tolerance by looking the other way when we met our former maid's younger sister tripping along the street hand in hand with her uniformed boy friend. We meet her now occasionally on the bus, hand in hand with a nondescript looking infant, part Japanese, part soldier.

Yes, the war left our city dirty and unkempt, and our clean-up campaigns, when we had to rely so long on ex-hula dancers and lei sellers to do the heavy work of sweeping the streets, did not get along very far or fast. We still pay 25 cents (though this excited the ire of a *Saturday Evening Post* writer) for an inadequate curbside shoe shine. We likewise pay eight dollars a day for our cleaning ladies, and a dollar an hour for our yard gentlemen; that is if we can afford to return to the American way of life in Hawaii that we enjoyed before the war, and have our houses cleaned and our lawns cut by hired help. These things are nothing to cry about, but it is a little hard to accept goodhumoredly the snide remarks of some of the officers and war correspondents for whom we emptied our one a week bottle of whisky, knowing all the time that the armed forces brought in for their consumption enough liquor to refloat all the battleships that were sunk in Pearl Harbor. As for food, we continued to hand out, unflinchingly, our hard won tidbits of hospitality to those who had butter when we had none, meat when there was no meat, and bacon to burn. Occasionally a civilian was lucky enough to have his hospitality returned by an invitation to dine at an officer's club. How his eyes glistened and his mouth watered over roast beef or fried chicken and vegetables not prematurely delivered from our bug-infested back yard, but fresh from the mainland.

A little while ago a correspondent of a Boston paper, who thought he knew us during the war, came through Honolulu on his way to Bikini. He wrote a story purporting to show how differently we acted now. This story had a moral to the effect that if we had treated the servicemen in the same way as the Bikini party, with hula girls and leis and Hawaiian music and Hawaiian cocktails, Hawaii would have saved itself its greatly deserved unpopularity with the boys. He implied nothing, but said straight out that if we had wakened up sooner and dished out the old Hawaiian hospitality, the soldiery would not have had us in such contempt.

Now Boston is a fairly large city with more than five hotels. It was also once the home of intellectuals. But if the whole population of New York suddenly moved over to Boston for four years, bringing with it scads of food and building priorities and refrigerators and cars and liquor — all of which the local population was fresh out of — then it is quite likely the New Yorkers would vote the Bostonese a cold, snooty, and inhospitable crowd. Much the same thing happened to Honolulu, only worse.

CHAPTER XII

Pakiki Na Kanaka Kauai[1]

I N 1942 no one in the islands knew whether
or not the enemy had plans for the invasion of the Territory. Their first blow had been so
unexpected and so astonishingly successful that no attempt,
however contrary to ordinary military strategy, was considered beyond their capacity. The quick fall of Hong Kong
after a ten-day resistance, the conquest of Singapore after
a few weeks, the swift overrunning of Java, the not long
delayed withdrawal from Batavia, and the surrender of
Corregidor all seemed to accord with a precise and over-
whelmingly efficient schedule of events. The rapid progress
of the Japanese in the Western Pacific and in the islands
north of Australia was equally breathtaking. Soon we heard
of the bombing of Port Moresby and Darwin and the impending invasion of Australia. With Singapore and all the
forward line gone, and even India threatened, Hawaii seemed
to be the chief hindrance to Japan's complete dominance of
the Pacific. There seemed no reason why she should not
by-pass Australia and New Zealand and attack us here.

Perhaps to the best military minds such boldness was incredible, but our confidence in professional soldiers' opinions,
if not destroyed, was badly shaken. The Japanese successes
looked to us at that time to be just as extraordinary as those
of the Germans in Europe. It seemed as if this were a new
kind of warfare in which all the old military principles had
been superseded. No matter how much confidence our

[1] "Tough are the men of Kauai."

military defenders professed as to the outcome of an invasion attempt, we watched, and approved, their hurried preparations against even the most unlikely chances.

Among these was the invasion and conquest of the outer
islands of the group, so ill-defended in the early days of the
war that a few submarine-borne commandos could well have
made almost unopposed landings. Kauai, as the northernmost
of the group, seemed to stand directly in the path of an invader, once Midway had been occupied. We know now
that Japanese strength had been strained to the utmost, and
that even with Midway gone, it would have been difficult
for Japan to stage any all-out invasion. We did not know it
then, and military and civilian preparations for defense of
all the islands went on apace.

It was Hemingway, I believe, who once said, with a flash
of inspiration, that in order to understand the essence of a
country and its people, you must first have some sense of its
terrain. Detailed description of each island may be helpful to
this end. Kauai, as the oldest of the group, is the most worn
down, though Oahu in point of erosion runs it close. Like
the rest of the islands except Molokai, it possesses two sets
of mountains, one being the residual backbone of what was
probably, in the beginning, a separate island. This is marked
on the map as the Hoary Head Mountains, no doubt with
reference to the air of antiquity that they bear. Mount
Haupu is the central and highest point.

On either side of Haupu, the range extends in a series of
rough eminences like an irregularly preserved and fossilized
lower jaw of some prehistoric animal, in which only the
broad molars with their broken cusps are left. These rocky
cusps are bare at their tops, and the rains of a thousand centuries have discolored them with the green of moss and
lichen and the dark colors of decay. The base from which
the molars have erupted is mantled with trees, lapped in
turn by the upward-sweeping green of sugar cane. The
eastern end of the range runs into the ocean, forming one

of the low heads between which Nawiliwili Harbor opens
The Huleia River parallels this part of the range and pro
vides an extension of the inlet. The harbor facilities have
been greatly improved by a breakwater pointing towards the
other headland, a low bluff of black lava upon which the
lighthouse stands.

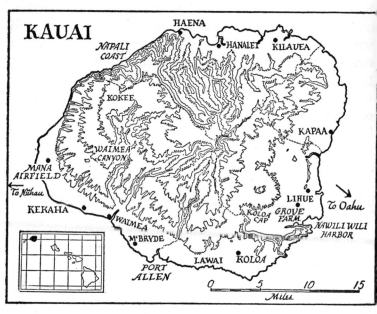

At its western end, the range has weathered down to low
hills, capped with forest, mainly eucalyptus, with some native trees such as the hau. Thus the western entrance of the
Huleia Valley is a gap through a connecting ridge that lifts
itself towards the central mass of mountains which culmi-
nates in Mount Waialeale. This Koloa Gap divides the
island's perimeter into two habitable halves, on the one hand
the east and northeastern rim, on the other the southwest
and western portion. The northwestern arc is the Napali
coast, too rough and steep to be inhabited except by wild
pigs and goats and the ghosts of old Hawaiians. On one
side of the Koloa Gap are the plantation districts of Kekaha,

Waimea, Olokele, McBryde, and Koloa. On the other side are Lihue, Grove Farm, the town of Kapaa, Makee, a long stretch of pineapple lands at Anahola, and the outlying plan-tation of Kilauea. Thus the Koloa Gap was a central point in any scheme of island defense.

The wide valley that contains Lihue, Grove Farm, and the Rice Ranch at Kipu is one of the most beautiful and fertile on Kauai. It is a rolling expanse of rounded hills intersected with gullies whose sides, until pre-empted by the cane, were covered with shady clumps of mangoes, eucalyptus, hau trees, ironwoods, and bananas. But what made it authen-tically Kauai were the tiny groves of pandanus palm exhibit-ing their strangely buttressed stems and awkwardly thrusting limbs, each crowned with its tufts of narrow four-foot strips of leaves like flat rushes bent in the middle that have some-how migrated into the tree tops. Pandanus palms spraddle rather than grow, disdaining most of the principles of tree architecture.

Beyond Kilauea, the mountains grow higher and wetter and nearer the sea. They draw back a little so as to contain the Hanalei Valley, a flat river plain parceled off in green plots, covered with what were once rice paddy fields and would have been so again if blockade had cut us off from California.

Hanalei is the mountains' last concession to fertility. Thereafter they close in quickly, leaving space only for little rivers to come flashing seawards, and for some of the most glorious beaches of the South Seas. Then the twenty-mile rampart of the Napali coast begins, sea-girt precipices, three to four thousand feet high swooping down from cloud-hung forests that back Waialeale, claimed as the wettest place on earth. This coast was considered inaccessible even to the craziest Japanese landing parties, yet even so, as we shall see, its defense was not overlooked.

On the landward side beyond the Napali coast, the great mountain mass of central Kauai slopes down gradually, but is gashed by a three-thousand-foot crevice, which is Waimea Canyon, the island's scenic pride. Its walls are red, brown and a burnt terra cotta, but these combined colors are soft-ened with the green of mantling forests and the faint purple of Hawaiian air distances. The broken plateau that sur-rounds the forks of the canyon is filled with streams and gullies, all covered with a natural forest of ohia and koa, under which passion vines, purple lasiandras, wild nastur-tiums, begonias, and blackberries find the shade they love.

The character of this terrain is most important because it was planned, if invasion came, to make this broken country a defensive core, from which an intensive guerrilla campaign might have been waged to prevent the enemy from having the unrestricted use of the rest of the island. So long as Kokee with its maze of gullies could be held, the only avail-able air field would have been open to constant attack and its use restricted.

This air field is just beyond Kekaha and occupies the Barking Sands area at the extreme tip of the crescent-shaped strip of low land between the mountains and the sea. At the other end of the 25-mile crescent is the Koloa Gap, which we have already described. Beyond the Barking Sands is the western tip of the Napali coast. Approaching the landing field from the air, the ground, as it rises behind the coastal plain, looks as if someone had taken a mass of brown putty and scored it irregularly with the tip of a knife. It would be arid-looking except that the flat plains between the gulches are green with irrigated sugar cane. Beside each field there is a plantation road leading to the higher levels. The problem in Kauai is to find level acreage enough for the cane. The soil need not be rich and deep; agricultural science and abundant irrigation do the job.

On the mile-wide strip of coastal plain you see Kekaha Mill, and four miles along the coast is the river, at the mouth of which stands the historic town of Waimea. It occupies the flat land on the right bank of the stream, where in

Cook's time the place was covered with the grass houses of he natives. On the other bank of the river at its confluence with the sea, the Russians built a fort but were ejected from he island before they could establish themselves firmly there.

Midway between the Mana Air Field and the Koloa Gap s a small bay which, with the aid of a breakwater, has been made into the harbor of Port Allen, big enough to accom-nodate small naval craft and medium-sized freighters. Flank-ing the harbor are two sugar holdings, the Gay and Robin-on Plantation (formerly Makaweli) and the McBryde sugar lands. The monotony of miles of cane is broken in one spot where the road skirts the side of Hanapepe Gorge, a minia-ture Waimea Canyon. You find here the same hot red cliffs filled with caves so characteristic of the lower reaches of the canyon, and on the ledges, bizarre, twisted shapes of prickly pear and ragged mesquite. From these the eye drops grate-fully to terraced taro patches on the river bottom, shaded by giant monkey pods. A mile or two inland the stream is fed with tributary waterfalls and the gorge dissolves into the purple of Kauai Mountains. Had invasion come, these gulches would have been important to military tactics. The plantation roads would have served for the removal of the civilian population to camps in the mountains, while the mili-tary fought along the sides of the gulches and across the fields to prevent enemy infiltration and the outflanking of the Koloa Gap positions.

Beyond Port Allen the land bulges to the south, making room for the oldest sugar plantation in the Hawaiian Islands. Koloa began its operations in 1835 but was itself preceded by a Chinese mill, the granite rollers of which have been re-covered from its site and set up as an exhibit in the Koloa Plantation office grounds. Any enemy force making its way towards the Gap would have pinched off Koloa, so that very careful plans for the evacuation of its population had to be made.

The sea coast on the south side of the Hoary Head range

was not very vulnerable except at the cove of Kipukai, owned by the Rice family, where once existed a small settlement of Hawaiians. From there, an old stone causeway leads through a pass in the mountains to the valley where Lihue stands. This pass too must be heavily guarded as any penetration there would turn the Koloa Gap position.

The next vulnerable point on the Lihue side of the Gap was of course Nawiliwili Harbor. That with Port Allen and a small landing at Ahukini a couple of miles farther along the coast from Nawiliwili make up the sum of harbor facilities, where heavy equipment could have been brought ashore. All along the coast, however, are many beaches where landings could be effected with special barges and landing craft. A couple of miles from Kapaa, Kauai's most populous center, the Wailua River is spanned by a concrete bridge. This would be important to the defense of the island as its destruction would forbid the use of the highway to the defending troops, who could not then be rushed to any danger point along the island's periphery.

The beaches near Haena are too much beset with reefs and currents to make landings feasible, unless the invaders had the assistance of people who knew the coast intimately. But the half-moon bay of Hanalei offered no such difficulties. Hence, as the Army had not sufficient men to defend all these landing places, it had to rely on extreme mobility to rush its repelling force to any threatened point. The guarding of bridges and roads would of course be vital to such a plan. Very important too would be the provision of irregular troops or scouts, who could act as a containing force until the heavily-armed regular troops could arrive. On the northern side of the island perimeter, the most important installation was the electric power works at Wainiha back in the mountains, on the banks of the stream of that name.

On the Waimea side of the Gap, the Waimea River and Hanapepe bridge bore the same relation to defense as the

Wailua bridge did on the Lihue or Kapaa side. The high-way there was also essential to a highly mobile scheme of defense. All of this talk of military defense by the Army assumes of course the presence of the Army on the island, but until nearly four months after war broke out, there were no soldiers there.

To recapitulate its military features, Kauai could be divided into four main areas.[2] The most important was Kekaha-Waimea, wedged in between the western extension of the Napali cliffs and the Waimea River, and backed on the land-ward side by the high land of Kokee. This contained the only landing field large enough for military purposes, though smaller strips had been formerly in use at Port Allen and at a place not far from Kapaa. If the Japanese had won the battle of Midway with the consequent withdrawal of the Navy to the West Coast base, the time may have come when invasion of the outer islands might have been not only fea-sible but advisable from the Japanese viewpoint. The knock-ing out of the airport at Mana beyond Kekaha would then have made the investment of Oahu easier. Blowing up the bridge at Waimea and the retreat of the defending forces into the Kokee highlands would undoubtedly have followed the capture of the airport by the enemy. The gulches lead-ing up through the sugar cane of the Kekaha area towards Kokee may have played an important part in attack and defense.

Next to the airport, the most important enemy objective would have been Port Allen and the utility installations of the four plantations nearby, Olokele, McBryde, Gay and Robinson, and Koloa. Here there is a larger area of country suitable for military operations, which would have necessi-tated wholesale evacuations to get the civilian population out of the armed forces' way. All this had to be most care-fully planned to avoid having the main highway cluttered up with civilian refugees. Included in the plan were total

[2] See map.

demolitions, a scorched earth policy, involving the destruction of harbor facilities, mills, machine shops, garages, warehouses, water and electric installations. With this area occupied, defense would have shifted to the Koloa Gap so as to deny enemy access on the landward side to Nawiliwili Harbor.

Had this been endangered, the same demolitions would have been carried out as at Port Allen, including the blowing up of the breakwater and piers. Port Allen would probably have been the easier prize, as unlike Nawiliwili it is not commanded by high ground near by, thus making assault from the sea easier.

Beyond Nawiliwili and Lihue, across the Wailua River, is the fourth area. This offered little advantage for enemy occupation, but on the contrary would allow of the retreat of defending forces so as to make communications with the troops holding Kokee. It would be difficult, however, to effect a real military junction since the mountain trails are extremely precarious.

As to where enemy landings could take place, we have already pointed out that the Haena area was unsuitable, the beaches being well screened by reefs often placed in echelon. The great Pacific rollers break over these, and in the process masses of water are temporarily imprisoned between the successive lines of coral, whence it escapes in all kinds of tricky cross currents that only the Hawaiian fisherman knows.

To discover the safest landing beaches would mean an excursion of inquiry into the days of sail, when there were no piers, and men and cargo came ashore in open boats. The Russians, well used to landings effected from whalers on the Aleutian Islands, chose two localities which they proposed to protect with forts. As we have seen, one of these, at Hanalei Bay, would lead to a hinterland of negligible military importance. The other was at Waimea, where beaches run for miles, all suitable for landings during calm weather, which is best between June and September. The old Ha-

waiians knew and used the safest spots where their war
canoes could be easily hauled up out of reach of the storms.
Only in southerly weather is this Waimea stretch of the
coast exposed. Hence this western arc of the island's circumference was the most vulnerable to attack, as well as
containing the greatest prize, the airport.

But if any determined attempt had been carried through
to take Kauai, then all the military could hope to do would
be to fight a delaying action until help could come. Where
that help would come from was a problem, dependent upon
whether the enemy was able to attack and capture Oahu
first, or whether they would merely invest that island, making diversionary attacks on the outer islands such as Kauai.
The invasion did not come, but by this time the Army had
learned the lesson which General Short admitted he neglected — to prepare for the worst. In the final defense of
the island, the Kokee area, as we have seen, was vital. It
offered several advantages — among them a sufficiently large
maneuverable area protected on both flanks and rear. On
one side lay the deep canyon of Waimea, its head screened
with almost impenetrable swamps. On its other side and
rear stood the almost unscalable cliffs of the Napali coast,
scalloped into a succession of half-bowls and breathtaking
ravines, separated by razor-back ridges that swoop dizzily
down to the Pacific surges three thousand feet below.

The officers of the 27th Division, after their landing on
Kauai on Easter Sunday, 1942, took one look at these precipices and pronounced them unscalable. So they were, to
men who came straight from Brooklyn and the Bronx to
Hawaii, but not for the wild pig-hunters and cowboys of
Kauai. Judging from what the Japanese had accomplished
in the jungles of Malaya and the mountains of New Guinea,
any assumption of invulnerability would be unwise. The
soldiers sensibly left the defense of this area to the men who
knew it best. In the meantime, they established their most
secret and valuable radar and wireless station in the Kokee

wilds, and no doubt began the storing of food and ammu
nition in the mountains in preparation for a possible la
ditch stand.

As we now know, the Japanese did not include in thei
plans any invasion closely following Pearl Harbor. That wa
discussed in the Japanese war councils, but turned down by
the navy spokesmen as being impracticable. If, however, ever
a later attempt had been anticipated, the task of the invader
would have been immeasurably easier if an active and
properly-organized group of fifth columnists had, on De
cember 7th or 8th, carried out a destructive campaign, cut
ting telephone lines, blowing up bridges and culverts, and
putting a few sticks of dynamite in the mills and under the
piers and in the electric plant at Wainiha. If also the water
reservoirs had been judiciously dynamited, the whole island
would have been thrown into the utmost panic and con
fusion. Consider also the moral effect on the rest of the
people in the Territory and on the nation at large. Such
sabotage would have been branded as the blackest treachery
and Hawaii would never have recovered from its disgrace
Every plan for the defense of the Islands and their use as a
base for a counter-offensive would have been changed there
by. Wholesale fifth-column activities would then, in the
eyes of America, have explained our military failure.

None of these things happened, but it would have been
purblindness of the most stupid character to have assumed
that they could not have occurred. The sugar plantations,
as we have seen, were strategically placed all over the habit
able parts of the island. They employed 2,000 Japanese
men, 900 of whom were enemy aliens. According to firm
belief in mainland America, these 2,000 were all potentially
or actually disaffected. They made up one-third of the sugar
industry's total male employees, and against them were arrayed 166 men of Anglo-Saxon blood, plus 450 Portuguese,
100 Hawaiians, and a large group of Filipino laborers devoid
of military training. How important the sugar industry is

to the island may be judged from the fact that of the total
population of 31,000 (figures for 1942) about half lived on
the plantations or were employed thereon. According to
the figures of the 1940 census the haoles,[3] Portuguese, and
Hawaiian males together totaled just about half the male
Japanese population of the island. If the Japanese were disloyal and determined, subversive activities on their part
would have been easy, unless careful precautionary measures
were taken. These measures could not be left to the regular
military forces on the island, which on December 7th hardly
amounted to a corporal's guard. With the exception of a
company of the National Guard, the U.S. Army had neither
military forces nor equipment on Kauai. The same was true
of the island of Hawaii. These facts should be remembered
when the armed services speak of the Territory of Hawaii,
as they are so fond of doing, as a military outpost. You may,
if you wish, consider the island of Oahu, with over 250,000
civilian inhabitants, an outpost, but the rest of the islands
in 1941 did not constitute even a splinter of an outpost of
defense as far as army protection was concerned. A single
enemy commando landed on the outer islands within a
month or two of December 7th could have played hell with
their defenses. Whatever measures for defense against such
attacks or for the suppression of subversive activities could
be taken had to be provided by the civilians themselves. The
story of how it was done has some interesting features.

At the time of the Japanese attack, a company of the
National Guard existed on Kauai, equipped with two old
French 75 mm. artillery pieces and two anti-aircraft guns.
Due to the fact that the per diem pay for guardsmen during
their training period was less than that offered for plantation
labor, there was no great tendency for responsible men to
enter the organization, though some did at considerable personal sacrifice. After the National Guard was taken into the

3 Haoles was the name applied to foreigners, mainly British and Americans,
who first settled in Hawaii. It does not mean whites, but strangers.

regular Army a territorial Guard was set up, but the people of the island did not feel particularly secure under the protection afforded. Soon after war broke out, the lights of a submarine were reported visible from Port Allen, and at once a truck with a gun on a trailer was rushed towards the scene from the airport 20 miles away. The driver drove like Jehu and covered the distance in record time, but when he drew up with a flourish into position at Port Allen, ready to open fire, there was no gun. The trailer had dropped off unobserved and the gun was lying in the ditch half way back along the road to Kekaha. Still, it was a matter of satisfaction to know that at least one of the French seventy-fives[4] would go off without killing someone, for it returned the fire of the Japanese submarine which shelled Lihue three weeks after the war began.

The story of Kauai's preparations to defend itself, with or without military support, began eighteen months before the war. The tragic events of the month of July 1940 aroused the island people just as it did the rest of the Territory's population. On September 4th, at the height of the German attack on Britain, Major Fitzgerald, army intelligence representative on Kauai, addressed the local planters' association, urging the formation of a civilian defense organization. Early in 1941, plans were set in motion under the leadership of Judge Phillip Rice, who had been named coordinator for Kauai. Enrollment forms were distributed, and volunteers were asked, among other things, to list any firearms they possessed. These provisional police were organized on the same general lines as similar groups on Oahu, and were to be subject to call on any emergency, with the specific exceptions of labor disturbances. Men of every racial group were at first encouraged to volunteer. The American Legion gave the plan their backing, and the Board of Supervisors voted funds for office equipment, badges, and armament for training in pistol shooting. This last consisted of

4 They were twenty-four years old.

Ben Franklin air-pistols, for the leaders decided not to wait for real weapons but to begin training in marksmanship with anything available. Perhaps this was wise, as at first many of the Filipino rank and file did not know one end of a gun from the other. The bolo was their weapon.

The Army, through its spokesman on the island, gave every encouragement to the Provisional Police plan but when it stressed the guarding of vital installations, a careful screening of personnel was deemed necessary, with finger prints, photography, and loyalty investigations in order. Some culling was done without making racial discrimination too apparent. A few trusted Japanese were retained but the enrollment was mainly from other groups. Many part-Hawaiians were already in the National Guard.

This gathering up of a force of a thousand men from every town and village on Kauai and giving them careful instructions on how to challenge a man before he gets within striking reach, whether or not the guard should place a hand on a suspect when making arrests, and all this shooting at targets with air-pistols seemed to some people unnecessary. The instruction was a trifle amusing in its scope. A woman suspect, for example, "if violent or apparently dangerous may have her hands tied or her arms held to her sides by a belt, etc., but she should never be searched — except perhaps her hat, and coat, if any — until there is another woman to do the searching." The suspect evidently was not to be given a chance to use a hat grenade. In any case the Training Bulletin counseled taking no chances. "A woman," it says, "may try to do something that a man couldn't get away with." How very true!

By the middle of 1941, Kauai was humming like a very disturbed hive. The women soon showed that they were not going to sit quietly at home while their menfolk went rushing about to drills or secret meetings, pored over topographic maps (restricted against feminine attention), or shot off their little air-pistols. First-aid courses were organized at

Waimea, Lihue and Kapaa, and two Japanese women's societies, the Fujinkai and the Asoka-Kai, volunteered to do
knitting and sewing and had material issued to them. In
April 1941, a women's volunteer motor corps was organized
and took instruction in changing tires, making minor repairs,
and practising driving over slippery dirt roads, of which
there were plenty on Kauai. This training was subsequently
put to good use.

Meanwhile, all women with nurses' training had been
registered and refresher courses instituted. The Red Cross
also began the training of Nurses' Aides, but from this, by
army orders, Japanese women were excluded, a ruling which
gave considerable offense.

Next came a period when Oahu was exercised about its
evacuation problem, and Kauai was surveyed so as to arrange for the placement of 5,000 Oahu residents if necessary. This scheme was carefully worked out so as to cause
a minimum of family dislocation and was under the newly
set up Major Disaster Council, directed locally by Charles
Fern. This body set about organizing air-raid and fire wardens, making blackout provisions, arranging for emergency
food supplies, and setting up transportation and communications systems. After December 7th, this became the Kauai
branch of the O.C.D.

By this time, everyone in the Islands was talking and
thinking in terms of the coming war. Measures, that had
seemed at one time far-fetched, were now seen as reasonable
precautions. Each plantation took stock of its food situation
and that of the Territory as a whole. By January 1941, over
3,000 acres in the Islands had been planted with vegetables
and papaias. Yet the University Extension Service reported
that the Territory was only producing 30 per cent of its food.
The Kauai planters agreed to set aside one thousand acres
for basic food crops, such as soy beans, corn, Irish potatoes,
and peanuts, while the banks of irrigation ditches were covered with sweet potatoes, which were to contribute our nu-

tritional standby. Compared with the Irish potato, the *uala* or sweet potato produced four to five times as much, and it took only two-thirds of the time to raise the crop. To scale down the amount of starchy foods, string beans and Chinese cabbage were also grown in large quantities.

Kauai plantations were on the whole in a fairly good position as regards food, some better than others. Kekaha for example had set up a hog farm, and Waimea, just next door, had an excellent dairy with ranch lands in the mountains, so that meat supplies were assured. The plantation stores doubled their inventories of food stocks and the small private stores were urged to buy flour, rice, etc., in large quantities. Special machinery for sowing and harvesting sweet potatoes was purchased, so that this community felt that even if the Waimea bridge were blown up and the district isolated, it had ample food for at least six months.

The story was much the same elsewhere. McBryde Plantation, as early as 1936, had gone in heavily for producing potatoes. By December 1941, the plan was in full swing with 65 acres in diversified crops, the plantation obtaining its seed from the H.S.P.A. crop committee and acting as distributor. Soon there were 452 home gardens as well, in a population of 2,500, or one garden to every three adults.

The communications system of the Kauai Disaster Council had been set up. It divided the whole island into six districts, each with its own director and clearing through a central office at Lihue. The Japanese, having been excluded from many other activities, volunteered for this service and were of all groups most faithful in their attendance at practice alerts. One morning in December, the staff happened to be at their posts for a practice demonstration. Suitable codes had been arranged, "J. B. Blue" was the signal for an alert; "J. B. Black" was evacuation; "J. B. Red" meant war. Suddenly "J. B. Red" came over the wires from the central station at Lihue, and the system went into immediate operation. It was December 7th.

The Sugar Planters Association had scheduled their annual meeting for December 8th, and some of the managers and other executive officers had gone to Honolulu early, in order to attend the football game being played for the bene-fit of the Shriners' Hospital for Crippled Children. On Kauai, the news of the attack was at first met with incredulity, but there quickly followed a sober realization of its truth. By some military inadvertence, the local wireless station KTOH was not ordered off the air as were all other stations. The prearranged plans were set in motion immediately, and rapid organization was helped considerably by radio an-nouncements. The O.C.D. director, in the absence of its organizer in Honolulu, took over the direction of the Pro-visional Police, and in a couple of hours a hundred per cent turnout of men trained for guard duty was reported. By noon the ambulance corps was mobilized, the first aid sta-tions manned, and the hospital ready to receive patients. Before nightfall every power installation, every water supply cistern or intake, every bridge and all side roads joining the highway were guarded. Eleven days previously, Judge Rice had reported to the Governor's Advisory Defense Commit-tee the receipt of 40 riot guns, 18 automatic pistols, and 10 Colt revolvers. These, with the privately-owned weapons, were all the armament available for a thousand men. Most of them for the first few weeks went armed with clubs, cane knives, anything they could find. The guarding of roads auxiliary to the main highway was important, for in this way all unauthorized travel was forbidden. Hence the gath-ering of potential saboteurs was made difficult, had there been any to gather. The hours of that night (and a good few following) were full of uncertainty. No one knew whether or not Japanese landing parties, guided by disloyal elements, were coming ashore on remote beaches. Rumors during the day had flown thick and fast, including a report from Oahu that Kauai had been captured. That, at least, these people knew was not true.

But the local Japanese population, some twelve thousand of them, had never been put to the test. The men guarding the mills and bridges, or the reservoirs in the mountains, could not guess what the darkness covered. Many of them had never watched all night before. Bands of saboteurs might be stealthily gathering, hiding in brush or cane, creeping up to a point from whence they could make an overwhelming rush. No one knew anything beyond the circle of his own vision. The general situation was dark. Oahu had gone silent, and if there had been good news it surely would not have been withheld. For the first time the word "invasion" had real and direful meaning. This war had brought about strange happenings, but surely nothing as terrible and confusing as this.

For the first time, since there is no big game in the Islands to be hunted, men became conscious of the strange appearance of things at night. Venus setting over the mountains could be a parachute flare, the reflection of stars submarine lights at sea. And if the foe lurked offshore, what about the women and children in unguarded homes? These were the disturbing thoughts of the watchers, in a blackout so complete that even the consolatory cigarette could not be lit. The men of Kauai were left to themselves. I do not know what happened to all the women but one at least lay out under the stars on Koloa Beach, her rifle and a box of shells beside her, determined to pick off any boatload of the enemy that came ashore. She would have done it too, for she was a dead shot and a woman of unflagging spirit.

Small wonder that there were incidents at which, in retrospect, we can afford to smile. Three men were sent up into the mountains at midday to guard Waimea's fresh water supply. Arsenic was used in huge quantities for weed eradication and poisoning the water was at once thought of as a prime danger.

In the hurry of organization these men, who were to have been relieved at midnight, were completely forgotten. When dark of the second night fell with no food or relief in sight, the men decided that nothing short of complete catastrophe could have befallen the town. Leaving his comrades on guard, one of the men crept down through the forest to the cane fields and thence to the building which was the Provisional Police headquarters. Crawling carefully a foot at a time, he reconnoitered the darkened building. All was so still that the scout decided that the Japs must have taken the town, so when he heard haole voices he burst in, asking anxiously, "Where are they? Where are they?" The subsequent relief at the reservoir of two desperate and starving men armed with shot guns posed some perils for the relievers.

Fortunately every man on Kauai, with the exception of many of the Japanese, had his assigned task and that forestalled panic. Though many of the key men were absent in Honolulu, their deputies took charge with complete assurance. The plantation set-up was favorable to effective organization, and each large commercial unit was quite familiar with the technique of the pooling of resources in a common cause. Another circumstance incidental to the plantation system was also fortunate. The men in the community outside of that system must possess outstanding initiative and independence to succeed. This matter of island defense being a community matter, these men were quite able to shoulder their full share of responsibility in the crisis. It is easier of course to show what the plantations contributed, each according to its size, as for example to say that Kilauea had 38 men on guard on December 7th, Koloa 210. The yeoman service contributed by the men outside plantation employment cannot be thus summated; but it was given, in full measure.

With the outbreak of war, the Provisional Police became the County Guards under the O.C.D. Lieutenant Colonel Fitzgerald, commanding a handful of National Guards, became the military governor, and the first fourteen of the hundreds of general orders issued under martial law were promulgated. These closed the Japanese language schools, prohibited public assemblies, shut down the civil courts, warned against spreading spy rumors, etc. One hundred general and 107 district orders were promulgated the first year.

The news of the "invasion" of Niihau, the privately-owned island whose cliffs may be seen across the nineteen-mile strait that separates it from Waimea, caused mixed feelings. The story has been told and retold, and in the process has acquired some embellishments. The first account was, however, obtained by a "Garden Island" reporter through an interpreter while Kanahele, the hero, was recovering from his wounds in the Waimea Hospital.

According to this report, the pilot of the Japanese plane that made a forced landing on Niihau after the attack on Oahu was dazed with the crash and was found by a man named Kaleohana, who took the precaution to get hold of the aviator's papers and his gun. The Japanese was then installed as a guest in the house of one of the absent owners, Mr. Alymer Robinson, who lives on Kauai. Free to move around, the pilot soon enlisted the assistance of the only two Japanese residents on Niihau. One of them, Harada, found and returned his pistol. The other, a man named Shintani, tried to bribe Kaleohana to return the papers, but the latter became suspicious over the flier's extreme anxiety and hid them securely, before setting out with five other cowboys on a sixteen-hour pull in a whaleboat to Kauai.

It was then that the pilot became desperate, and meeting Kanahele, forced him at the point of the pistol to make a pretended search for Kaleohana. When the latter could not be found, the pilot became enraged and shot Kanahele in the groin, stomach, and thigh. It was then that the Hawaiian got mad, and seizing the Japanese by the legs swung his head against the stone wall. Harada then shot himself in the stomach.

"I wasn't feeling too good with all those bullets in me,"

Kanahele was reported to have said. "My wife ran to the village for help. But while they were coming out to me on horseback, I walked to the village."

This occurrence had contrary effects. It raised the fighting spirit of the Kauai folk, but at the same time seemed a very bad omen as to what might happen if the island were to be invaded. The only two Japanese on Niihau — one hundred per cent — threw in their lot with the enemy. On the other hand, many of the younger Kauai Japanese — the Nisei — were most bitterly ashamed.

Soon afterwards there appeared a new danger, the threat of interracial clashes between Filipinos and Japanese. When Corregidor fell and the Americans surrendered, some of the alien Japanese did not conceal their elation from the Filipinos, again to the great perturbation and shame of the Nisei. Some of the Filipinos became enraged and openly sharpened their surreptitiously manufactured bolos, eying their nervous Japanese neighbors in the camps and villages most malevolently. A Filipino with a grievance and a knife can hold himself in very uncertain restraint, but only for a limited time. On the other hand many of them became most discouraged. "The war is over for us," said they. "General Wainwright has told the Filipinos to give up."

Then someone in the Territory got hold of the bright idea to collect the Filipinos into military units under white leadership. The effect on their morale would be good. Their fears would be allayed, their sense of self-importance be re-established, and at the same time they could be used as a force against invasion. There was another consideration not stressed unduly at the time. A dispirited Filipino made a poor plantation worker; indeed he didn't care whether the cane or the weeds grew higher — it was nothing to him. The suggestion was carried to General Emmons, who gave it his enthusiastic blessing, promising both arms and military instructors in its support.

On March 9, 1942, when 1,200 volunteers were called

for, 2,400 enrolled. Night drills and four hours' training
each Sunday, practice with rifles, pistols, and machine guns,
soon molded these men into an effective fighting force. By
Rizal Day (June 19th), they were ready for their first review — hardly a full-dress affair, but in whatever fatigue
uniforms were at that time available. All had taken the oath
of loyalty, signifying also their willingness to be at once inducted into the American Army, if and when invasion or its
threat appeared. Of this unique volunteer army we shall
hear more anon.

But soon there came to the people of Kauai the greatest
possible lift to their spirit, the arrival of two regiments of
the 27th Division under General Anderson, on Easter Sunday, 1942. The men and women of the island felt no longer
left to themselves. To G.I.'s from New York State, this
island in the Pacific was as foreign as the Philippines or New
Guinea. The people seemed to be of all breeds and colors
but equally unintelligible. Even the whites didn't know
north from south, but uttered some strange gibberish about
"mauka" and "makai." No wonder that when one group
came in to Honolulu and saw an armed Japanese home guard
watching the Hawaiian Electric Power House, one of them
yelled, "Hell, boys, let's go home. They've taken the place."

Of course the unintelligibility was not all on the one side.
One white child, the son of a former missionary to China,
was completely mystified. "Father," he said, "those men
from Brooklyn speak the strangest pidgin you ever heard."

To add to the difficulties in pronouncing and locating such
names as Eleele (El-e-el-e), Polihale, Haena, and the like, it
was raining on the day the troops arrived, just as though
some of the cloudbursts common to Waialeale had slipped
off the shoulders of the mountain and were sluicing down on
the lowlands. But the female gardeners of the Garden Island
were not to be daunted by sub-tropical rains and slippery by-
roads. The Women's Motor Corps had been doing all kinds
of jobs, transporting army doctors and nurses to first aid

classes, teaching 500 men to be litter bearers, carrying medical supplies, picking up surgical dressings and driving whenever and wherever the need occurred, often in pitch dark blackouts — so why should they stand aside when a real military job was to be done. So they turned up in full force and all day long drove the heavy army trucks here and there and everywhere, getting the soldiers under cover in schools and public buildings, where other women fed them until they could get their bearings and their own commissariat working.

The canteen service which, from the beginning of the war, had served coffee and sandwiches to 500 guards nightly, rose to the occasion, and many a soldier, wet, fatigued, and mentally confused by this strange experience, was warmed mentally and physically by this cordial reception at the hands of the people of Kauai. It did not matter what their organization, Red Cross, O.C.D., U.S.O., or nothing, the women did their utmost to make the men comfortable. Thus was cemented from the beginning a very warm aloha between the Army and civilians on Kauai.

With the arrival of these regiments, events moved rapidly towards the organization of defense, and the army officers received many surprises at the efficiency of civilian co-operation. Five miles of winding tracks joined the airport at Mana to the highway at Kekaha. The plantation was asked to help put the road into usable condition for military transportation. Bulldozers, scrapers, tractors, and all necessary labor, including carpenters and other mechanics to work on the bridges, moved out, and in three days a serviceable job was completed.

From any responsible defense job, the Japanese, at the Army's insistence, were carefully excluded. In the face of frustration, the Japanese-Americans could easily have been resentful and sullen. Instead they looked around eagerly for work to do. Word was passed that evacuation plans must be completed by the building of camps. Sites within reach of

water and back roads were selected, brush was cut, latrines
dug, house foundations built, and water piped in. Here was
work the Japanese could do, even though they could not join
the County Guards or the Kauai Volunteers. Under plantation leadership they did an excellent job. The only trouble
was when some high ranking officer came along and approved a camp so highly that it was immediately taken
over for military use.

Red Cross activities provided another outlet for this
dammed up patriotic spirit. After a year of war, 3,185 volunteer workers had given 175,000 hours to production alone,
spent mainly on surgical dressings, garments for evacuees,
various hospital articles, and bunny masks for infants. Many
of these Red Cross workers were Japanese.

Next came the clearing of fields of fire, obstructed in
many places by the thick cover of kiawe or mesquite. This
tree forms a rather ragged screen over the lava-strewn slopes
of the foothills, but in the richer soil of the lowland benches
it flourishes like the green bay tree. Hacking down the
prickly branches with cane knives, heaping the stuff and
burning it off was no easy job, but 200 men, all used to plantation labor, can make quite a clearing on a single Sunday.
When the weekly turn-out increased to 1,600 men, the progress was extraordinary. Even then General Brush had to issue
an appeal for greater efforts to do away with kiawe cover for
infiltration tactics of which the enemy were so fond. "Cutting brush for Brush" became quite a popular activity; soon a
couple of hundred Filipinos joined in, army trucks provided
transport to critical points, the girls came along as water carriers and brush gatherers, 250 high school boys formed a
special corps to string barbed wire along the beaches, and a
new community effort was added to the list of Kauai's co-
operative enterprises.

With so much to be done and so much enthusiasm in the
doing of it, civilian spirit rose wonderfully. But many of the
older Japanese were still confused, and many of the younger

ones had not recovered from the shock of refusal to accept them as Americans, and allow them to take their places in the first lines of defense. It had never occurred to them since their school days that the nation did not mean what it said when it called them citizens. But there was a small group of young people who refused to take refusal. "It should be our job," they said, "to mend the bridge that is broken between our parents and the rest of the community." So with suggestions from the Oahu Emergency Committee and careful advice from a small advisory council of leading haoles, the Kauai Morale Committee was born. It began to function in May 1942, under the chairmanship of Charles Ishii. In two months they met with 43 groups, representing 1,600 families, all over the island, talking over the war and its implications with the older Japanese. Here are some typi-cal reactions.

"This clears our hearts," said one family head. "We have lived here for over forty years. We love Hawaii. Because we are Japanese - — alien enemies — we were afraid. Hawaii is now un fire. We can't think of race or blood. We must all put out the fire, or else we all perish." Said another: "Most of us have lived longer in Hawaii than Japan. We have an obligation to this country." A third declared, "We are Yoshi (adopted sons) of the American Government. We have children growing up as Americans. We want to do our part for America, and it is the only right thing for us to do."

These statements were made among themselves and not for public consumption. If any American can read them and not feel a thrill of pride that it was his country that called forth these simple declarations of gratitude and trust, then there are some cracks in his own armor!

So the Committee did not worry about the meaning of morale but helped establish the Kiawe Corps, stimulated the purchase of $800,000 worth of war bonds by Japanese on Kauai, plus substantial contributions to the Red Cross, U.S.O., and Welfare Funds. They fostered the idea of setting up classes in simple English, so that all could learn to speak the language of their adopted home. The Committee, being Japanese, met with all kinds of distrust and suspicion, but gradually grew in favor as a community-welding force. Kauai is a half-inhabited island away off in the Pacific. It has a plantation-dominated economy. Its politics are sometimes pathetic. But I cannot think that there can be much wrong at heart with a community where such whole-souled service was possible.

Meanwhile the Kauai Volunteers (Colonel Townsley of Lihue in command) were taking an increasingly important part in the military plans for island defense. Their role as guards and guerrilla scouts was revised. The excellence of their machine gun practice and their rifle marksmanship caused them to be given the job of manning the coastal pill boxes and patrolling the beaches. They, not the soldiers, were to be the first line of defense, the shock absorbers of invasion. But this business of night patrols along rocky foreshores was risky, and Captain Alan Faye of Waimea decided to put his men on horseback. Horses see better at night and cover more ground. From this grew the corps of mounted troops to be attached for special duty to the K.V.'s.

The notion gained immediate favor with the Portuguese and Hawaiian cowboys who felt out of place in the ranks with the smaller Filipinos. An army general, who watched with amazement the evolutions of this troop of thoroughly skilled horsemen, saw at once their potential value; they must be withdrawn from beach patrol and sent to maneuvers in the mountains as an effective screen for the Kokee defenses.

But maneuvers were too much like playing soldiers to these cowboys, for they were to a man wild-pig hunters. Even such a small-brained animal as the pig, after a few generations of freedom, develops an astonishing aversion to man and his murderous intentions. These men thought little of following their dogs in pursuit of wild boars into wilder

gorges where no sensible man would ride. Then they dis-
mounted and clambered down precipices and finally, knife
in hand, plunged into a dog-pig melee — not to save the
beloved hounds but to save as much of the pig as possible
from the jaws of the dogs which were notably half-starved
and savage. The trick was to seize the pig by the hind leg
or by both ears, flip the animal over on its back and stick its
throat before the tusker could get back on its feet and slash
you. To these Kauai hunters riding through the forest
armed with pistols, pretending to find an imaginary enemy
had little appeal.

But the captain saw that there was no reason why military
maneuvers could not be organized as a pig-sticking campaign, or vice versa. So two men with the best trailers left
camp before dawn, followed by a squad of eight others with
the rest of the dogs, their mission being to support the scouts
and act as liaison with the main troop, which stopped behind to strike camp and load the equipment on the spare
horses. The dogs gave tongue, the detail galloped forward,
sending back dispatches at intervals to indicate changes in
direction to the officer in command, while the main troop
followed at full speed, leaving a rearguard to bring up the
led horses and mules.

Reports were supposed to be made in proper military style
but sometimes excitement was too much for newly-practiced
discipline. On one occasion a dispatch rider galloped up to
report. "Jeezus, Alan," he yelled, "make queeck, we've put
up one hell of a beeg peeg!" Then training asserted itself;
"Captain Faye, sir," he said as he saluted, "a large force of
the enemy is retreating rapidly towards Halemanu Gorge,
and for Chrissake, get goin', or we'll lose the beeg booger!"

Army officers attached as observers got an eyeful, whenever they could keep close enough to observe. Except for a
mug of coffee in the morning, the Pig Stickers Brigade
needed only one meal a day, but that was a full one. They
refused to open their K-rations, preferring to take them home

to "the keeds." To their families also went the best part
of the pigs. But scraps and chitlings roasted at night with
all kinds of edible roots and greens gathered from the forest,
garnished with pheasant picked off from the saddle with
pistols, made most delicious meals. Characteristic of the
captain's report was: "Met the enemy, captured him, ate
him." Finally, the troop impressed the general so much that
he issued them, of his own accord, Browning automatic
rifles.

Getting the island in condition for defense was a problem
for the U.S. Engineers, and for this work they had to depend on plantation equipment. There was no other. Koloa
for example, contributed 2,000 man days and 5,000 unit
hours in trucks and tractors, with an additional 2,500 man
days to the O.C.D. for building evacuation camps. For
general defense purposes, the Koloa quota was 16,000 man
days, with 5,000 man days of volunteer work in the Kiawe
Corps. In connection with evacuation plans, a motor pool
of plantation trucks and cars was formed, every man,
woman, and child knew the proper assembly points, knap-
sacks were kept packed, stacks of vital foods were kept just
inside the doors of the retail stores, and for practice a "dry
run" was staged, evacuating the people of a whole district.

McBryde Plantation supplied the military with 80,000
cubic yards of cinders and crushed rock, 150 million gallons
of water for military domestic use, $217,000 worth of elec-
tricity and power. It was because civilian enterprise had
made these things available, besides roads, bridges, etc., that
this so-called outpost of defense was defensible. Kekaha had
an impressive record; being near the airport, its heavy equipment was constantly in demand. Grove Farm near Lihue set
up evacuation camps and also conducted dry runs for 10 per
cent of the population, and underwrote the growing of rice
crops — a lost industry on Kauai due to Californian competition. The springs near Kilohana fill the cisterns from
which water is piped down to Nawiliwili Harbor, where

millions of gallons were taken on board L.S.T.'s to supply the troops attacking Tarawa. The assistant superintendent of Grove Farm supervised all the finger printing of the whole population of the island.

The work of organizing the K.V.'s centered about Lihue. Twenty-six thousand dollars was raised for uniforms, shoes, and insignia for the Volunteers and plantation trucks conveyed them to and from training and to their various defense posts. The Filipinos made excellent soldiers, the more so when permission was given by the Army for them to manufacture bolos, their traditional weapon. There is no doubt they would have made excellent jungle fighters though their ideas of military procedure were a little naïve. One man, who had been instructed to be very careful about identifying men in cars, held up the general and made him get out of his car in the pouring rain to show his credentials. When the Filipino saw what he had caught, he threw his rifle into the bushes and fled. It took some hours of search and a great deal of persuasion before he could be induced to return to duty. He was sure the general would order him shot.

The greatest difficulty in describing Kauai's part in the war is that which plagues the presentation of any of the Islands' activities. It is knowing where to stop. So many worthwhile projects must be scantily treated, so many leaders' names omitted. After all, 31,000 people averaging sixty to the square mile are not so many. This means that the same people duplicated responsibilities over and over again. I would be loath to make a roster of all the leaders' names, whether or not they were connected with plantation work, for that would neglect the rank and file. Some Tony Rodrigues stood guard every night at some lonely post; Sebastiano Ramos dropped his plantation hoe to hurry home to get ready for drill; Shigeki Okayama had two sons fighting in Italy and worked each morning at the Red Cross; fifteen-year-old Mary Holokea did a man's work in the sweet

potato patch, Ah Sung Wong was a boy scout and did mes-
senger work night and day at the O.C.D. center — and thus
it went. These names are fictional, the services were real.

There are so many activities unmentioned, so many ac-
complishments unrecorded, such for example as the Sons of
Mokihana, nearly a thousand strong, whose members all
offered their blood to the Blood Bank, organized Farmer-
ettes to save the food crops, plaited coconut leaves as screens
for gas contamination units, worked on evacuation camps,
acted as air wardens, firemen, canteen workers — and were
all Japanese. Every such list of activities or organizations
must be ended by an honest et cetera, not because the writer
has run out of facts, but because they are too numerous to
mention.

Some large organizations, such as the Red Cross and the
U.S.O., are merely listed, the reason being that they are
branches of national services and have published their own
records of accomplishment. Most glaring of all omissions
is the contribution of the teachers who finger-printed and
registered, and reinforced by example and teaching the loyalty of the young people in their charge; and in their spare
time did scores of odd jobs. Their schools were occupied,
their classes scattered, but they never faltered in undertaking the most thankless or monotonous duties. The whole
public school system of Hawaii earned a military citation
at the hands of the commanding general.

Finally a few lines must be given to the "Tired Fliers" or
Air Force Morale program, the idea of which came from
Oahu but was enthusiastically taken up on all the "outside"
islands. The people who took part threw open their homes
to the men who flew those long-distance, near-suicide missions in the Pacific, such as the attacks on Japan which were
staged from Saipan in the last years of the war. The men
of the big bombers, not so much the pilots, but non-com
bombardiers, gunners, radiomen, after so many missions
came to the best homes on Kauai for five- to ten-day visits.

No efforts were made at formal entertainment — the men were free to swim or play, sleep or read, and above all discard their uniforms and for a moment forget the war. Some played with the children or the household pets, some even went into the kitchen and tried their skill on favorite dishes. Others drove with their hostesses or pedaled bicycles into the nearest village, just for the fun of being arrested — and instantly released — by the M.P.'s for not having passes, or for being dressed in unmilitary fashion. The same woman that guarded the beach with her rifle on the first night of war was the official or unofficial head — I don't know which — and she was backed by women who knew that the most gracious part of hospitality was to force nothing, not even kindness, upon their guests. Perhaps the men recognized kindred spirits, but these women of Kauai were saluted by more men about to die than was any Roman emperor.

Out of 30 men in one squadron only six survived. The rest were shot down, made forced landings, or disappeared in the stormy eastern waters. Strangely enough, these six came back between missions to the same house. They came to believe that this home somehow drew a magic circle around them, a charm against disaster.

CHAPTER XIII

Isolation Versus Isolationism

A MAP of the island of Hawaii, even if drawn to large scale, lacks reality, mainly because it will make too much of the sea. Being an island, it is necessarily surrounded by water, but to the dweller on Hawaii the sea has ceased to be of lasting significance. Now and then it catches and holds your attention, but briefly. One such occasion is when you look down from high cliffs onto a small green platform, called by the Hawaiians Laupahoehoe, the leaf of lava. It was quite recently the scene of tragedy, for the tidal wave wrought destruction here, taking a toll of twenty lives. But at any time the sea resents Laupahoehoe. The great Pacific swells smash themselves on its foreshore or retreat in sullen backwash. The land is equally savage, baring its black lava fangs at its enemy. On a tiny green flat, backed by the cliff and beset by the seas, the little settlement rests.

At Onomea also, a small mountain torrent tumbles into the sea in a cliff-lined bay, with one headland pierced as a savage pierces his nostril for a nose bone. Elsewhere the sea is seldom out of sight but holds no place in attention.

In Hawaii it is the boldly swelling land, not the flat sea that claims your interest. Four mountains make up the island's elevation. The first in view, proceeding around the island from Hilo, is Mauna Loa, the long mountain, nearly 14,000 feet high, that does not dominate so much as contain the southern half of Hawaii. For almost a hundred miles the road skirts the base of the mountain and then only spans the half of it.

The longest slope is to the southwest bounded by the arc of the South Kona coast. Down this slope have poured the lava flows of 1857, 1868, 1919, and 1926, thus visibly

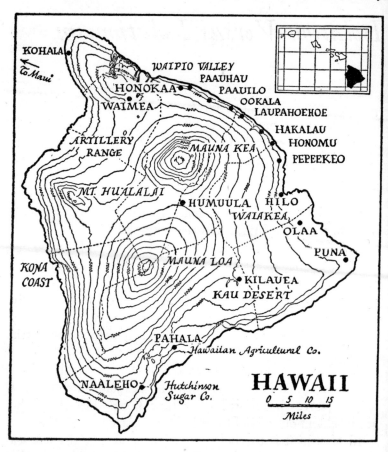

extending the land. A very old man in this district might preface an account of his life with the phrase "geologically speaking." He could have witnessed several times the recurrent phases of earth-building — the outflow of new material, its disintegration and reforesting, its obliteration under an-

)ther flow. In three score years and ten he might see as much of changes in the earth's surface as elsewhere might :ake a thousand years to accomplish.

Any one of these flows has enough wonder for a lifetime. At first, high up above the mountain's summit is the pillar of cloud, beginning with a light spume of smoke, so thin that it scarcely stains the blue of the Hawaiian skies; but at night, the cloud is red and angry, the pulsations of color indicating the live lava beneath. Perhaps within twenty-four hours the activity may reach its height. The mile long crack in the mountain's crust is now lined with fountains of fire, many of them playing 500 feet in air. It is as if Mother Earth had suffered a jagged, deeply punctured wound from which the red arterial blood issues in spurts. The lava flows like blood also; at first a rapid mobile stream, then becoming slow and viscous, spreading in dark pools and tentative rivulets, finally coagulating in ropy masses and waves like a confused sea.

And that is how the flow ends, unless the wound remains open and the lava channels itself, searing its way through the forest, tumbling boulders and rafts of slag down its course, pushing its way over small eminences and finally cascading in one glowing, exploding, lightning-attended cataract into the boiling sea.

But the results, as far as man's occupancy is concerned, are small. Flows fifty years old sometimes look as though they had come down the mountain a few months ago. What is called "aa" lava is like chocolate fudge, the fragments piled in endless confusion. Most flows begin as smooth "pahoehoe" lava, but because of some gaseous or chemical change turn into a slowly-moving front of slag, incandescent only at night. This finally cools as aa.

Naturally, land that is subject to periodic inundations of this kind has little military or other value. Campaigns can be waged across deserts but military operations over new lava beds would be short-lived. A fishing village or two on the coast contains most of the population in this area. Emptiness is its best protection. But sixty miles from Hilo where the road leaves the lava beds and swings north, it skirts the steep slopes of a region where Nature has tidied her domain a little, sweeping the volcanic ashes together into pockets, wetting it down with frequent afternoon showers, and sowing ferns and forest in the interstices. These pockets have a fine though shallow fertility, and have been converted into scores of small coffee farms. Aside from the fact that most of the farmers are alien Japanese, the Kona area is of minor military importance.

At Kailua, another forty miles along the coast, you are opposite Mount Hualalai, a westward extension of the main volcanic rift that runs northeast and southwest through the long axis of the island. This subsidiary crater built itself into an 8,000-foot mountain, and before sealing itself off sent a number of flows down to the sea, the latest from 100 to 150 years ago. However, in 1923, constant quivering of the ground seemed to presage another outbreak at Hualalai, but the giant finally turned over on his side and went back to sleep.

Beyond the lower flanks of Hualalai, the road enters an area that lies opposite the wide trough that separates Mauna Loa from the island's other great elevation, Mauna Kea. Here, despite former recurrent flows, disintegration has proceeded far enough to support a cover of coarse grass suitable for ranching. These empty miles provided space for artillery ranges and a great training ground for marine divisions. The lessons learned in the broken volcanic flows down near the coast were applied in Saipan, Iwo Jima, and the Bonins. Cool camps at Waimea at 3,000 feet elevation insured that the men would not be over-trained and exhausted before the real fighting began.

From time to time during the past hundred years, great flows have broken out on the side of Mauna Loa and have ponded in the saddle between the two great mountains before turning either west towards the Kona coast or east towards Hilo. Since 1859 the flows have gone in the latter direction, threatening the city. From one such experience a striking lesson was learned that might conceivably have had a bearing on the Japanese scheme for attacking Pearl Harbor.

In November 1935, lava broke out on Mauna Loa near the summit, but after flowing for eight miles sealed itself off. But the pressure of the lava column was too great for the crust of the mountain. It again burst out 4,000 feet lower down and a greater flow resulted. Presently this came against the barrier of the 1843 flow and, turning towards Hilo, made an advance of a mile a day, which soon threat-ened the city's water supply.

Molten rock, it should be known, congeals very quickly on the surface while retaining its heat underground. Thus you can walk lightly over lava an hour after it has flowed, yet kindle a stick in its cracks five years afterwards. Some distance from its source, a flow begins building a covered way for itself which, like an extended hose, emits liquid lava some miles farther down. When the flow finally stops, these tunnels or lava tubes create caves of remarkable ap-pearance. In the old days the tubes were used as burial caves or as secret avenues of escape from invading enemies.

Following the suggestions of the volcanologist, Dr. Jaggar, the Army determined to try and stop the flow by dropping 600-pound bombs on the tunnel near the source of the flow, in order to block the channel, relieve the gaseous pressure, and cause the lava to spread out in great sheets, where it would quickly cool. The army pilots did a fine job of pin-point bombing, and within a hundred hours the flow ceased.

The Japs, who are also familiar with volcanoes, may well have recognized that Pearl Harbor was the channel through which the great might of America must be funneled before it could spread into the distant reaches of the Pacific. If the channel could be pinpointed with bombs, the flow could be dispersed, its force dissipated. That was, in essence, Japan's strategy. Our strength in ships suffered tremendous damage but the Harbor with its installations was not knocked out of usefulness. Had the battle of Midway provided the enemy with an air base from which the roof of the tunnel could have been reopened, the whole course of events would have been different. One more attack on Pearl Harbor on the same scale as the first and the Navy must have withdrawn; Hawaii's army garrison and its people would then have been left to defend themselves until America could have gathered her strength in West Coast bases for a decisive counterattack. That might have taken years. In 1942 the army situation in Hawaii was such that adequate preparations for defense had to be perfected before the Islands could be used as offensive bases in the great Pacific push. Our forces in occupation were scrutinizing carefully every means of improving Hawaii's defensive positions.

As far as the Big Island was concerned, Waimea constituted a very critical point. The Kohala Mountains, worn down to mere five-thousand-foot stumps, form a north-western protuberance which is for all military purposes a peninsula. On its eastern flank its sides are cut into by the huge Waipio Valley, inaccessible except by a bridle path. On its other side is the wide curve of Kawaihae Bay, on whose beaches landings would have been easy. If these were in force they would have cut off the Kohala peninsula, which with its airport was of some military importance. Nevertheless, to waste men in its defense would have been foolish, and so for some months the people of Kohala were left very much to themselves.

When the Army landed on Hawaii in March 1942, one of the first things they did was to wedge themselves tightly in the gap between the lower slopes of Mauna Kea and the Kohala Mountains, so that if invasion came via Kawaihae

Bay they could forbid the enemy access to the richly-productive Hamakua coast on the island's other side.

Once you have passed through this Waimea Gap, which is swept continuously by blustering northeast trades, you dip down the slopes to Honokaa, where you get your first sight of the Hamakua coast. Here the plantations lie contiguously — Honokaa, Paauhau, Hamakua Mill, Ookala, Hakalau, Honomu, Peepeekeo, and Hilo Sugar Company — 50 miles of rich sugar land. This land lies between the 300- and the 2,000-foot levels along the lower slopes of Mauna Kea, the fourteen-thousand-foot volcano, presently extinct, that occupies this northern end of the rift.

Sugar planters are farmers, but on the grand style. Those of this Hamakua coast live their lives along one geographical axis bounded by the sea on the one side and the huge bulk of Mauna Kea on the other. This latter has at its summit a succession of burnt cones and brown ash fields, bare except for the snow which lies for a couple of months in the winter. The next three thousand feet is given over to clinkers and lava, an area disowned by the vegetable kingdom save for some inconspicuous mosses. Then comes the zone of straggly bents and twisted shrubs that drip coldly in the fogs. At about six thousand feet altitude small ohia trees appear, their stems blackened and gnarled like old hands that have labored too long and hard. Not until you are more than halfway down the mountain is there real forest, great koas and ohias and ferns filling the rocky wrinkles of old lava flows. Lower still the tree population becomes cosmopolitan, eucalyptus and grevilleas vying with the native trees; and then comes the cane. Finally the land ends abruptly, in three- to five-hundred-foot cliffs, cut by the sea.

The cultivated fields, commonly two to four hundred acres in extent, form an irregular green parquetry, a series of inclined planes, divided by deep gulches that score the mountain's sides. All unevenness of the ground is screened by the cane, thus accentuating the wildness of the gulches.

For in these sheltered depths, tendrils of the forest above reach down to the sea.

Thus we have two worlds: one, the upper world of man's effort, of ordered growth, of machines drilling their careful furrows, of irrigation ditches following their exact contours, of all the bustle of sowing, reaping, and harvesting. The other is the underworld of the gorges, where nothing is ordered, where kukui trees pre-empt the streambeds, leaving guavas, wild bananas, breadfruits, mangoes, and the native hau to struggle for lodgment on the ledges. To screen this disorder from his sight, the planter borders the gulches with rows of ironwoods and eucalyptus.

Regularity and discipline set the keynote of plantation life. Labor on this mountain slope meant at first the clearing of every rock or stump that stood in the way of drilling the cane in perfectly parallel rows. This precision, this order, is characteristic of all plantation life. There must be no bottlenecks in operations, but an ordered procession of activities, planting, harvesting, transportation, all in time with the turning wheels of the mill. Timing and spacing are of the essence of plantation work; no lost motion, or that bugaboo of managers — increased cost of production — begins to haunt their waking and sleeping hours. They and their helpers spend themselves untiringly if only they can keep the rhythm of activity unbroken.

Just as in military operations, logistics is of great importance. The moving of men and machinery and supplies, the making of roads and building of bridges are essential considerations to the plantation, just as movements and alignment of troops, order of battle, maximum use of equipment are vital to military campaigns. The semi-military organization on the plantation has already been referred to, and the fact that it was but a short step forward to a defensive set-up. The military commander, when he arrived in Hawaii, found not only roads, communications, bridges, railway lines and equipment, electricity, warehouses, domestic water sup-

)lies, and heavy machinery ready to his hand, but a stream-
ined organization of personnel which he could use as an
extension of his own command.

A single instance of this will suffice. When the Army
:ame in March 1942, their most urgent need was an airfield
big enough to accommodate their big bombers. The civilian
airport being inadequate because of short runways, the army
engineers thought they would begin all over again with new
airstrips. From the air the country between Olaa and Hilo,
or off towards the Puna district, looks deceptively level. A
few bulldozers and scrapers from the plantation could, so
the engineers thought, do the trick of preparing the surface
in record time. But they soon learned, after a few minutes
of consultation with the plantation engineers, that an old
lava bed cannot easily be converted to use. The ropy out-
pourings of pahoehoe, or smooth-flowing lava, congeal into
all kinds of bulges and billows, the mass turning viscous
before it ceases movement and developing gas bubbles big
enough to bury a bulldozer. Finally the troughs are filled in
with ash and cinders, and with copious rainfall a thick
vegetation springs up, so that what is really a frozen sea of
stone thrown into the worst confusion, appears as a level
alluvial jungle. But a closer inspection reveals the difficulties.
The soil may be six inches or six feet deep according to
location, while the pahoehoe will yield only to rock drills
and blasting. The Army decided very quickly to take over
the commercial airfield near Hilo and extend it for military
use.

The engineers had no heavy equipment and so had to
depend on what the island plantations could supply. One
day there was great need for a caterpillar tractor, so the
responsible officer telephoned the request to Olaa Plantation
eight miles away. The answer was a cheerful affirmative and
the officer sat down to write out the necessary requisitions
and orders against the arrival of the machine the next day.
As he was at work, he was disturbed by the unmistakable

clank-clank, clackety-clack of a tractor going by his office on to the field. He rubbed his eyes with amazement — i was his equipment ready to begin work.

The seeming miracle was soon explained. The tractor had already been loaded on a flat car ready for transporta tion to the Puna end of the plantation. All that was neces sary to do was to reverse the engine, rattle down the sever miles of railway to the airfield, unload the tractor and be ready for work. There were many such instances when the eyes of the military widened in amazement at civilian effi ciency. They found, for example, that terrain determined so many lines of plantation activity that the most detailed contour maps were available for each district. These were invaluable for military use.

Then, too, amphibious activities on a large scale were still remembered from the days when all the planting, the har vesting, and the milling of the cane culminated in the critical effort involved in getting the sugar down the cliffs and into the hulls of the ships anchored insecurely below. Built in the solid rock in the shelter of some tiny headland were concrete platforms onto which cable cars ran, down the steep pitch of iron rails. Far below, fending their whaleboats off the cliffs with long sweeps, Hawaiian seamen waited for some abatement of the swells, to give the signal for the crane to swing out its load of sugar bags and drop them in the row-boat. The ocean is always restless off the Hamakua coast and it took landsmanship and seamanship of a high order to get the year's crop safely away. Civilian enterprises had their big moments and their risks, and a military emergency could be met in the same way.

We have already suggested that there are military difficul-ties when the defense of the island must be served by a single highway, which in the case of Hawaii went quite around the island. This end-to-end arrangement of villages made the organization of defense each community's individual respon-sibility. The task was, of course, complicated by the loosely

conglomerate population, of whom the largest group were
Japanese, many of them born in Hawaii, but a substantial
number born in Japan and therefore enemy aliens. A considerable proportion retained their dual citizenship which
was as good as none.

But there is one tie that binds the people of Hawaii. They
were, outside of Hilo, nearly all connected directly or indirectly with the fourteen plantations that grew sugar and
partly processed it. These plantations were set up for that
purpose, and, war or no war, producing sugar is what
they continued to do. This did not mean any lack of
patriotism on these people's part, but quite the reverse. The
plain truth is that this was all they knew how to do, and
moreover the nation wanted the plantations' product and
wanted it badly.

The circumstance about Hawaii itself that is of importance
is that it is literally the "Big Island." To say that Hawaii
has somewhat less than the area of Connecticut (4,015
as against 4,820 square miles) or twice the land area of
Delaware, does not help us to realize the situation; for Connecticut with two million inhabitants, and Delaware with
a quarter of a million people represent much closer concen-
trations of human beings than a population of 70,000, especially since the 27,700 who live on plantations live end to
end, so to speak, so that 200 miles separate the first and the
last along the line. Obviously such extended lines of communication make any social organization much more difficult
than in restricted population areas such as Delaware or
Rhode Island. There is always safety in numbers, but what
the individual loses in the comfort of the crowd, he gains in
independence by living on the outskirts.

The outstanding fact that the white population of Hawaii
had to face, in the event of war, was that there were so few
of them to do so much. On the plantations for example, 667
whites of North European ancestry faced a total population
of 14,161 Japanese, a ratio of one to twenty-one. The pro-

portion of haole males was 230 to 4,103 Japanese,[1] two thousand of the latter aliens. A few people who were on very familiar and friendly terms with these older Japanese foresaw no trouble with them if war should come; others thought this trust entirely unjustified, and feared that the loyalty of many of the younger Japanese would not stand much strain.

Of other employees there were 718 Portuguese men and 212 part Hawaiians, all of undoubted loyalty but requiring efficient leadership. The largest group consisted of 5,000 Filipinos, who also would render loyal service if they were shown how. Thus the burden of preventing sabotage, or of organizing other measures for defense, fell mainly upon the 230 haoles in plantation employ, for it was on the plantations where the greatest opportunities for sabotage existed.

In addition, as we have seen, a more actively nationalistic spirit on the part of the Japanese was apparent on this island than elsewhere, and this had been fostered by the network of Japanese associations that covered every district. A great fillip to this pro-Nipponese feeling had also been given by the visits of Japanese warships to Hilo. These associations kept the ball rolling by sponsoring drives for collecting scrap metal, rubber, and tin foil, for the support of the Japanese Red Cross, and the buying of Japanese Government bonds. Here, if anywhere in the Hawaiian islands, was there a danger of subversive or fifth-column activities. Many of the haoles still believe that they were sitting on a powder keg and the only reason why it didn't explode was that they sat so tight that no one could get near it with a match. As proof of this, they pointed to the fact that many of the Japanese returning from internment as suspicious persons were welcomed home with more acclaim than were some of the A.J.A.'s from the battlefields of Europe. The same Japanese Chamber of Commerce that stood behind the Nipponese Bonds sale had to be

[1] H.S.P.A. "Census of Plantation Employees and Families." June 30, 1944. Throughout this book haole is used in the Hawaiian sense, meaning North European stocks. We repeat the warning that it does not mean whites or Caucasians.

firmly discouraged from setting up a public committee of welcome for the internees. What would have been the reactions of many of the Big-Island Japanese if invasion had come about is any man's guess. Fortunately, the matter was never put to the proof.

Quislings in Norway, collaborators in France, fifth columnists elsewhere naturally turned people's attention to our local situation, lest there be among the Japanese some determined nationalists who would not stop at anything to advance their country's cause. Long-time residents discovered how little they understood the psychology of their Oriental neighbors. Instances of servants leaving their white employers with lying excuses after twenty years' service were discussed freely. "You never can be certain of these Japs," was the conclusion. "You never know what they are thinking." The haoles, on the other hand, felt no urge to restraint in expressing their most inconsequential thoughts. Few people understood that to a Japanese who found it advantageous to change his employer, it was much more polite to invent a sick or dying grandmother than to embarrass the boss by asking for more money. "Me too much shame speak boss more money," was the explanation proffered, if as was rarely the case, the Japanese would explain at all. So the whites spoke of "the dumb Japs" and the Japanese among themselves countered with "the gabby haoles," and mutual misunderstanding continued.

Soon wild tales went the rounds. Typical were the rumors of a wholesale poisoning plot, the haoles of course to be the victims. The scene of the story was usually a dinner party where the poison plan came up for discussion. The hostess is supposed to have remarked to the maid of many years' service, "You wouldn't do that to us, Mama-san, would you?" "Oh, no," was the alleged reply, "that the yard-man's job." The story was reported on every island and for a half dozen different parties. It seemed to have happened most often on Oahu, but that is natural. There are more dinner parties there. It was probably pure invention.

In the meantime, the military representatives were doing their best to alert the civil population to the dangers of air attack. Apparently they had no qualms about unduly alarm- ing the people in 1939 and 1940. That tender solicitude was, according to the testimony of the generals, as recorded at a Pearl Harbor inquiry, reserved for late 1941, when it prevented them from calling a general alert. On May 18, 1939, the first practice blackout was called, while another was held in 1940 and a third in 1941. Instead of becoming panic-stricken, the populace co-operated in the calmest, most efficient manner.

Towards the end of 1940, the news from Europe disturbed the people on the Big Island as it did those in the rest of the Territory. By November, England had weathered the storm of Luftwaffe attacks, but was still hanging onto the ropes when winter sounded the bell which ended the round. In Hawaii, concern was reflected in the calling of a meeting in Hilo on November 8, 1940, when measures for defense against sabotage were discussed by plantation managers, heads of utility companies, and business men, and an emer- gency organization planned. A month later a local chapter of the "Committee to Defend America by Assisting the Allies" was formed.

There is a record of the swearing in of plantation em- ployees as early as November 19th, but the formation of the "Emergency Guards" seemed to have proceeded slowly. At Olaa the whole Puna district was divided into 14 sub- districts with a squad of ten men under a leader selected to supervise each. As was the case on the other islands, the turn for the worse in the Allied situation in early 1941 set off a whole flurry of civilian preparations. Possibly the cementing of the bonds of the Tripartite Pact through the visit of Matsuoka to Berlin and Rome contributed most to the heightening of apprehension here. On May 20th there was an island-wide blackout under civilian supervision, followed by a number of single plantation blackout rehearsals.

As yet no one thought of invasion, but hit-and-run raids were quite within the range of expectation. The fact that so many of the old Japanese were thoroughly familiar with the use of dynamite and that there was plenty of the stuff left over from road-building and tunneling worried the plantation men considerably. Any man who wanted to do a little dynamiting of fish knew where to get a few sticks. Arsenic in large quantities was also distributed to Japanese who took contracts to raise cane on plantation lands. This was used to keep the weeds under — and most of the cane contractors were aliens. Even the most complacent white residents were perturbed, so that the proposal to set up emergency police was taken up vigorously. Maps were prepared on each plantation showing the position of all critical points, guards were allotted to each, and enrollment went on apace. At first, young Japanese who seemed completely trustworthy were enlisted; Paauhau's unit for example had 50 per cent Japanese and these were most enthusiastic at drills and rifle practice. Some even purchased their own .22 calibre rifles.

Strangely enough, it was isolated communities like Paauhau, which accepted the news of war so much more readily than many people in Honolulu. Paauhau is not only on one of the "outer islands" but its situation on Hawaii is one of the outermost. Whoever first used the phrase "a branch road" evidently conceived a highway system in terms of a tree. The road around Hawaii is more like a creeper, twisting and turning around the heads of gulches, and bearing on its main stem stiff spikes that run, wherever the terrain allows, down to the sea. One such spike road leaves the highway about forty-five miles from Hilo and descends swiftly to the little plantation village of Paauhau. A gulch coming down from the mountain determines the position of road, mill, village, and boat landing, if a tiny cove with rusting railway lines dipping dizzily down to a little concrete platform can be called a landing. On a flat bench in an elbow of the gulch, the mill and plantation offices and store form a little cluster of buildings surrounded by the workers' houses. So isolated is this small settlement, that in the old days, when the manager wanted to bar the coming of labor "agitators" all he had to do was to block the road with a guard and the place was hermetically sealed.

When the news of Pearl Harbor came, the manager called a meeting of all "key men." "Something had to be done," he wrote in his diary. "Here we were, faced with the gravest emergency; communications were overtaxed, there was no strong positive guidance we could seek, and we knew we were on our own."

But a community tucked away a mile and a half from a country road and perched on the edge of a precipice overlooking a harborless sea, a community united by a common peril, will not be panic-stricken if left "on its own." It is used to self-dependence. The first move was, as the Scotch say, "to mak' siccar," to make assurance doubly sure. The plantation office became the emergency headquarters. Guards were assigned on eight-hour shifts to watch the mill, the hydroplant, the railroad bridges, and to supervise each of the plantation camps. The older Japanese were called together, "scared, but outwardly co-operative." Stern warnings were given against tolerating any untoward moves by them or members of their families. One man, for many years an irrigation "luna" or overseer spoke, echoing the sentiment that was heard many times in the Islands. "I have lived longer in Hawaii than Japan," he said. "My children have been raised and taught here in our school. You can count on me." If anyone has doubts as to what the schools had accomplished in cementing loyalty, they might ponder this simple declaration.

Once the telephone lines were cleared, orders from Hilo came thick and fast. No more gasoline, no more liquor, and food to be sold from plantation stores in only very limited amounts. Inventories of everything in the world from towels to toothpicks were called for incessantly. "I suspect," said the manager, "that 90 per cent of the inventories submitted were never looked at." This, I believe, was a very optimistic estimate. Everyone knows how to make lists, and how nicely they fit into files. Judgment Day will undoubtedly find some redeemed clerk making up lists of the resurrected by age, sex, nationality, and dates of interment.

By the following Thursday, orders had become so in-volved or contradictory that the manager felt constrained to brave a visit to Hilo, a trip without incident except that he records being "held up at the point of a gun at every bridge by emergency police of every nationality."

A story, possibly apocryphal, is told of another planta-tion manager who had been brought up the hard way and believed that that was the only way that should be trodden by all of his subordinates. He did not hold with the appli-cation of the Golden Rule as much as of the brass ruler. Suddenly, at one of the bridges, he found himself confronted by one Joe Souza, armed with a double-barreled shotgun. In all Joe's life he had never had such an opportunity. He knew he would never have it again.

"Git out an' be reckernized," Joe ordered. "You know damn well who I am, Joe Souza," the boss complained testily, as he crawled out of the front seat of his car. But this made no difference to the guard who kept his lethal weapon cocked and pointed directly at the manager's plump belly.

"Don' geeve me no bullsheet, Mister," warned Joe. "How the 'ell I no know you no goddam Japanese spy, huh?"

The first of many calls for plantation equipment soon came, and bulldozers went trundling up the hill to plough deep furrows on the local golf course to discourage Japanese pilots from attempting to land. In a few days the situation eased somewhat, since no further attacks came. Gasoline was rationed and the number of military passes allowed for cars to be on the road was increased from ten to a more reasonable number. The mill could run if fuel could be obtained, provided it could be blacked out so that no chink of light was visible from 5,000 feet. Fuel oil was a prime shortage. From a weekly consumption of 1,000 gallons on Paauhau Plantation, it had fallen to 65 gallons weekly.

The first drill of the Hawaii Rifles, whose formation will be described later, is recorded for March 8th. Up to this time the Emergency Guards had patrolled the cliffs day and night and kept a close watch on all places where the Japs might possibly make commando landings from the submarines which had been sighted off the coast. One of these carried out a little desultory shelling of gas tanks at Hilo. Now the sea had taken new significance in the lives of these people.

The only other entry of consequence in the diary is concerned with the water that came pouring off the roof of Mauna Kea in the week following the first landing of our troops on the island. Every gulch, of which there are hundreds, was literally spouting. At the plantation office the week's rain totaled 32 inches; at the manager's house, about 800 feet higher up on the mountain slope, 45 inches fell, or 6½ inches a day. What the army division straight from New York State thought of this deluge could probably not be recorded.

One other entry skates very fearfully over a horrifying prospect that brought bleakness beyond measure to every managerial soul. This was the program of demolitions if invasion came. "The 106th Infantry," says this note, "somehow felt that scorched earth meant complete destruction of the entire mill and all the canefields." Such a scorching each manager knew would have to begin with himself topping the funeral pyre. No Scotchman would have wished to survive such wanton waste.

What happened at Paauhau was repeated at all the other outlying plantations, but on a somewhat larger scale. Paauhau's neighbors on either side, Hamakua Mill and Honakaa, had greater calls on their heavy equipment because they had more. They also conformed to the general pattern of guarding their own critical points. This is easy to say but difficult to realize for men who had never stood guard. To get some idea of what this duty meant, the writer visited the powder magazine at Paauilo (Hamakua Mill). It was a little cement building a couple of hundred yards from the highway, down a winding slippery track lined by ghostly white-trunked eucalyptus and ten-foot sugar cane almost over-arching the path. Beside the powder hut was a deep gulch filled with the usual wild growth of vegetation. Outside the single padlocked door someone had put up a piece of roofing where a man might huddle away from the rain, sluicing down six inches at a time. When the wind on a dark night rustled the eucalyptus branches, or whistled through the gorge, or the march of the torrential showers could be heard like a ghost army across the canefields, it was a spooky place. And against more material marauders the only protection was a few strands of barbed wire, loosely strung. Even the plantation diary spares a kindly thought "for those who spent many a wet, dreary, and lonely night at their outposts." And for wetness, dreariness, and loneliness commend me to a wintry gulch in Paauilo. Incidentally, we may remark that that was really an *outpost* of a very different kind from populous Oahu, which the military so designate.

One is constantly surprised by the thoroughness of civilian organization, with headquarters, subsections, outposts, etc. When the O.C.D. took over after the 7th, there was no need to look for volunteers. At Paauilo there were already 10 area wardens and 25 block wardens in addition to armed guards who served 27,000 hours up to October 1942. Twenty-five thousand unit hours were contributed by bulldozers, jackhammers, dump trucks for the purposes of military construction and 5,000 hours used in hauling marines to and from Camp Tarawa at Waimea, forty miles distant.

One hundred eight acres were devoted to food crops, and dairy and beef cattle were kept on the ranch. Besides the 340 men needed to keep over 5,000 acres in sugar production, 45 women and 89 teen-age children were employed. The mill kept 61 men busy while 97 men and 14 women worked on other jobs.

So this was evidently not a war for men only. Other women gave 9,000 hours in this small district to Red Cross. Haoles and even Japanese had worked in the "Bundles for Britain" project in 1939–40, and at once switched their activities to the American Red Cross. Japanese women in the village and camps had sons at the front. From the old mama-san to the high school girl who wrapped her new hair-do up in a bandana while she wielded a hoe in mud and hot sunshine, all did their part. These were no talky-talky clubs, adorned with madam presidents, such as were common on the mainland. Few of these people indeed could give any reasoned or coherent account of what they were fighting for, except that it was for their homes, their work, and the place where their children went to school — but they all knew they were fighting.

It is, of course, impossible to list all the contributions of all the people to the war effort. Perhaps it would be worth while to illustrate the fact by a condensed account of one community. When war broke, the first thing that was done on this plantation was to call the leaders of both the Japanese and Filipino groups together to explain what had occurred, and to impress on them the need for self control and obedience to orders. Boy Scouts were sent out into every camp to deliver printed pamphlets and to explain the emergency instructions to the older people who could not read. They continued to do this with every general or district order issued from Hilo.

The worst hardship was the restriction of auto travel. For 135 motor vehicles on the plantation there were 15 military passes. The men had become accustomed to riding to work in the fields, which were sometimes a couple of miles distant from their homes. When the food purchases were limited by military order to 35 cents daily, that imposed a great burden. Single men, forbidden to pool their purchases, were compelled every day to walk several miles from the higher level camps down to the store, and walk all this distance back again, carrying their scanty purchases. Finally community cooking centers were set up, and when the plantation got its trucks back from the military, stores of food were sent up to the distant camps. But 35 cents would only buy the plainest food such as rice, and the burden of keeping accounts that was put on the storekeepers by these small day-by-day purchases was a very heavy one.

Until blackout paper and know-how were available, the whole community except the night guards went to bed at dark. Here families were at a disadvantage. To get the children bathed and fed and put to bed and then prepare meals for the adults before dark, meant an upsetting of routine that harassed greatly the overworked housemothers who must also be on hand when the menfolk returned from their night vigils.

To keep up with the endless stream of military orders was another great burden on plantation personnel. First, all firearms had to be collected. Next, all short-wave radios were to be impounded if owned by an alien or if there were an alien in the family. Cameras also were forbidden. Collecting poisons from all individual owners was quite a facer for plantation authorities. Without it the weeds would outgrow the cane, and as poison could only be used under white supervision, and the only free days the haoles had were Sundays, another responsibility had to be shouldered. It had taken four men three days to collect all the poison, weigh it, and give credit to the owners.

In June every man, woman, and child had to be inoculated against typhoid and smallpox. Work was abandoned while the people stood in line at the hospital where 170 persons received their inoculations per hour. Previously every individual had been registered and finger-printed.

The Army certainly introduced complications in these people's daily lives. There existed among men from the mainland a natural distrust of the Japanese. They could not of course distinguish between aliens and citizens, and the soldiers could not understand that though all Japanese looked alike, they might think differently. Yet the 27th Division was largely composed of men whose parents or grandparents came from Poland, Italy, Ireland, and all the countries that were engaged in conflict in Europe. These men had acquired the arrogance of Old Americans.

The results were awkward. On March 15th, the plantation diary has this note: "The soldiers are puzzled and suspicious, having just arrived from the mainland on their way to fight Japan, and they arrive at Honomu and receive a great welcome from a population of about 30 per cent Japanese. They have itchy trigger-fingers and are shooting at lights and sounds. Our night flumers left the fields at 11:30 P.M. after being fired at by a sentry. The workmen are afraid to leave their houses to come to work before broad daylight in case of being shot at."

The mention of night flumers has reference to the fact that the plantations near Hilo, which have an abundance of water, convey their cane down to the mill in narrow water-flumes. If at any time the cane gets twisted and a jam occurs, an overflow results, the water is cut off from the mill and the cane is spilled into the fields. To break these jams at night, men with lanterns must find the stoppage and go to work to get the cane moving again. No matter how well hooded the lanterns may be, flashes of light are now and then apparent. The whistle of a bullet over their heads never failed to disperse these men to their homes. They could not understand why it was that, having carried on quite safely for months before the Army came, they should now be under fire.

By March 1st, much of the island was organized in a more definite scheme of defense. The Filipinos were getting very restless and every success of the Japanese in the Philippines raised their blood pressure considerably. Military organization would provide an escape valve and the necessary discipline. Hence a rash of local defense units broke out everywhere.

When the Honomu unit of 127 men and 5 officers was organized, the men were most enthusiastic. After working in the fields all day, they drilled for four evenings on week days and a half-day on Sundays. Until the Army could spare instructors, the local officers, mainly men with experience in the previous war, must carry on. Some Japanese with National Guard training volunteered to help as non-coms, and their offer was gratefully accepted. Then came the military order that all Japanese were to be rigidly excluded from the Hawaii Rifles. The local officers knew that these men were to be completely trusted, but they had no recourse save to drop them from the roster. However, when the unit had a banquet, these Japanese were specially invited and publicly thanked by the manager.

As far as the haoles and the military were concerned, minor differences existed but were soon ironed out and good relations established. The manager, a canny Scotsman, notes that this cordiality "was a little expensive and made quite a dent in our reserve liquor," but it was worth the cost.

No special mention is made here of the loans of heavy equipment to the Army because Ookala, Hakalau, Peepeekeo, Onomea, Hilo Sugar, Waikea Mill, and the rest all gave, not what they could spare, but all they had. To keep a constant supply of labor and machinery on hand for military purposes, A. T. Spalding was named co-ordinator for the whole island. One single instance will suffice to illustrate what kind of "kokua" or co-operation he received.

At 8:00 P.M. on March 7th, just at the beginning of the rains that drenched the island, the call came to Spalding for

100 trucks to be at the dock by 8:00 A.M. to move men of the arriving 27th Division out to their stations in various parts of the island. Four hours on the telephone were necessary to rouse the managers, most of them from their beds. Plantation phones began to ring, the communication system relayed messages to the personnel of outposts on watch. Besides the drivers and their families, garages were alerted and from all the plantations the heavy trucks, some of them from Kohala a hundred miles away, began trundling out onto the highway and rolling towards Hilo. Gradually the line grew so that by 9:00 A.M. 87 trucks were at the docks with the rest reporting a little later.

Then a difficulty arose. The military officers took one look at the drivers and their "swampers" or helpers, most of whom were Japanese. "Thank you very much," they said to the co-ordinator, "we don't need these men. Our drivers will take over. No Japanese will be allowed near the docks when the troops land."

"But," said the co-ordinator, "these trucks are private property and our roads are tricky at the best of times, and in this tremendous downpour they are positively dangerous. Both the troops and the trucks will be safe if you use our drivers."

"Sorry," said the officer in charge, "those are military orders."

"Sorry," returned the co-ordinator, "those are civilian trucks. No drivers, no trucks."

The matter went up through channels, now brimming with a real Hilo he-rain, to higher authority, who humphed and snorted and threatened but finally gave in to an obstinate co-ordinator who knew right well that his co-ordinating would go immediately sour if any of these precious trucks had been dumped in a gulch by an inexperienced army driver. When these military drivers saw the roads, they were the most relieved men in the Army. "More better you watch scenery. Me drive," was the Japanese driver's advice

o the sergeant who tried to give him some directions. But
hat night every truck load of those thousands of army boys
reached their destinations safely.

The co-ordinator has this little restrained comment in his
report. "A good deal of diplomacy had to be exercised with
he military authorities, as these people were all new to our
methods of operation and ways of life. It is gratifying to see
how quickly newcomers change their attitude of mind
towards us, after living in our midst a short time." The story
from every island is the same. Cordiality grew between the
armed forces and the civilian communities. Autographed
photographs of marines, fliers, soldiers, and sailors from
general and admiral down to buck privates, adorn the walls
of many an island home.[2] Lasting friendships were formed.
On the outer islands you speak kindly of General Short and
the rest of the high-ranking officers — or not at all. Some
civilian administrators were not nearly so popular.

The progress and usefulness of the Hawaii Rifles was remarkable. From ragged companies armed with knives made
from automobile springs, to two full regiments equipped by
the military with the latest weapons; from a morale-building
organization to a most valuable auxiliary service fit to go on
regular maneuvers with the Army makes a good record. To
tell that story except in the barest outlines is impossible here.
One outfit from Waiakea Mill could not shed their blood
in the field, but they gave it — 100 per cent of them — to
the Blood Bank. The 2nd Battalion of the 2nd Regiment,
with plantation assistance, built four rifle ranges and fifty
per cent of the regimental rifle team came from that battalion. The 3rd Battalion had no plantation to assist them,
but they blasted a rifle range through the lava beds of Kona,
following this work by what the report calls *laborious* pick

[2] The four-year-old son of a plantation manager had as his only playmates
two older boys, sons of the Japanese servants. Each day they played "marines,"
who bombarded the enemy in his dugout with ripe guavas. The white child
complained to his mother that he always had to be "the Jap." The Japanese
boys insisted on being the marines.

and shovel work. The writer confesses he didn't know there was any other variety of pick and shovel exercise. There was, however, one acknowledged blot on the record of the 1st Regiment Headquarters Company. In three years of activation its commander sadly notes that there was one month in which the attendance fell short of one hundred per cent.

The story of the mounted troops of the 1st Battalion, 2nd Regiment is of special interest. It was the only unit that regularly had *over* 100 per cent attendance. These men had their headquarters on Kahua Ranch overlooking the beach at Kawaihae, and the commanding officer reports that a number of mounted men who had been turned down by the doctors because of age or physical defects attended regularly all drills and maneuvers. "What the hell," they said, "if the Japs come we'll be fighting, fit or unfit. May as well go through this whole training business anyway." Two other ranches, Kukaiau and the Parker ranch, also had mounted troops, and as these men knew every inch of the back country, they would have been invaluable to the military as scouts or guides in the mountains.

Both the 1st and 2nd battalions of the 1st Regiment underwent special training, including ranger courses and maneuvers with the Army. The best proof of the value placed on the Rifles is the fact that the Army was ready to equip them thoroughly. General Richardson, in command of the Mid-Pacific area, told the Rifles on their third anniversary that the regular army "look to you as comrades-in-arms ready to assist us in any emergency which might threaten these islands. We consider you an integral part of the strength of these islands."

It is impossible here to do even scant justice to the other districts and their contributions to the war effort. Outlying plantations such as Hutchinson and the Hawaiian Agricultural Co., which lie beyond the Kau district, simply incorporated the army units there into their own communities, rendering a great amount of unrecorded service as well as answering cheerfully every official request.

Two plantations, as has already been mentioned, were in positions of special peril, if invasion was to take place. Olaa and Kohala stand at either end of a defensive line dividing the island in two. A new military road, constructed through the saddle between Mauna Loa and Mauna Kea, provided communications between these two pivotal points. Getting the civilian population out of the way would be vital to the unrestricted movements of troops in defending this line. Hence both districts had extremely detailed evacuation plans.

Olaa, for example, had sketch maps prepared which showed the position to be taken up, in a motor pool, of each unit of motor transport. A detailed census was taken of every man, woman, and child in the Puna and Olaa districts. The 7,455 residents were then divided into companies with leaders who had their designated assembly points, from which they would be evacuated to special camps.

By September 10, 1942, every man over 18, numbering 2,573 adults, was allotted a defense job, either transportation, maintenance of equipment, fire fighting, or military service with the Hawaii Rifles. Others were given the jobs of road maintenance, civilian evacuation, and first aid work. Every man was instructed as to the part he should play. Such schemes of organization were of course not peculiar to Olaa, but through all the plantations the whole able-bodied population were assigned some useful task. Honokaa, which also had a special evacuation problem, was similarly organized.

Kohala also had its comparable evacuation plans. Organization of the district had been carried out prior to the war for blackout purposes. When hostilities broke out, every adult in the district had his set of written instructions, stating the area to which the evacuee should proceed and the name of the person responsible for the area. From these the people would be picked up and transported to their assigned evacuation camps.

Because of the vulnerability of the district, there would be no time to waste if invasion of the Kawaihae beaches or other focal points came about. Each person prepared, therefore, an evacuation kit with four days' supplies of canned food, 2 blankets, a raincoat, spare towels, soap, etc. Certain groups of men were to remain behind to serve as fire fighters, air raid wardens, motor transport drivers, etc. A picked group had secret demolition orders, which would render useless every bit of machinery or facility of value to the enemy.

The racial composition of the male employees' roster is interesting: 261 Japanese (99 aliens), 606 Filipinos, 83 Hawaiians, 49 Porto Ricans, 47 Portuguese, 38 Anglo-Saxons. Thus the task of organization fell on $2\frac{1}{2}$ per cent of the total. Obviously this small group could not assume the burden unaided. As a matter of fact, 4,000 people were included in this district's co-operative effort, indicating the finest kind of social integration.

Before Pearl Harbor, there was no writer on the situation who had not pointed to Hawaii as the Achilles' heel of national defense because of the danger from the large Japanese population resident there. All dire expectations having failed of fulfillment, wild tales of subversive activities were at first widely circulated. When these stories were refuted by the highest military testimony, there were no amends made or retractions offered. Frank Knox, for instance, made no withdrawal of his initial Hawaii fifth-column accusations. In the minds of many, the Japanese in the Territory still stand convicted of these utterly baseless charges.

I believe that there were two reasons why there was no sabotage on these islands. The first was that the measures for prevention were too thorough; the second was that the alien Japanese were not sabotage-minded and two things contributed to that. One was that in the evacuation plans

he same provisions were made for the safety of every individual, citizen or non-citizen, haole or otherwise. The second
was the universal distribution of gas masks. Here were two
proofs offered to the Japanese that they *did* belong, that
their lives and the lives of their children were considered
of value to the community, and that when the real crisis
occurred they would be given equal consideration with the
rest. There is nothing that warms the heart so much as this
recognition of individual worth. Democracy is functioning
at its best when this is apparent.

CHAPTER XIV

Maui No Ka Oi[1]

PEOPLE who live on an island develop
some peculiar psychological characteris-
tics. Among the distinctions of insularity is a heightened
self-consciousness, which may come about either by thinking
more of themselves or less of other people. Countries, states,
cities, towns, and villages display this egocentrism in ascending degree. The people in each tend to the belief that their
home is the jewel of the piece, the rest of the world its setting. But this feeling is tempered by contiguity, which makes
travel easier. Self-centered as the New Yorker is, he must
accord a little significance to the rest of his state, and must
at least recognize the existence of New Jersey, Connecticut,
and Rhode Island, even though Philadelphia may seem a
little mythical. Furthermore, his ardors of self-admiration
are moderated by the fact that some of the things he is most
prideful about are possessed by other cities such as London
and Paris, and, possibly, by Chicago, which admittedly has
bigger and better gangsters. The man from New York soon
discovers that in terms of geography its aura of acknowledged supremacy does not shine very far. That is why he
feels that to leave his home town is to invite insult.

The island-dweller does not suffer these rude correctives.
What is sea-contained is self-contained. He is eager to be
hospitable to the stranger but always he retains something
of the importance of the host, and along with this goes an
unwillingness to be himself the guest. He somehow loses

[1] Maui over all.

stature when he leaves home. The foolish person who first declared that the whole is always greater than the part, never lived on Maui or Kauai. Life there includes the American way of life and much besides. Hawaii is part of America but much more than the whole.

The men of Maui have this pleasant insularity of outlook quite pronounced. It is shown by their motto "Maui no ka oi," which means "Maui over all," a boast that is not supported by history either ancient or modern. But being a matter of faith, it requires no evidence.

The island certainly has its advantages. In the old Polynesian legends of the brothers Maui, who together or separately went fishing and hooked up the various Pacific islands from the bottom of the sea, there was need to distinguish them, since all had the same name. In several of the traditions, mention is made of Maui-the-First, Maui-the-Last, and Maui-in-the-Middle. This is where the island of Maui is today. It bears the distinction of being so centered in the group that five other islands can at times be seen from some part of its surface. Molokai is well within view, although largely screened by the bulk of the West Maui Mountains. The other two islands which with Molokai make up the political subdivision, the county of Maui, are also plainly visible. Lanai lies just across the Lahaina roadstead, while the island of Kahoolawe helps to shelter the wide gap in the outline of Maui which is called Maalaea Bay. Lanai is given over to pineapples, Kahoolawe to red dirt, volcanic debris, solitude and menehunes, the mythical "little people" of Hawaii. But whatever did exist on the island was considerably stirred up during the war. Kahoolawe is by all odds the most artillery-battered island in the Pacific. It has been stated that more gunfire was poured into this place than into either Iwo Jima or Okinawa. For it was here, on what was called "Little Tarawa," that the full-dress naval rehearsals of invasion were staged, as many as 800 vessels, from battleships to destroyer escorts, taking part from time to time in the bombardment of its beaches and hills. The middle of the island afforded a fairly safe spot for gunfire observation.

From the top of Haleakala, ten thousand feet above the rest of Maui, you can look across a deep strait, as translucent as a glass dish, its bottom a misty blue which might be

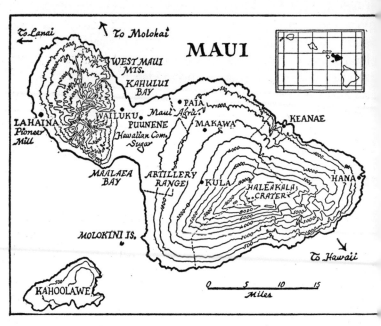

either air or sea, its surface clotted with broken clouds. Above the farther rim of the dish you see Hawaii. Its two great heights of Mauna Kea and Mauna Loa, when they are covered with snow, stand out in either sunlight or moonlight because they outshine the clouds. If you want a nearer view of Hawaii, you may get it from Hana where only a 20-mile strait separates the two islands. In the clearest weather Oahu is dimly visible from the top of Haleakala.

As was the case with some of the other islands of the Hawaiian group, Maui was probably built on the two-island plan, one centered about the great mountain mass of Haleakala, the other representing a smaller outpouring from the crater of Eke which surmounts the West Maui mountain block. Finally successive flows, aided by silt from erosion, filled up the channel between the two heights of land and they were consolidated into one island. The low land between, representing the waist of the island, is occupied by two towns, Wailuku, spread along the lowest fringe of the West Maui Mountains, and Kahului which occupies the low point of the ten-mile isthmus connecting the two original land masses. Wailuku is much the more picturesque, lying at the mouth of the deep gash of Iao Valley and circumscribed by the green of the plantation fields which extend up each minor gulch, taking advantage of its fanwise deposit of silt laid down on top of the sandy plain. Here are some of the most fertile fields, and as you fly over to the landing field, the trade winds ruffle the sugar cane like the deep pile of green velvet.

The gentle slopes of the farther side of the isthmus, stretching eastward to the base of Haleakala, have all been enriched by the denuded material from the old volcano. Two plantations, the Hawaiian Commercial and Sugar Co. (H. C. & S.) and the Maui Agricultural Company preempt this area for their sugar lands, though the Naval Air Base has taken a huge bite out of the holdings of the former company. This still remains one of the most profitable of the Hawaiian plantations. Before the war it was rich; it still hopes, if labor will allow it, to remain profitable. But its richness did not reside in the fertility of its soil, for the rainfall hereabouts is far too small for profitable production. Prosperity had to be literally flooded into and out of the soil through the carrying of ditches and flumes from around the windward, well-watered side of Haleakala, thirty miles distant. It took both brains and brawn to make this profit. To say that either labor or management was alone responsible would be like ascribing it all to the mules which were the original beasts of burden.

The huge bulk of Haleakala effectually blocks off the

trade winds, so that only the heaviest rains can sweep partly around the western side. All the slopes on the southwesterly side are dependent for their moisture on the Kona or southerly winds, which reverse the conditions of the trades. The clouds bank up between the three- and five-thousand foot levels and heavy downfalls result. On the bench below the mountain, the climate is hot and dry. The land is thick with boulders set in deep red dirt and given over to kiawe trees. This is part of the Harold Rice Ranch and his cattle live on kiawe beans and prickly pear. It was this area that was made into an artillery range for the army and marine divisions, with rather heavy casualties among the cattle which later learned to avoid the fields of heaviest fire.

The slopes of the mountain farther north above the little settlement of Makawao are occupied by the Haleakala Ranch, and down below are the Maui pineapple plantations. On the far side of the mountain is the isolated community of Hana, reached by a single highway which rollercoasts its way up and down across the gulches between the mountain and the sea.

In following the plan adopted in this book of sketching in the physical background of these island peoples' lives, some brief mention should be accorded Lahaina which lies in West Maui, almost directly across the mountains from Wailuku. But the mountains are not crossable and you reach Lahaina by means of a road that skirts the burnt, dry palis on the leeward side of the mountains overlooking Maalaea Bay. Because of their isolation, the people of Lahaina were in a similar position to that of the residents of Kohala on the island of Hawaii. They knew that the military would attempt no serious defense of their district if invasion came — which knowledge may account for the thoroughness and enthusiasm that were behind civilian plans for their own protection in both places.

Naturally it was the wide isthmus, the waist of the island, indented on one side by Kahului Bay and on the other by

the beaches of Maalaea, that was most vulnerable and essential to military operations. There, towards the middle of
the isthmus, the Navy built their Air Base while on the
Kahului side the Army constructed a large airfield. On the
northern slope of Haleakala above the bulge of Haiku, the
marine divisions made their camp, where the climate is
cooled by the frequent showers that sweep around the
shoulder of the mountain.

It has been stated, not without fear of inter-island contradiction, that the military found themselves more at home
on Maui than on any other island. Certainly a very sincere
aloha sprang up between them and Maui's civilian population. The fact that there was no large city on the island,
only the small towns of Wailuku, Kahului, and Paia, probably meant that the servicemen did not expect the type of
entertainment that more populous places like Honolulu
promised, but did not provide. No one was getting rich on
Maui on exorbitant prices charged the men in uniform.
Marines, soldiers, aviation crews, pilots, and Seabees all
knew that they must rely on themselves for a large part of
their recreation. The civilians showed a decided disposition
to join in and enjoy themselves with the men, who felt that
whatever was offered was the utmost the community could
provide. This made for an excellent feeling, so that a
civilian petition for the return to Maui of the Fourth Marine
Division from Iwo Jima for their rest period had considerable influence on the decision to bring the men back here.
If this had not met with the marines' own approval, no
notice would have been taken of any civilian request.

Perhaps one reason why the servicemen found the island
so congenial was because the recreational facilities it possessed were so completely organized. For many years Alexander House Community Association has covered the island
with a network of clubs for the service of youth. Boy and
girl scout activities, baseball, football, basketball teams,
swimming, tennis, dancing and social clubs were all included

in the association's program and were directed or assisted by its 1,500 volunteer workers. Even the smallest and most remote communities received attention.

With the outbreak of war, the whole organization swung into a greatly increased tempo of activity. The program was no different except that it centered around the servicemen. At first the level of entertainment was in some ways very amateurish. The writer had a very small part to play in this program, having been invited to come from the University and lecture with moving-picture films on expeditions to Northwest and Central Australia. Some of the men were going "down under," and the director of the U.S.O., who had accompanied me on one of these expeditions, thought that some information on the outback country and its wild aborigines might be of value. A Jap invasion of Australia was at that time thought imminent and some of our fliers expected to be based in Alice Springs or Port Darwin, around which parts of the continent these pictures had been taken.

Since there were no blacked-out buildings available, the men had made their own out-of-door theaters in the middle of thick groves of eucalyptus trees where the screen could be well hooded from observation from the air. The seats were tree trunks and a carefully-guarded flashlight the only illumination. As an occasional shower drifted over us, the screen showed a vast country smitten with a six-year-drought and a strange wild kind of life to which it seemed we were rapidly reverting. A general alarm, occasioned it was said by enemy submarines off the coast, put an end to the program of lectures. Driving in the dark with only an inch-and-a-half slit of light directed at the ground a dozen feet in front of the car was hardly restful, especially as we were held up at the point of machine guns four times while coming down the mountain roads. Our passes were scruti-nized most carefully, and I had reason to be thankful I had a haole driver.

The feeling of complete co-operation and a common responsibility was greatly strengthened by joint military and
civilian committees, who arranged all programs a week in
advance. The Alexander House set up a canteen, a lounge
with reading and writing rooms, kept four bowling alleys
open and provided swimming pools, tennis courts, and gym-
nasiums available for servicemen's use. Dances were arranged
with hostesses and supervisors provided. Discipline seemed
to be no special problem, as the armed services did what
policing of these gatherings was necessary. General Cates,
in a letter to the director of the Alexander House (also of
the local U.S.O.), gratefully acknowledged that the relaxation provided was of the greatest value to military discipline.
The tough marines of the 4th Division displayed on the
whole remarkable gentleness in their dealings with the civilian population.

Every ball field, every club house on the island was given
over to military use with $3,000 worth of sports equipment
donated by the Alexander House Association, until the men
could get their own supplies. Civilian officials were provided for all service games and sports competitions. Dances,
plays, and moving-picture shows, arranged by the local
moving-picture theater company, were held in all military
areas. The Seabees particularly enjoyed informative lectures that gave accounts of Hawaii, its history, scenery, volcanoes, political system, etc. I believe that Maui County
was among the first to close the houses of prostitution, with
no marked increase of sex crimes in consequence.

That over 30,000 men could descend upon an island
population of about one-third as many males and cause a
minimum of dislocation of civilian life is surely significant of
the capacity for adjustment in both groups. The credit must
be equally divided.

Special commendation is due to another joint military and
civilian effort, which was directed towards allaying unrest
or anxiety among the Japanese and Filipino populations.

This plan, more than perhaps anything else, exemplified a principle which said that, war or no war, this was a democratic community where every right of the individual, consistent with public safety, would be respected. The method was for Maui's only woman magistrate to visit the large schools and, in an assembly of the senior pupils, endeavor to answer whatever questions were handed in, particularly those pertaining to civil rights and liberties under martial law. Thus also freedom of speech, or at least of inquiry, was emphasized. If Judge Jenkins could not give the answer, the question was submitted to the proper military authorities. From the pupils of one school 89 problems were reported, mostly concerned with the financial status of the family due to increased cost of living, freezing of alien assets, removal of the alien breadwinner from the home, while other questions had to do with the future status of the Japanese or asked for definite information as to military regulations.

A survey of these questions is interesting as uncovering the various fears, anxieties, and resentments that afflicted the minds of these young people. Some of those fears are extremely natural — for example one boy was very anxious about the welfare of his alien parents in the event he should join the Army. Many were very fearful of the fate of the Japanese after the war — would they, as a consequence, be discriminated against, in seeking jobs or promotions. Others were afraid that as the war situation became more serious, there would be wholesale dismissal of Japanese, whether citizens or otherwise. Some were perturbed about Filipino threats. As one student put it: "Since the attack on the Philippines, Filipinos around my area are worrying about the war and are just mad at the enemies' ancestors. I think something should be done to calm their minds toward the people around the same place."

Cropping up again and again was the question about Japanese being forbidden to work on defense jobs. In some cases there was a genuine patriotic concern, as shown by the

following very typical question: "Can we of Japanese ancestry have equal opportunity in working on defense projects? We, too, are proud of America, and want to participate in defending these islands." But in others the motive
was clearly rather mercenary, shown by resentment at being
prevented from earning the prevalent high rates of pay.
Typical of such queries is this:

"The great question is: what are you going to do about
children with Japanese ancestry trying to get into defense
work. Even if they went into the Army it is known by all
that they can not rise over, maybe, even corporal. Most
of them would be buck privates and cannot rise even if they
wanted to. After we get out of school what kind of work
can we get?"

The above question and comment obviously came from
one of those youths who took the gift of American citizenship at its face value, and found that the certificate, under
certain circumstances, fell considerably below par value.
They did not understand — and no one had told them —
that the privilege was unintentionally bestowed by the 14th
Amendment to the Constitution, which aimed particularly
to protect the Negroes already resident in the United States,
and for whom many Americans felt the burden of responsibility. It hardly contemplated its results in non-contiguous
territories of America. The final justification for making
American-born individuals citizens was of course the declaration in the Preamble to the Constitution, which stated
that all men were born free and equal. There, again, the
bewildered American-Japanese did not comprehend that to
most of those who signed the Constitution this meant "all
white men are born free and equal," the word white being
understood. It took almost a hundred years of argument, a
civil war, and a million lives to clarify half that sentence,
and in a large part of America the question isn't settled yet.
The other half, about being born equal, is, unfortunately,
a sociological and psychological joke.

To speak quite frankly, when these Hawaiian-born Japanese had been sold the idea of Americanization, they were not told of these clouds upon the title. Otherwise they would have spared themselves the trouble of asking such questions as: "Will natural-born citizens with enemy-alien parents have opportunities equal to those of American children with American citizen parents?" Some others added their own question mark, as witness the following: "Why is the opportunity for all kinds of work open in many cases to all other nationalities except the Japanese? Many of the American citizens of Japanese ancestry are just as loyal to America, aren't they?" The basic resentment crops up in such queries as this: "Shall there be preference to 'haoles' just because they are better talkers, etc." The gist of the matter of course lies hidden among the et cetera. The whole situation would be more adequately described if, instead of saying that Hawaii is the land of equal racial opportunity, we made the more moderate claim that it is a country of less unequal racial status. Our hypocrisy would be at least less barefaced.

Some of the questions indicate a very stupid inability to realize that precautionary measures must be taken to safeguard a community at war. Sample queries were: "Why are rights of the aliens so limited while the citizens' rights aren't so limited? As in blackouts, aliens are not to stay out as long as citizens." "What is wrong about hearing Japanese programs over short wave?" "If an alien is proved unguilty of sending information to our enemy, can that person ride an airplane?" "Why did the Army take some Japanese enemy aliens away?" "Must we put away the picture of the Japanese Emperor?" Another question was certainly forward looking. It asked, "Can officials be tried for their unnecessary infringement of rights during martial law, after the emergency?" Another read: "We have two defense bonds in our home. Do you suppose these bonds will still be profitable, or rather, good, after the war?" Some questions asked by adults were naïve but by no means simple. Here are examples: "Can a citizen of Japanese ancestry hold a bow and arrow?" "My girls are afraid to go to the outside toilet at night — the boys are not. What shall they do for light?" "What will happen if at midnight we go out to toilet and get caught by the guard?"

Among these "Information, Please" sessions were some that were held at Filipino camps. In the early days of the war, these people were mentally confused and considerably perturbed. They needed leadership badly. One asked: "Should there be an air raid with incendiary bombs, and my neighbor's house is burning, shall I follow instructions and stay within my own house, letting his burn, or help him?" Others read: "What can we do in case of an invasion — we are helpless and know not what to do." "Why can't the Filipinos join the Army when we all want to so much?" The outcome of these meetings was a series of bulletins printed in Filipino dialects explaining the military regulations and counseling the Filipinos to "keep cool head."

The following letter presents a serious dilemma. It was addressed, rather appropriately, to the Oriental Benevolent Association of Wailuku:

First of all is my wish for a good health to you all. I hope I shall not be criticized to consult you about my trouble. I am asking your advise if it would be possible just to hit a Japanese if he does not pay me for what I have worked for. (my wages) It would be all right with me if it is only a matter of $1.00 but it amounts to $150.00 more. I depend upon your advise. If possible, I would like to hit him, but have to get your advise first in order not to act against the law. It had been my intention to bring this matter to your attention last January, but he (the Japanese) promised to pay me after his crop is harvested. But now he is acting fresh because they are winning the war. He said he will pay me after the war, because he has no money now, and further said that even if he goes to jail he would not pay me, that is why if possible I would like to hit him. Awaiting for your advise. J. M. R.

Life in these Hawaiian Islands had its lighter side, even during the first days of war. As a counterbalance to this specimen of Filipinese, I would like to offer this equally weird example of Militarese, published for public information in the *Hawaii Press* of December 23, 1941.

"Release No. 104. To clarify much talk, that is all right in itself as news going around concerning things that are being done all over the territory about the war and emergency measures, it is felt that a clarification will be helpful to everyone to know just what the people of the Big Island are going to do about all this — whether they are required to do everything that is talked about or not." Anyone who can read the above and feel clarified should be congratulated.

That the problems of English can be really acute and should be shouldered by everyone is borne out by Military Release No. 143 which said:

"In order to put everybody on the same basis in sharing and sharing alike the problems and necessities of the emergency all motion pictures shown on the island of Hawaii will be in English."

As on the other islands, there was some firing over and above the call of duty, as witness this stern warning apparently addressed to wandering canines.

"In recent nights Army guards have challenged noises in the dark and three times no one has answered. Three shots have been fired and three dogs have been found dead. Everyone is sorry for the dogs, but the point is — answer when challenged." Perhaps the sentries should have changed their warnings to "Bark, or I shoot!"

One of the best spy scare stories came from Maui. There, the usual baseless reports were phoned in to the intelligence center, Venus herself being accused of dropping flares into Iao Valley. But just after the enemy submarines shelled Kahului, a message came to the effect that Morse code signaling could be observed coming from a house occupied by a Japanese school teacher and his family. Moreover as the signals were being given every night and the house fronted

Kahului Bay, it certainly looked as if information was being sent to the submarines lurking off shore.

The intelligence officers were very smart. Instead of raid' ing the house, they braved the submarine menace and sat out in a boat on the bay, night after night, attempting to copy the messages and break the code. The flashes came regularly, one series after 7:00 P.M. and another just before lights out at 10:00 P.M. They appeared very rarely at a later time in the night. They seemed to follow one general pattern but conformed to the principles of no known code. So the military raided the house.

They found that the large plate glass window of the living room faced the ocean and as blackout paper was scarce, the owner of the house decided to screen only the kitchen and a back bedroom. Unfortunately the bathroom was across the hall from the living room, and the fact that a swing door led from the kitchen provided the key to the mystery. Every time one of the family felt constrained to go to the toilet, the kitchen door emitted two or three dashes followed by a series of dots. The length of the message was propor' tionate to the urgency of the call, and the regularity of the time sequence reflected the going-to-bed habits of the chil' dren and their parents.

All this, however, was not at first apparent, and at night when the place was raided, the young Japanese was so taken aback with the shock of accusation that his very innocence bore the appearance of guilt. He foresaw for himself noth' ing less than internment and possibly the firing squad. He was on the verge of collapse and asked to be escorted to the bathroom. Suddenly the sharpwitted intelligence officer, a local man, also collapsed — but with mirth. He stood in the living room and recognized the strange pattern of flashes from the swing door that they had studied so carefully from out at sea. The building of a screen in front of the kitchen door solved the whole difficulty. Safety sometimes hangs on a thread; here it swung on a hinge.

Because we have turned aside briefly to record such trivial occurrences does not mean that Maui did not take its war seriously. The strategic importance of the island was soon recognized, so that the military construction engineers came early to Maui and stayed late. One of the first groups to arrive was a navy outfit, bearing the rather mysterious designation VJ-3. These men were charged with developing the flying field as a naval air base and a proving ground for robot planes. One never forgot the war on Maui — it was going on all the time under your nose. Grumman fighter planes from one of our sunken carriers made this their base, and fliers returned here from their missions. Hence, heroic names like Butch O'Hara became household words on Maui, for Maui households knew their presence. Every battle and every large scale mission in the South Pacific brought its toll of sadness and sense of personal loss to many island families. They mourned the passing of the gay, the composed, the witty, the brooding, the carefree, the serious, the hopeful, the foreboding — all the young men for whom the sands of time were running out so swiftly. The people knew them by their first names, by the nicknames they called each other. They cared for them drunk or sober, elated or low in their minds, bade them a quiet Godspeed, when the inevitable grapevine brought hints of departure, and if and when they came back welcomed them with open hearts and houses. When some did not return, these people told you, "Micky the Finn and Jerry Snip are gone" — as though all the world would know these names and share their sadness. Some households specialized in marines, others in fliers, while in still others army men held the place of affection. The more mature Seabees, who seemed the most concerned to find out what we were fighting for, earned everybody's respect. The claim is made for one ranch on Maui that its guests during the war numbered thousands.

Perhaps it is because of these personal relationships and the sense of tragedy that followed the loss of so many men who had been stationed on the island, that Maui is less inclined to speak of its material contributions to the war effort. Plantation men there look somewhat surprised when you question them concerning land that was taken from them, heavy equipment on loan, or labor enlisted for military projects. These contributions were matters of course. Fine relationships grew up also in Hawaii where marines and army men made themselves very much at home, but the island was too big, the servicemen too scattered and the local Japanese seemed more uncertain in their reactions. Kauai, too, had a warm aloha for its soldiers and marines, but just as on Hawaii the haole group, upon whom fell the main burden of hospitality, were strung out around the island, and possibly there was less rank-and-file rapprochement there than on Maui. These opinions are of course open to question and will be quite firmly disputed, but that is how the situation appears to an observer who has tried to cast up accounts for all three islands.

Perhaps this view is related to the fact that everything seemed more concentrated on Maui and the war appeared nearer at hand. You could be waiting for your plane at the civilian airstrip and watch the heavy shells throwing up red geysers of dirt in almost ceaseless gun practice on the range at the foot of Haleakala. Right overhead the navy planes would come dropping out of formation to make their landings, or swift Corsairs would go streaking across the sky. Perhaps someone would whisper to you the rumor about the four Corsairs that dived out of a rainstorm in follow-my-leader fashion straight into the sea. Unfortunately the rumor was authentic news; it really happened. Everything was there for everyone to see. There were more military secrets told, and rigorously kept, on Maui than on any other island of the group.

Of course the Maui plantations contributed very materially to military projects. The Hawaiian Commercial and

Sugar Co., having the airport on its lands, lost 3,827 acres of land to military service, 1,384 acres being sugar producing. For construction purposes it supplied on the average 50 men a day to P.N.A.B. (Pacific Naval Air Base contractors) and housed and fed the men sent by the other plantations to work on this project. It installed a deep well to pump half a million gallons of water a day for the air base, supplied electric power to all military posts on its properties, installed a siren and air-raid system, located and constructed ammunition dumps for the military, and did countless jobs of repair work in its machine shops. In short, this plantation is an excellent example of how the small military outpost was grafted onto a large and healthy commercial stock.

The Maui Agricultural Company, in its turn, contributed over three thousand acres of its lands for training purposes and charged the military no rent for two years and a nominal rent thereafter. Two hundred fifty of its "key personnel" were sworn in to serve as armed guards until the Army arrived to take over. Hence, for months, plantation activities virtually ceased. Fire-fighting units were set up in every plantation settlement, and hedges and fences were torn down to allow freedom of movement in combating possible incendiary bomb attacks. An abandoned tunnel was converted into a fully-equipped secondary hospital. First-aid stations, under plantation doctors and nurses, were also established and hundreds of employees took Red Cross instruction. Public air-raid shelters were constructed, etc. Undoubtedly, all of this consisted of nothing more than measures for protection for their own people and their own property. As was mentioned, the plantation personnel seek no special credit. These things are listed here merely to show how the war welded these Hawaiian island communities into smoothly-functioning organizations, functioning co-operatively under combined military and civilian leadership.

A few extracts from the diary of the manager of Wailuku Plantation will serve to sketch in lightly a few more lines of the total picture.

December 7th, 1941. On this day the Engineering Dept. moved all Wailuku Sugar Co.'s explosives from the Iao Tunnel job to the Spreckelsville powder magazines where a constant guard has since been maintained. The mill did not run but steam was maintained constantly in one boiler so that the mill whistle could be blown as an air raid siren.

Dec. 8th. There was quite a run on the grocery stores; most of them were closed at noon to take inventory. No news was received from Honolulu, even over the radio, but Monday night the bombing was described over Army stations, and 3,000 dead and wounded were reported.

Dec. 10th. Provisional Police started working eight-hour shifts. 49 guards at eight stations.

Dec. 11th. Mrs. Allen and I, also Mr. Jennings of Hana with his family returned from Honolulu by special plane. It was an unusual trip in that the pilot had orders to fly at 500 feet, and came up without any radio contact. Nothing happened, but we momentarily expected that something would.

Dec. 15th. At 6:00 P.M. one submarine (some say two) shelled Kahului, firing from eight to eleven shots, aimed either at the S.S. "Maliko," which was in port tied up at Pier I, the Standard Oil tanks, or the Maui Pineapple Company water tank. Whatever the target was, it was pretty good shooting, as two shells hit on the north side of the pier, several in the water between the pier and the shore, and several in the cannery yard. The cannery smokestack was badly damaged. One shell hit in the backyard, demolishing the chicken yard and killing two chickens, these being the only casualties in this our first attack.

Dec. 16th. Public reaction to this shelling was very good. There was no hysteria whatsoever, but many people commented on the fact that no planes took to the air during the shelling.

Dec. 21st. 30 survivors of the S.S. "Lahaina" landed at Spreckelsville after having drifted for ten days. An interesting sidelight on this was that the boat was able to land before anyone knew that anything unusual was happening. The comment was that the Japs could have done the same thing.

Dec. 23rd. The annual Christmas party for plantation children was held, but with this deviation from the usual: each camp was visited by Santa Claus with gifts loaded on a truck. This change was necessitated by the fact that the military authorities would not allow large gatherings in any one place.

Dec. 29th. It appears to be necessary to have 729 guards, exclusive of those required for private property. Cost, $900,000 of which approximately $600,000 would be the sugar industry's share, or about $3.00 per ton of sugar. In addition to this, we would have to guard our own properties at a cost of two or three dollars (per ton) more. It is essential we have Federal assistance.

Dec. 31st. At 1:53 A.M. Kahului was shelled again but no damage was done. Incidentally, our armament on this date consisted of two 75 mm. guns which, from the name plates, were built in 1917, and we question whether or not anyone had ever shot them. Later reports showed that all of the ten or twelve shots (from the sub) were duds. We retaliated with eight shots from one of our 75 mm. guns, but no planes took to the air. The public took this shelling very calmly also, but the reaction would have been better if a plane or two had gone up.

Jan. 28, 1942. Forty-two survivors of the S.S. "Royal T. Frank" came in to Hana. The vessel was torpedoed just outside of Hana; twenty-two were reported missing. We have it on pretty good authority that a destroyer got the submarine.

(According to a Japanese account by a Captain Omae, the Japanese submarine aimed, not at the "Frank" but at a barge loaded with half-a-million dollars' worth of heavy equipment, being towed to Hilo Harbor. They fired a second torpedo at the barge just as it reached Hilo, but missed it again.)

Feb. 10th. Sinking of the S.S. "Royal T. Frank" was officially announced. People were worried over the possible loss of Singapore and wondered if Hawaii would be next.

March 16th. Troops are arriving fast — 2,000 in one lot.

May 29th. Rumors are running wild. Midway gone, China Clipper down, Humuula sunk. Local forces are very much on the alert.

The foregoing excerpts will serve to suggest the anxieties of those early days of the war and how many responsibilities had to be shouldered by the civilians until the arrival of the troops brought them some feeling of security.

* * *

In accordance with our plan of paying particular attention to the outlying centers of population, not because of their military importance but as illustrating the self reliance that was engendered by isolation, we might give a brief account of events in Lahaina. This warm and rather sleepy town was for a time the royal capital of the islands, and is spread along a couple of miles of foreshore facing the island of Lanai. It is shaded with breadfruit trees, mangoes, and monkeypods, and has at its back the bare ridges of the West Maui Mountains. These are cut here and there by deep gorges, out of the mouths of which comes fertility, a little stream, and stray breaths of coolness. Perhaps the old town would go fast asleep except for the Pioneer Mill Plantation, around which its life is centered.

The leaders of this community knew quite well that the Army did not consider Lahaina defensible. Its one communications road across the steep slopes of the palis that lay between it and Wailuku could be too easily cut. Hence, the military force which held the town was reduced from 76 men to four and, if invasion came, it was understood that the road would be at once blown up.

But knowledge of this plan of no-defense did not deter the Lahaina folk from taking measures for their own defense. When the Provisional Police were enrolled in July 1941, the manager of the plantation collected all the firearms he could buy or borrow. He also devised a shoulder stock for the semi-automatic pistols, thus increasing fire accuracy and giving the men the feeling of being better armed. By January 1942, Lahaina had 200 fully trained men, with weapons for 80.

So that the community would know in advance if it was to be invaded, the manager set up a whole chain of observation posts, manned, and occasionally womanned, by Lahaina volunteers. From these posts 35 miles of coastline were kept under constant surveillance. Each post was built by plantation labor, miles of wire were laid, and a telephone, a mattress (so that one of the guards could rest), a firearm for defense, and a home-made sighting device were provided. This last consisted of a length of one-inch lead piping fitted with an eyepiece and cross-hairs and mounted so that it could be swung over an accurately orientated chart. On this, azimuth readings could be taken on any ship or plane that came within sight. Bearings from the next observation post were then co-ordinated in the telephone center and the position and course relayed at once to military intelligence. Sleepy or not, Lahaina was not to be caught napping. Husband and wife sometimes teamed up as watchers on either of the two six-hour day shifts or any of the four three-hour shifts at night. The burden on planta-tion cars and drivers of relieving watches at night in the blackout was a very heavy one, but the vigil was not re-laxed until the danger of invasion was over.

In a few months the 1st Battalion of the 1st Regiment of the Maui Volunteers was organized at Lahaina under the manager's command, and by September 1943 had reached a strength of 424 officers and men. The Army's attitude towards the defense of Lahaina reminds one of the remark made by Lord Beaconsfield (Disraeli) when he was asked if he would attend a political opponent's funeral. "No," he said, "I'm not going — but I approve of it." Defending Lahaina was not going to be the Army's funeral, but they approved of it. Hence they encouraged all the volunteer battalion to undergo the special infiltration course, the main feature of which was to crawl 75 yards on your belly through two barbed-wire entanglements with a stream of machine gun bullets whipping less than a couple of feet overhead.

The possible results of an air raid on such an isolated community were fully realized, and special attention was paid to Red Cross organization. Soon 200 individuals en-tered training courses with two to three hundred more wait-ing to enroll. There followed a most interesting develop-ment. Practical courses using only verbal instruction were instituted for those who could not read nor write, and no less than 385 persons took this training. Special certificates were issued to the best qualified. By March 1942, 600 individuals had taken these courses under 80 leaders and helpers. In the local evacuation scheme, 5,841 people were listed, so that this may be taken as Lahaina's total population. To have more than one adult trained in practical first aid to every ten men, women, and children was surely something of a record in community self-help. Counting 250 more individuals who held standard certificates, the ratio of trainees was one in seven. Had air raids occurred, I doubt if any other community could have looked after its casualties as well as Lahaina.

The manager of Pioneer Mill in his report pays tribute to the assistance given by high school students, pointing out that 275 boys earned $47,000 in 15,000 days of work, while 171 girls in 5,700 days earned nearly $13,500. In addition to these students, 350 grammar school pupils worked 11,500 days. The high school boys did 71% of the hand weeding on 4,400 acres of cane and 50 per cent of the chemical spraying on 4,200 acres. The manager estimated that through this help he had been able to keep 820 acres in production that otherwise he would have been compelled to abandon. In Maui it was the children who kept the home fires burning. The adults did more important work.

One other thing deserves mention as coming fairly close to the highwater mark of a democracy's functioning. The manager organized alien work battalions and these paraded side by side with the Lahaina battalion of the Maui Volunteers, the review being held before General Mittelstaedt. No doubt the army officers blinked a little when the enemy aliens marched by. Perhaps such an occurrence was only possible in an isolated community where everyone's sentiments were well known.

Of course, all was not complete trust and harmony. Had the record been perfect, had there been no weeding out of the disloyal, such a procedure would have been foolishly optimistic. The manager was also chairman of the Alien Internment Board which conducted hearings for detained persons and made recommendations to the military authorities. Every individual brought for a hearing had the right to engage counsel and to give testimony in his own defense.

Of 72 Japanese arrested, 29 were interned, 16 released on special parole, and 21 released unconditionally. In three cases there was disagreement between the military and civil boards; three other individuals were apparently caught in flagrantly disloyal acts and did not come before the Board. The essential matters on which decisions were made concerned military service in Japan, connections with the Japanese consular service, enemy bond purchases, marked activity in Japanese drives for scrap metal, etc., Shintoism, and criminal records. I can find no iota of evidence that the internment of a suspect was ever opposed on the ground of his usefulness to the sugar industry. For men who were working night and day in defense of themselves and their communities thus to play fast and loose with national safety would have been the height of stupidity and inconsistency. The men running the sugar industry have their faults, but arrant stupidity is not one of them. The charge recoils on the general who was stupid enough to make it.

I would be loath to end this account of the impact of war on the various islands of the Territory by casting too much weight in the balance on the side of the intelligence and patriotic devotion of the various community leaders, such as the managers and officers of the sugar and pineapple plantations. There was leadership of a high order but it could have accomplished little or nothing without the loyalty of the led. There is no Ernie Pyle here to do justice to the courage and patient effort of the common worker. Perhaps the best proof of that loyalty was that it spread by contagion from him to its most unlikely exponents, the enemy alien.

Here is the concluding paragraph of a report of a meeting,

called by the Maui director of publicity for the purpose of explaining in simple language the contents of the various military orders which were flooding the island. The meeting was attended by representatives from the various Japanese camps on the H. C. & S. Plantation.

"One of the old men then spoke: I have been working for this plantation since 1907. I came here because I wanted to. My children, grandchildren, have been born here. I will live here and I will die here. I am a good citizen. I want to thank you for coming here today and saying these things to us. I want you to know that we are doing all we can to help. We will work harder than before. All we want to know is what we shall do. I shall live here and shall die here."

No matter who said this or under what circumstances, it bears in itself the impress of dignity and truth. But its sentiments were not plucked out of the air. They grew in 35 years of work and good citizenship. This statement was no sop to the bosses, but a tribute to the good life that was possible for this man and his family in Hawaii. The plantation authorities may quote it. They have a right to. But it should also be remembered that there is a whole lot of living crowded in between contacts of the boss and the Japanese laborer. Teachers, law makers, neighbors, fellow workers, and, possibly, even the land and Hawaiian skies contributed to this warmth of good feeling, which is summed up in the somewhat overworked word, aloha. "I shall live and die here" signifies truly where this man's allegiance lies.

CHAPTER XV

They Blew Not the Trumpet

IN DAYS long before the atomic bomb, the prophet Ezekiel set forth the destruction of the cities of Egypt, No, Sin, and Memphis and the fate of Tyre and Sidon. He was particularly bitter about Tyre, "in the heart of the seas," and its rowers, pilots, mariners, and calkers. "Shall not the isles shake at the sound of thy fall," he asked, "when the wounded groan, when the slaughter is made in the midst of thee?" He could almost have been inveighing against Pearl Harbor.

But Ezekiel also told how a watch should be set, and what should be the punishment of the unwary watchman. "But if the watchman see the sword come and blow not the trumpet, and the people be not warned and the sword come, and take any person from among them; he is taken away in his iniquity, but his blood will I require at the watchman's hand."

In telling of the watch that was set over Pearl Harbor, the writer of this brief preface to history proposes to avail himself of a device favored by authors of movie scripts. This is the cutback which, after depicting the crisis, goes back and picks up the threads of events which led up to it. In this case we can then judge whether the trumpet were blown and the watchman guiltless. As far as our adversaries, the Japanese, and ourselves are concerned, it will, I think, be apparent that on the one side there was a remarkable combination of daring planning, bold execution, and extraordinary good fortune; on the other side was an equally

272

remarkable failure to carry foresight to the point of action, combined with bad luck and considerable ineptitude. The watch was well planned but ill-kept.

The sources of information relied upon for this chapter are the three most concerned with the Pearl Harbor disaster. First place will be accorded to the enemy's account, as given to Captain Peyton Harrison of the U.S. Navy in interviews with Japanese naval officers, particularly with Captain Genda, former Chief of Staff to the Japanese admiral who led the victorious attack; the political version was obtained by Captain Harrison in an interrogation of Kurusu, the Washington envoy, as late as January 28, 1946. The American side of the story is taken from the published reports of the Army and Navy Boards of Inquiry which investigated the debacle. It may be said that all three accounts are somewhat biased, but it is not difficult to detect the lines of partiality and the directions in which they lean. Another account is that of a supposedly neutral board, the Congressional committee, but that proved to be as biased as any. But in the main, if we give most weight to unwilling admissions, the picture becomes fairly clear and reliable.

According to Captain Genda, the idea of a surprise attack on Pearl Harbor was first formulated by Admiral Yamamoto in a discussion with Admiral S. Onishi, commander of the 11th Carrier Division. This discussion took place long before Cordell Hull's declaration of American Far Eastern policy. If Hull's statement was the instantaneous match, then the laying of the trail of gunpowder was begun by Yamamoto as early as February 1, 1941. Ambassador Grew apparently knew that there was talk of such an attack, for it was on January 27th, four days earlier, that he reported to our Department of State that a plan for a sudden onset on Pearl Harbor was under consideration by Japan.

Yamamoto, in common with most of the other admirals, was fully convinced that in order to have any chance at all of winning, Japan must strike a blow at the outset of the war that would cripple the American fleet. Either the war must be won in the first year, or the foundations of victory firmly laid. As far as Japan's resources were concerned, its naval strategists claimed that they knew war with America was a shoe-string adventure. They understood the vast industrial potential of the United States. Indeed, it was the help that she was already able to give Great Britain that convinced them that Japan must strike before that potential became properly geared to war.

The technical difficulties in the way of a successful attack on ships in Pearl Harbor were the shallowness of the water and the short run that would be available in which a torpedo must arm itself before striking its target. The Japanese had no illusions about the difficulty of the task but realized that the torpedo would be far more destructive than any aerial bomb. According to our Naval Board's statement, it had been accepted that a torpedo dropped from a 300-foot height would take an initial dive of 75 feet, and the bottom of Pearl Harbor was only 45 feet down. It is true that the British had reported that torpedoes had been launched which required only 42 feet of water and a 75-yard run, but no one seemed to take much notice of this fact. It apparently was lost in the shuffle of naval defensive planning.

Perhaps the Japanese knew of the British torpedo, but in any case they went to work. Three of the best aviators were set aside for experimental work, which was carried out in Japan's Inland Sea under conditions approximating those at Pearl Harbor. At the end of August 1941, a successful technique and type of torpedo had been evolved and constituted what the Naval Board called the Japanese secret weapon. With the technical part of the plan proved feasible, the whole general scheme had then to be worked out. Accordingly on September 1st, war games were instituted with great secrecy at the Imperial War College, in which all details of the attack were planned as well as the over-all features. By November 15th the scheme was completed and approved by Yamamoto.

All of Harrison's naval informants were agreed that the Navy was from the beginning opposed to the idea of war with America, but that the Army was always able to dominate the situation. This is probably a bit of Japanese yen-passing, or whatever takes the place of the stratagem of buck-transfer in Japan. However, some confirmation of the statement came from Kurusu. The enmity between the Army and Navy was, it seems, part of a struggle for power between the two clans, the Chosha, made up largely of Army personnel, and the Satsuma, with which most of the Navy group were identified. The Chosha — according to the Navy story — were both aggressive and scrupulous, and did not balk at assassination to gain their ends. They gained great prestige because the Emperor in his public appearances wore army uniforms. On one occasion when he appeared in an admiral's attire, the naval officers openly wept with joy. According to Kurusu, the Japanese Cabinet was also dominated by the army Chief of Staff, the Director of Military Education, and the War Minister. These "Big Three" could force a cabinet out of office simply by one resigning and the other two refusing to approve his successor. They had the right to do so, and this was how they put Admiral Yonai out of office.

In an Imperial Conference held on September 6th, it was decided that if negotiations with America had not come to a point satisfactory to Japan by October 1st, the Army should proceed with its plans for war. The Navy declared that it was not ready for war and was opposed to the idea, but agreed to abide by Prince Konoye's decision, knowing that he also was against hostilities. On October 1st the admirals again said they were not ready for war, but Tojo insisted that they should declare this publicly and officially. This they declined to do, stating again that they would follow Konoye's leadership. Konoye was then forced to resign on

October 16th and Tojo took office as Premier. This meant that the die was cast in favor of war.

The above statement seems to be borne out by subsequent happenings. Konoye, it will be remembered, committed suicide when he was placed at the head of MacArthur's list of war criminals. It has been suggested, probably with truth, that the U.S. Army did not expect to convict Konoye and was relying on the effect of his acquittal as proof to the world of the impartiality of the trials. They could then more plausibly ask for the death sentence on those who were found guilty. If all the accused were convicted, it would make it appear that accusation was equivalent to sentence of death.[1] If that was the strategy, it seems a pity that Konoye did not understand it that way. For him accusation *was* equivalent to death.

Another statement to Captain Harrison may or may not have been due to protective bias, though its general purport was confirmed by Ambassador Grew. Kurusu and the naval informants agreed that the Emperor was averse to war, until Hull's Ten Points were presented in the closing days of November and interpreted by the Cabinet as a virtual ultimatum. They say that the ruler of Japan agreed to war, but that at the close of the Cabinet meeting he told the military leaders that he presumed the ordinary formalities of a declaration of war would be followed. The navy informants claim that the Army double-crossed the Emperor in this respect, because they controlled the communication system and delayed the declaration until after the Pearl Harbor assault. This claim, in view of the obvious advantages of surprise in staging the attack, may be taken, if not with the proverbial grain of salt, at least with a considerable dash of soya.

The plan was for the fleet to take the northern route to Hawaii, as that way there was less danger of detection. In

[1] Since this was written, the results of the Nuremburg trials have confirmed this hypothesis.

addition, the Japanese guessed, and guessed right, that our Navy would be watching what was called the suspicious southwest sector. The enemy fleet assembled at Tankan Bay, off the island of Etorufu, northwest of the main Japanese island of Hokkaido, on November 22nd. For secrecy's sake, fueling was carried out at sea, and on November 26th, ac' cording to Genda, the task force set out on its mission. According to our Navy Board's statement, the date of de' parture was "27th–28th November," but neither the text nor a footnote makes clear whether this means the 27th or 28th, or whether it means the 28th by the Japanese calendar, 27th by ours. The Army Board's statement reads: "The assembly was completed and the Task Force departed on November 27–28, Eastern Longitude Time, which was ap' parently after the date that the counterproposals (consid' ered by the Japanese as an ultimatum) were delivered by the President of the United States to Japan through Secretary Hull on November 26, 1941." [2] But this statement still leaves us very much in the air, as it is impossible for the reader to determine whether the 27th or the 28th was the date of departure, or whether the fleet began moving out on the earlier date. It also forgets to say that Hull's message was delivered on November 27th, Japanese time. It is not at all "apparent" that the Task Force left after the date of Hull's counterproposals. But as we have previously re' marked, the point is of little importance except politically; the fleet was assembling for the attack from November 22nd, and plans had been completed two months previously.

It is also true that the final orders, "Climb Mount Niitaka," the signal for attack, were not given until after the Japanese rendezvous had been reached, and that, if word had been received before midnight of December 6th that the United States had backed down, the attack would have been called off. But Roosevelt did not back down, so — if you like the

[2] Full Text of the Official Reports Concerning the Attack on Pearl Harbor. *United States News*, Sept. 1, 1945. (Extra Number.) P. 34.

reasoning — he and he alone was responsible for the war.

In any case, the Japanese fleet reached their rendezvous undetected, and proceeded with the rest of their plans in exact accordance with an "estimate of the situation" signed by General Martin of the Army Air Force in Hawaii, General Bellinger of the Naval Air Force, and approved by Admirals Kimmel and Bloch, and General Short, in April 1941. This estimate the Board termed "prophetic in its accuracy and uncanny in its analysis of the enemy's intention." The portion quoted in the Army Report begins: "In the past, Orange (Japan) has never preceded hostile action by a declaration of war." It anticipated a dawn air attack from fast carriers, since this was the type of assault that could be delivered most probably as a complete surprise. The estimate also suggested that attack by a single submarine might indicate the presence of a fast surface force. Among its other assumptions were that Japan could employ a maximum of six fast carriers (they used six), early morning as the best time for attack (correct), that the task force would cross a circle 881 nautical miles from Oahu at dawn of the day preceding the attack (they did so), and should launch its planes at dawn 233 nautical miles from Oahu (250 miles was the actual distance). The estimate ends with the following pregnant declaration with regard to the assumption of Hawaii's supposed invulnerability: "Plans based on such convictions are inherently weak and tend to create a false sense of security with the consequent unpreparedness for offensive action." Here we have an extraordinary situation — the military predicting an undeclared war, setting forth a blueprint of the attack which the Japanese followed exactly, reminding themselves of the dangers of complacency, and yet failing to meet the crisis when it came.

The army report states in one place that "we were preparing for war by the conference method," of which no doubt this estimate was one outcome. It sounds like Hono-

lulu's favorite plan for solving a social problem; elect a committee to consider action; in turn elect a subcommittee to
write a report; then all go home imagining we have taken
all necessary steps to settle the issue. Could it be that Kimmel and Short, who had the problem of defending Hawaii in
their hands, had been infected by this Hawaiian weakness
for the resolutionary "whereas."

On the other hand, there was nothing dilatory or impractical about the Japanese except that they overestimated the
opposition. Genda's account gives the number of planes
launched as 370. (The Army report said 424.) Of the 81
fighters, 39 remained to protect the fleet, the rest partici-
pated in the assault. The Japanese expected to lose one-
third of their planes, and thought they would be lucky to
escape with the loss of one-third of their surface ships.

They lost no ships and only 29 planes, though about 50
others were either destroyed or damaged in landing on the
carriers because of rough seas that had worked up during
the morning. This tribute to our enemy was proffered by
the Army Board:

"Japan evidently brought to bear on the attack the best
brains, the best equipment, and the finest intelligence, with
the most expert planning, which it had." Yet in another
place the Board, with typical self-contradiction, speaks of
"this extraordinary chance-taking characteristic, due to the
violent and uncivilized reasoning of the Japanese mind," as
being the basis of the success of the attack. It is to be sin-
cerely hoped that the Oriental mind will not take these statements as typical of the reasoning of the Occidental mentality. They are not so.

That expert planning was helped immeasurably by reports
from the Japanese consulate. These daily bulletins were
based on a scheme which divided Pearl Harbor into three
zones, ship movements to and from each being given. It
should be remembered that there are miles of hills behind
the Harbor, from which clear views of its surface may be

obtained. Captain Genda claimed that the Japanese played no favorites in sending these reports — half went by the Mackay Radio and half by R.C.A.

Even more exact information was furnished by a two-man submarine launched from the deck of a 3,000-ton underwater craft. This midget submarine entered Pearl Harbor a couple of days before the seventh and made the complete circuit of Ford Island, noting the positions of all capital ships. The captain reported a little difficulty with the net at the entrance, but he managed to get free in time to enter after the net was opened at 4:00 A.M. to let the garbage scows through. He went out again the same way. We certainly left the front door wide open while we carefully barred the bedroom window against possible saboteurs. What with other details supplied by the planes that were over Pearl Harbor at dawn on the morning of the attack, the Japanese knew all they needed to know to launch a most successful blow. Moreover, the Navy, according to Admiral Mc-Morrow, knew that the Japanese were fully informed of all military activities in this area.

We can now leave the Japanese reports and direct more careful attention to our own sources. The report of the Army Inquiry Board is an edifying document, beginning with a declaration of highmindedness that must have been very satisfying to its authors, and ending with a similarly satisfactory pronouncement which reads, "Recommendations: None."

The Board, it says of itself, was "conscious of the deep spiritual and moral obligation, as well of its professional and patriotic duty to present an impartial and judicial investigation and report." Probably, to paraphrase Damon Runyon, it does not contain all the mental confusion and buck-passing in the world, for some is to be found in the report of the Navy Board. If its second chapter is not one of the worst public documents extant, it surely should be up among the contenders. As was said of a book by an angry reviewer —

it contains much that is new, and much that is true, but what is true is not new and what is new is not true.

The chapter begins with a true picture of the state of the nation in 1940–41. "The winds of public opinion were blowing in all directions; isolationists and nationalists were struggling for predominance; public opinion was both against war and clamoring for reprisals against Japan: we were negotiating for peace with Japan, and simultaneously applying economic sanctions that led only to war." In short, America was Alice in Wonderland, wondering whether it was on its head or its heels. All this may be admitted, but the Board's summation of the final causes of war does not help at all in enabling us to see through the murk. "Such," they say, "was the confusion of war and events, largely unorganized for appropriate action, and helpless before a strong course of events, that ran away with the situation and prematurely plunged us into war."

The writer must confess that he has read this statement backwards and forwards and either way it seems to make as much sense. Was it the men, the events, or the confusion that was unorganized and helpless before the strong course of events? And who or what was it — the confusion, the men, the events, or the strong course of events — that plunged us into war? I had always believed it was the Japanese.

General psychology, as set forth by generals, is somewhat weird in its pronouncements. They state that there was "a distinct lack of a war mind in the United States. Isolationist organizations and propaganda groups against war were powerful and vital factors affecting any war action capable of being taken by our responsible leadership. So influential were these campaigns, that they raised grave doubts in minds of such leadership as to whether they would be supported in the necessary actions for our defense by requisite moves against Japan." And the report adds: "There was little war spirit amongst the general public or in the armed forces, due to this conflicting public opinion having its influence."

The writer holds no brief for isolationists and their cam-paigns, but he would find it hard to believe that Lindbergh, Wheeler, and even Gerald Smith would have opposed "necessary actions for our defense by requisite moves against Japan." What was requisite or necessary is not stated. They could not surely have meant aggressive naval action against Japan without Congressional authority, and certainly the isolationists would not have objected to long-distance patrol reconnaissance from Hawaii or the issuing of live ammuni-tion to our mobile batteries in defense of Oahu. Here is Alibi Number One, a thumping big one. We were unpre-pared on December 7th because of the doubts in the minds of the leadership (sic) as to whether the public would sup-port defensive measures.

However, the generals' reading of the Japanese mind car-ried no tinge of uncertainty. Japan's people and govern-ment, it seems, "were psychologically and physically geared to war and were implemented with a polished plan of action and equipment to do the job. It was animated by cunning hatred and patriotism in a land where life is cheap, and nur-tured in an atmosphere of insane nationalism and oriental intrigue. Japan was a nation united for a single purpose of world conquest based on more than a thousand years of conflict."

The Japanese might, of course, retort that this is mainly bunk, nurtured in an atmosphere where words are cheap, and that in the past hundred years America has engaged in wars with Mexico, Spain, two World Wars and a Civil War, while Japan has waged at least one war less. And as regards national unity, the Board should have avoided quot-ing (six pages later) Ambassador Grew's report on October 25th to the effect that the Emperor had ordered a meeting of the Privy Council and "instructed them that there should be no war with the United States." Grew added: "This was the final effort by conservative Japanese to avoid war." In other words, Japanese unity in its intention to conquer the world, "based on more than a thousand years of conflict," dated from about six weeks before Pearl Harbor. All this amounts to Alibi Number Two. The little yellow men kicked us when we had our psychological pants down.

The third major alibi is concerned with the Japanese fortifying their mandated territories, which gave them "a string of naval and air bases across the lifeline to the Philippines, and rendered futile and impotent any fortification of our own islands, such as Guam, Midway, Christmas, Palmyra, etc." When the attack came, the Navy was actually convoying planes and other equipment to the "futile and impotent" fortifications of Wake and Midway. If the above quoted observation were the result of foresight, then it would have been much better to have left the planes, etc., in Hawaii. If it is a matter of hindsight, then the failure to fortify our islands loses its value as an alibi for defeat.

Alibi Number Four has to do with the reports that the Japanese consul was supplying Tokyo with information as to our naval dispositions. If the Army, Navy, and F.B.I. had been allowed to tap the consul's lines, much important information, so it was contended, could have been gathered, "which would probably have prevented in large measure the Pearl Harbor disaster." But leaving on one side the ethics of such line-tapping, which might have savored of "oriental intrigue," the military authorities certainly knew of this diplomatic immunity. They also knew that anyone with a pair of binoculars or with the naked eye could see from Aiea Heights the number and position of ships in Pearl Harbor. They were certainly not naïve enough to trust that the consul, "animated by cunning hatred and patriotism," would fail to send on this information at a time when our own ambassador in Japan was transmitting to Washington all the information he could gather about Japanese military plans. There was no need to tap any wires — any lieutenant j.g.

could have driven up Aiea and written the gist of the messages which the consul was sending. In any case, we paid no
attention to this immunity stuff. The Navy went ahead and
tapped the consular lines, all except the line to the cook's
quarters which they overlooked, and which was tapped by
the F.B.I.

Summed up, this alibi is not very strong; it amounts to the
claim that if the military could have actually seen the messages without surmising their obvious content, Pearl Harbor
would not have happened. If, for example, the Navy and
Army had actually read the orders to the Consulate to burn
all their papers instead of knowing that they were being
destroyed, we would have been better prepared. If the
enemy had been foolish enough to have sent the consul the
date and hour of the attack, we might also have been ready
for it, provided word could have reached Washington in
time. But the Chief of Staff might have been out horseback
riding, or General Short might have been going to a party.
This happened when the latter was shown a highly suspicious message to a newspaper in Japan that the F.B.I. had
obtained by wire-tapping. As the General couldn't decipher
its meaning, he went on to the party anyway. As for General Marshall, he could not be reached in Washington with
the news that a break in diplomatic relations with Japan was
imminent, and so this vital information was not relayed to
General Short until after three hours' delay. If, as people
have suggested, President Roosevelt left the fleet in Hawaii
as bait for a Japanese attack, he certainly should have told
General Marshall about the idea. In this whole matter of
exchange of last-minute information, General Short was certainly short-changed.

Now we come to Alibi Number Five, one of the biggest
of the group. It concerns the danger from Japanese residents
in Hawaii, and in this matter we must let the Board speak
for itself.

"It is significant that it had been the national policy of the

United States to exclude Japanese nationals from the United States and its territories, both for self-protection and to protect American labor against cheap foreign labor of the yellow races. *Yet in Hawaii, our fleet base and one of our most important defense outposts, we permitted the introduction into the population of the islands of Japanese to the extent of 30 per cent of the total population, or 160,000.*" (Italics ours.)

Since the members of the Board were so conscious of their "deep spiritual and moral obligation," we cannot accuse them of deliberately falsifying the facts; it is more charitable to assume that the gross error in the above statement was due to their ignorance. Since the Gentlemen's Agreement of 1907, Japanese immigration has been governed by exactly the same restrictions as applied in continental America. The Federal Government, not Territorial officials and not even the Big Five, since that time has been in full charge of immigration to Hawaii. We did not "permit" the introduction into the islands of Japanese "to the extent of 30 per cent of the total population, or 160,000," since this statement itself is contradicted by the figures given in a footnote on the same page of the report, which states the number of alien-born Japanese as "about 37,500." The rest of the 160,000 or 122,500, having been born in Hawaii, immigrated, without passports, from Heaven or wherever young Japanese-American babies come from.

Thus the implication contained in the next paragraph of the report, that Japanese laborers and artisans "highly prized in sugar cane, pineapples, shipping, and other interests of the islands" were imported by those "interests" against the national policy of the United States, is entirely a false one.

It is hardly worth while to criticize the strangely phrased statement that the purpose of our immigration policy was "both for self-protection and to protect American labor" as though American labor was not included with ourselves. Let the labor unions make of this what they will; we prefer to ascribe it to mental confusion, and to believe that like so much of the official report it doesn't mean a thing. But we should allow the generals to develop their case without futile objections to their use of English.

It seems that "it was the urgent desire of these commercial interests apparently both to enjoy the protection and profits from the basing of the fleet in Hawaii and also to have no disturbance of such labor or to be led into any situation that would disturb these profitable labor-relations." Surely none but the most muddle-headed men would regard profits from the fleet, enjoying its protection, and profits from labor as incompatible. But if they are, which would the generals advise should be given up? Should the commercial interests sell to sailors at cost, or disdain the fleets' protection, or give up using labor so as to make profits in their business?

War with Japan would, above all things, have tended to "disturb these profitable labor-relations." Hence if the report makes sense, the men in sugar, pineapples, shipping, etc., should have been the most arrant pacifists and isolationists in America. The truth is that, excepting one local newspaper columnist,[3] the breed was hardly represented in Hawaii. As to protests from these interests against removing dangerous Japanese from their plantations, the cold facts are that these had all been marked down beforehand by plantation personnel acting as "contact men" with the F.B.I., and were taken into custody by that same personnel on December 7th. Plantation managers also served on the internment boards and did not, I believe, consider at all the sugar interests in making their recommendations.[4] Rarely

[3] He was not so mildly pro-Axis as he was violently anti-British.

[4] Senator Hill of the local legislature was asked about this so-called unwillingness of the interests to have dangerous Japanese taken care of. He either didn't know the answer or possibly didn't hear the question aright. Occasionally plantation managers did oppose hasty or unjustified action. On one occasion, a newly arrived intelligence officer wanted an old Japanese interned on the grounds that after living forty years in Hawaii he could speak no English. With the aid of a little "pidgin" interpretation, the man was able to establish his innocence of any subversive tendencies. Two of his sons were at the front and he had bought all the U.S. Bonds he could afford. It was the military who appointed the managers to these boards.

has a more damning and damnable charge been leveled against the patriotic spirit of any section of Americans as this accusation of the Army Board.

The so-called Big Five, companies which serve as agencies for the sugar industry, have been frequently condemned for their alleged political control of the Territory, but no one has ever before suggested that they were powerful enough to set aside citizens' constitutional rights to vote and run for office. That kind of intimidation belongs only in some of our Southern states, such as Georgia or Mississippi. But this is evidently what the Army Board thinks the political strategy of the Big Five should have been. Here is their pronouncement.

"This policy (of the great commercial interests) of encouraging the Japanese and permitting them to become dominant in the affairs of the islands has even gone so far as to *permit* the Japanese to become important political factors with membership in both the Senate and the House of Hawaii, and to dominate, by way of majority, the island-governing councils in some of the islands of the Hawaiian group." Perhaps if a few of the Japanese-American citizens had been shot for attempting to vote, the situation would not have come to this sorry pass.

The report further speaks of "propaganda pressure on the subject of doing nothing to offend the Japanese in the Islands, and to let them alone so they could work for these Island industries and agriculture, *which must have been imposed heavily upon General Short*." (Italics added.) No single instance of this propaganda was adduced, and the cold facts of the matter are that it was as imaginary as Japanese sabotage. For an impartial and judicial body such as the Army Board claimed to be, this was a most unwarranted assumption. If this pressure had been imposed on General Short, why did he not himself complain of it? This was not one of his alibis.

However, from assumption the Board rapidly proceeds to

certainty. "The constant application of such pressure for a period of nearly a year upon General Short *doubtless had a material effect upon his mind* and upon his anxiety about the Japanese population." (Again, our italics.) What a pity that some of these generals, who read the mind of General Short so clearly, had not exercised some of their clairvoyance on General Tojo.[5]

The only evidence before the Board, apart from some doubtful testimony by a local politician, which supported the above statements was that given by General Burgin, who commanded all the coast artillery and all the anti-aircraft batteries in the Hawaiian Department. He testified that he could not put his mobile batteries into position on December 7th because of "resistance of landowners to letting the artillery go on the land or lease it for the placing of battery positions." This testimony was so contrary to the facts that it deserves a military citation as the greatest buck-passing exploit of the whole war. His own department's files would show that there was not a single instance of a refusal by any plantation for the use of its land for military purposes prior to December 7th.

The record as compiled by Colonel E. C. Moore on behalf of the H.S.P.A. is clear. In the period from 1939 onwards, the Army made 179 written requests to Oahu plantations for right of entry, use of land, granting of leaseholds of acreage for gun emplacements, maneuvers, or other military purposes. "Every request," says Colonel Moore's report, "regardless of its nature . . . was granted with promptness." Letters attached to that report show that in addition to these specific requests blanket permission was granted to

---

[5] On February 1, 1941, General Herron, on relinquishing his command in Hawaii, wrote an appreciative letter to the H.S.P.A. expressing his gratitude and bespeaking for his successor, General Short, "a continuance of the generous assistance you have always given to the Army in Hawaii." In another letter General Herron wrote: "I have lived in many American communities in my long service, but never in one so intelligently and whole-heartedly patriotic as Hawaii."

he Army to use all roads and lands under their control by
Kahuku Plantation (November 8, 1940), by the Oahu Sugar
Co. (February 11, 1941), and by the Honolulu Plantation
(November 21, 1939), while as late as September 11, 1941,
Ewa Plantation granted the 13th Field Artillery similar
entry to its lands.

Waialua Plantation, through its manager Mr. John Midkiff, reports that 42 separate permissions for 178 occupa-
tions were granted between January 9 and December 4,
1941, plus blanket permission to occupy certain strategic
points as well, including access to the whole plantation during maneuvers. Thus what Midkiff calls "a very close and
cordial relationship between the Army and the company"
had been set up prior to 1941, and for three years it was an
unusual month in which the Army was not holding some
exercises on the plantation. He also quotes a letter (June 6,
1941) from General Short, the man whose mind, according
to the Army Board, was affected by the constant pressure
from the industries to let them alone. In this letter Short
thanks the company for "a splendid co-operation" in acced-
ing to a request to strengthen and reconstruct its plantation
railway lines so as to make them usable for military purposes.[6] Major General W. H. Wilson also wrote saying that
the success of five days of maneuvers, November 24 to 29,
1941, on plantation lands was facilitated by the co-operation
of private landowners. Previously, on April 1st, 3rd, 8th,
and 14th, permission was also granted to the Army to carry
out "practice alerts" on Waialua lands.

This carries the record up to seven days before Pearl Harbor, yet Burgin was moved to testify that all his mobile
batteries had never been in the positions they would occupy
in case of hostilities on account of landowners' resistance.[7]
Considering that all the evidence to the contrary was in his

[6] Letter from John H. Midkiff, manager, to C. B. Wightman, September
28, 1945. H.S.P.A. File No. 1239.
[7] Official Reports, United States News, p. 40.

own records, is it not strange that the Board was not kind enough to suggest that his anxieties might have affected *his* mind?

But this is not all. General Burgin felt he should come to Short's defense as well as his own. He pointed out that "if General Short had gone to Alert No. 3, there would have been great opposition from important and influential civil-ians on the island and particularly those who compose what is known as the Big Five." We have been a long time com-ing to it but now we have the nub of the situation. It was not the generals nor the admirals, not Mr. Roosevelt nor Mr. Hull, not even isolationists nor the Japanese that were responsible for Pearl Harbor — it was the Big Five.

Yet in spite of this conclusive footnote to history, there are several minor mystifying circumstances with which the connection of the Big Five is not quite clear. Burgin testi-fied (Official Report, p. 41) with regard to his artillery that "they were all ready to go into action immediately, with the exception that the mobile batteries did not have the ammu-nition." With regard to the fixed coastal batteries, they had ammunition nearby, Burgin having "insisted on that with General Short in person." But it was packed up in wooden boxes and had to be taken out. The ammunition for the mobile batteries was, however, stored in Aliamanu Crater, a mile from Fort Shafter. The batteries had to send and get this ammunition and then move out into their positions. In short, they needed six hours' notice before they would be ready to fight. This unpreparedness, however, according to the General, was really a great blessing in disguise. He said: "If they (the mobile anti-aircraft batteries) had been out in the field without any ammunition, they would have been worse off than they actually were." That, it must be ad-mitted, seems quite reasonable. Guns without ammunition wouldn't have scared the Japanese aviators a bit.

But why didn't the guns have ammunition? As General Burgin summed it up: "It was just impossible to pry the

mmunition loose from the Ordnance, the G-4s, or from
General Short himself." It seems that the men of the Ordnance Department, like good housewives, object to letting
ammunition out of their hands, having it all dirtied up in
the fields, and then be required to take it back to clean and
renovate it. This attitude, it seems, belongs with "everyone
who has the preservation of ammunition at heart." No
doubt this anxiety of Ordnance was due to pressure from the
Big Five who didn't want their laborers scared away from
their work by loud and unexpected reports. Later, however,
in a couple of sentences the whole matter was put in a nutshell, and the Board might have concluded their report right
there. "I asked for ammunition for the anti-aircraft. We
were put off, the idea behind it being that we would get our
ammunition in plenty of time, that we would have warning
before any attack ever struck."

To illustrate further the state of the generals' minds, we
might mention that they quote with approval Burgin's idea
that if we had copied Japan's efficient methods, the Japanese
in Hawaii "would have been locked up before the war
started and not afterwards." To feed, imprison, and guard
160,000 Japanese would have been a large order and would
have employed most of our military forces in Hawaii. Using
a little hindsight of our own with regard to the absence of
any sabotage, we can point out that that would have been
a very wasteful plan.

As a crowning touch, General Burgin let out the fact that
for six weeks prior to December 7th the anti-aircraft batteries were in field positions every Sunday morning, so that
they could practice repelling, with simulated fire, attacks
from the carrier-based planes of our Navy. "And," he says,
"we were out just one week prior to December 7th . . .
on Sunday; but, *by some stroke,* we did not go out on
December 7th. The fleet was in the harbor." Could it have
been a *cerebral* stroke?

The Navy Board of Inquiry was much cleverer than the

Army Board in that it said less, published no testimony, and therefore made fewer damaging admissions. There were less directions also in which it could pass the buck. For example, it could hardly blame the Big Five for their type of alert or for what happened at sea. The Navy's strategy was apparently to pass the buck directly back to Washington. The chief alibi is that Admiral Kimmel's fleet suffered its historic defeat mainly because the Navy Department did not let him know the Japanese were coming. But this line of defense is certainly weakened by the statement that our Pacific naval forces were too feeble anyway to match the Japanese fleet, and that the attack was "unpredictable and unpreventable." Captain Layton, Fleet Intelligence officer, was asked what would have been the outcome if the Japanese task force had been discovered and attacked at sea. His answer, as quoted by the Army report, was: "I think the American forces here would have taken the licking of their life, first, because the American people were not psychologically prepared for war." This would indeed be a delightful "non sequitur" if the subject had not been so tragic. To prove this psychological unreadiness, he cites the fact that part of a squadron of our carrier planes flew into Ford Island in Pearl Harbor during the Japanese attack, but though armed there was no record of them firing a single shot against the enemy. There are other names for such inaction than psychological unreadiness.

Nor is it possible easily to follow the line of reasoning behind the Naval Board's statement that even if Kimmel had had two hours' warning of the attack "there was no action open, nor means available, to Admiral Kimmel which could have stopped the attack, or could have had other than negligible bearing upon its outcome."

Other alibis relied upon by the Navy were the neglect of the Army to have its anti-aircraft guns in position and to set up a 24-hour, shore-based, warning system. Other than these, the Navy Board's most important excuse is that the

Japs were too smart — they had specially designed plane torpedoes of which naval intelligence was unaware. The secret weapon bubble seems, however, to have been pricked by the Secretary of the Navy, who stated in his "endorsement" of the Board's findings that the British had reported in 1940 the successful launching of aircraft torpedoes in 42 feet of water.

The report criticizes the messages to Kimmel as being of the "Do-don't" character, but its own conclusions savor of the "It was — it wasn't" type. For example, while it condemns Admiral Stark's poor judgment for not sending Kimmel proper warning of an expected attack, yet it held that no serious blame had been incurred by anyone in the naval service.

Boiling down the Naval Inquiry Board's report and the comments of the Secretary of the Navy and Admiral King, we seem to be left with the following salient considerations:

(1) The Army was theoretically responsible for the defense of Pearl Harbor, but the Navy knew that Short's defensive resources were entirely inadequate. Kimmel didn't know or didn't care what type of alert the Army kept.

(2) Long-distance air reconnaissance was Admiral Bloch's charge, but as commandant of the 14th Naval District he had absolutely no patrol planes. This was entirely a paper defense. The Navy Department should have supplied the wherewithal for him to carry out his responsibilities.

(3) On the other hand, Kimmel had 67 patrol planes, 60 of them available for duty on December 7th. Normally, he used these planes to protect the fleet while it was carrying out training operations. But the ships needed that protection even more when they were in Pearl Harbor lined up, as was said, "like sitting ducks," except that only wooden or feebleminded ducks would line up that way. There were also installations absolutely vital to the fleet that required defense.

The force at Kimmel's command was admittedly too small to have given complete protection, but it might at least have patrolled the very suspicious northern sector. Besides air reconnaissance, a sea patrol would have been possible. Such patrolling had been carried out by Admiral Richardson in 1940, by Kimmel in the summer of 1941, and discontinued by the latter on November 27th! [8]

(4) Whatever Kimmel did *not receive* in the way of warning from Washington, the records show that he *did* receive the following:

(a) The "war warning" message of November 27th . . . the day he ordered long-distance aerial reconnaissance discontinued.

(b) Another "hostile action possible at any moment" message on November 27th.

(c) Information that the Japanese were destroying their codes. (December 3rd.)

(d) Instructions to outlying U.S. Pacific islands to destroy secret and confidential material. (December 4th and 6th.)

For a man who claimed to have been kept in the dark about the general situation, he did not treat his own subordinates very well in the way of giving them important information. The "war warning" message of November 27th was not relayed to Admiral Bellinger, who commanded the sea planes, nor to Admiral Newton, who was at sea with a carrier and other important units of the fleet.

(5) From December 1st onwards there was no intelligence forthcoming regarding the movements in the Pacific of the Japanese carriers, though it was assumed that all except four were in Japanese waters. This radio silence should have been considered most suspicious. Because not a single carrier service call had been identified in late November, the fleet intelligence concluded that carrier traffic was

8 "Daily reconnaissance was made after December 7th using Army B-17's and Navy P.B.Y.'s and 'anything they had'." Official Reports, p. 49.

"at low ebb." At the actual time when Japan's six carriers were headed for Hawaii, Kimmel was prompted to say to his intelligence chief on December 2nd:

"Do you mean to say that they (the carriers) could be rounding Diamond Head and you wouldn't know it?" Captain Layton testified, however, that the Admiral had a twinkle in his eye, yet the sober truth was that this boldly conceived carrier threat, then no more than a twinkle in Kimmel's eye, had already been launched against Hawaii.

One comment of Admiral King will hardly meet with a trace of dissent. He affirmed that after all was said and done, "The Navy cannot evade a share of responsibility for the Pearl Harbor incident. That disaster cannot be regarded as an 'act of God,' beyond human power to prevent or mitigate." That is not only true, but a triumph of understatement.

(6) The Secretary of the Navy in his "Endorsement" deals a shrewd blow of his own at his admirals' alibis, especially at the rather plaintive plea that the Navy was handicapped because, unlike the Japanese, they could not initiate hostile action before a declaration of war. As Secretary Knox pointed out, such constitutional restrictions or inhibitions "did not preclude either long-distance reconnaissance or a sortie by the fleet." Nevertheless, they did sink a Japanese submarine outside Pearl Harbor the morning of the attack, a fact which the Navy did not think important enough to communicate to the Army commander.[9]

Comment has already been made on the fact that the so-called "secret weapon" was already known to the British who had experimented with shallow-diving aircraft torpedoes, reporting that they did not require any more water

---

9 On this matter of Army-Navy co-ordination, perhaps one of the neatest tricks of the war was reported by Assistant Secretary McCloy, after an inspection visit to Hawaii. The respective commanders, he said, "were practically sitting in one another's laps." We rather doubt the practicality of the operation, and in any case such overlapping of authorities was hardly necessary.

for successful launching than the depth at which they made their normal run. (Official Report, p. 82.)

All in all, the story of Army and Navy foresight prior to Pearl Harbor is a sorry tale. Whether the glorious redemption of our military reputation by later heroic exploits and the final winning of the war are to be considered as offsets to this sadly tarnished record is another question. Men of the professional military class, plus many reserve officers, augmented by millions of former civilians turned airmen, soldiers, and sailors, won the war. To all who shared in that triumph, the whole nation as well as the democratic world owes an unpayable debt.

But in this writer's opinion it is of no use advancing puerile alibis, such as that it was "the violent and uncivilized reasoning of the Japanese mind" that misled us to our near-ruin — in short, that the enemy was successful because they didn't reason our way. That is a ludicrous statement.

Our former national complacency, which included a too thorough trust in our professional military leaders, is not in any sense a cause of military incompetency. The nation at large has acknowledged its sins of foolish optimism and its failure to provide our military forces with adequate fighting equipment. It would have been equally becoming for the Army and Navy to have frankly admitted their derelictions of duty. It was particularly ungracious for the Army in Hawaii and the Army Board of Inquiry to try to shift the blame for ineptitude and unpreparedness onto the shoulders of the civil population. However, it is to the credit of General Short that he appears to have taken no part in this piece of discreditable buck-passing.

The people of Hawaii, recognizing that Short was responsible for stimulating much of their preparedness program, have a fine aloha for him and many of his officers; they regret exceedingly that his fine reputation was marred by a last-minute relaxing of vigilance. It is to the credit of all those who suffered by that unwariness that they complained hardly at all. Nor would you have heard in the dark days of 1942 any bitterness of complaint against Kimmel. Furthermore, the population as a whole accepted the inconveniences and some of the minor injustices of martial law quite tolerantly, and endured them patiently until long after the period of necessity for martial law had passed. Perhaps the same civilians were too busy doing their little bit towards winning the war to bother about making complaints.

Everything — martial law, Army and Navy alibis, general ineptitude and complacency — is in process of being rapidly forgotten. It is because we do forget so quickly that it has seemed worth while to write this chapter. We can forget Pearl Harbor, but it is a little too early for the nation to forget the mistakes that led up to that inglorious defeat — mistakes in which we all shared, and which should not be repeated.

"Then whosoever heareth the sound of the trumpet, and taketh not warning; if the sword come, and take him away, his blood shall be upon his own head." Perhaps the trumpet is already blowing, but with muddleheadedness in high places, and all this domestic clamor and dissension, how can we hear or heed?

Notes and References

GENERAL REFERENCES

"Report of the Pearl Harbor Investigations" (Navy Board of Inquiry, Army Pearl Harbor Board), *New York Times*, August 30, 1945.

Honolulu Advertiser Files, 1937–1942. World events leading up to war in the Pacific.

Honolulu Star Bulletin Files, 1937–1942.

Hawaii Home Guard in World War II. History of activities after December 7, 1941. Deals with training, service, discharge of Japanese members, etc. By Col. P. M. Smoot.

"Emergency Medical and Ambulance Service Diary." O.C.D., Oahu. Activities in first months of war.

"Civilian Damage on Oahu, December 7, 1941." Locations and extent of damage (with photos). By Dr. Chester K. Wentworth, Board of Water Supply.

Census of Plantation Personnel. Distribution by race and marital status as of June 30, 1944. Total, all islands, 78,952 men, women, and children. H.S.P.A. Report.

"Japanese Plans for Pearl Harbor Attack." Lecture and interview, Captain Peyten Harrison, Reserve Officers' Club, May 1946. Statements given by Japanese admirals and diplomats.

Analysis of Japan's War-Time Conditions. Deals with military control, reaction to victories and defeats, industrial planning, administration of conquered territory. By Loraine E. Kuck.

"Why a Diversified Crops Committee, H.S.P.A." Review of movement since 1917. By Dr. Harold L. Lyon.

Emergency Food Production Plan for Islands and Territory of Hawaii. Voluminous and exhaustive report on activities of eighteen subcommittees in charge of diversified crops program. H.S.P.A. Report.

Report of Department of Entomology, H.S.P.A. Experiment Station, 1904-1945. Historical summary of insect-pest control.

The U.S.O. in Hawaii. Account of activities throughout Territory. By F. C. Atherton and Sewell Turner, chairmen; Mrs. J. Platt Cooke, Territorial director; Edwin E. Bond, director of operations.

Hawaii at War. Summarizes Territory's chief contributions to war effort. Hawaii Equal Rights Commission.

U.S.O. Report on Final Year of War.

The War Record of Civilian and Industrial Hawaii. Factual summary of civilian contributions. H.S.P.A. Report. By Col. E. C. Moore.

History of Organized Defense Volunteers in the Territory of Hawaii Public Relations Office, Central Pacific Base Command.

Pacific Affairs, Vols. VIII to XIX, 1935–1941. Articles, reviews, and comments on Far Eastern situation.

Honolulu Advertiser, February 15, 1940. Report of Speech by Tetsui Oi, manager, Japanese Chamber of Commerce, Honolulu. Exposition of Japanese aims and foreign policy.

Honolulu Advertiser, October 9, 1940, Article — "We Helped Japan Arm."

Hawaii Hochi, October 18, 1940 Report of address in Tokyo by Lt. Gen Hamada to conference delegates including representatives of McKinley Alumni Association and other student clubs in Japan.

Letter from H.S.P.A. to Governor Poindexter re enlistment of Filipinos. Reports 10,000 fewer laborers employed in 1942 on plantations than in 1940. To March 31, 1942, sugar industry had furnished 270,000 man-days for military defense projects. H.S.P.A. File 1239.

Memo to Mr. Chauncey Wightman from General Briant H. Wells (retired) re General Burgin's testimony in regard to civilian non-co-operation with military. Relates to statement that civil leaders such as Wells, Dillingham, and Walker would have opposed Short's calling of Alert No. 3.

Letter from Major General Thomas H. Green (military ex-governor) to Ernest W. Greene, H.S.P.A. Declared civilian population always prompt to co-operate with military.

Report of Office of Civilian Defense to Interior Department, United States. By T. G. S. Walker, Co-ordinator. Describes Disaster Council's prewar activities, work of committees and O.C.D. divisions, lists general orders, persons in charge of O.C.D. agencies, also recommendations looking toward the next emergency.

"Statement of Prewar Civilian Preparedness Activities, Island of Oahu." Report to H.S.P.A. by T. G. S. Walker, Cor-ordinator.

"Memorandum re Seventh Air Force Morale Program." Report by Col. Harold T. Kay. Covers period from inception under Major General Tinker and continuance under Major General Hale.

Describes work of subcommittees. (Mrs. Peggy Baldwin, Maui; Mrs. George Cooke, Molokai; Miss Hill, Hawaii; Messrs. Caleb Burns and L. Faye, and Mrs. Flora Rice, Kauai, chairmen.) Arrangements for rest periods for flying officers and crews.

"The University Extension's War Record." Address by H. H. Warner, director, July 8, 1946. Summarizes wartime services of Extension personnel.

"Instruction in Survival Lore and Jungle Living." Report by Kenneth P. Emory, Bishop Museum. Describes training courses, demonstrations, and research on Pacific Island survival for military castaways, under which over 100,000 men were instructed during 1944.

"War Never Ends for the Red Cross." Article on continuing Red Cross activities, by J. Howard Ellis, in Magazine *Hawaii*.

Report by Robert P. Patterson, Secretary of War. Emphasizes Hawaii's contribution to war effort by pointing out the critical dearth of labor and mechanical equipment for defensive construction during early years of war.

Philadelphia Record. Vol. 6, 1945. Points out that the American people hired professional military and naval officers to guard against just such an attack as the Japanese carried out, but neglects to mention that the press which calls itself the eyes and ears of the world was similarly unalert.

Report on Red Cross Activities. Summary by Dr. M. Hollenbach. Co-ordinated services with military, U.S.O., and O.C.D. Preparedness program, motor corps work, canteens, emergency food supplies, welfare services at advanced base, Grey Ladies, Home Service, Nurses Aides, Junior Red Cross, assistance to Blood Bank. Military Locator Service arranges communications between men in service with friends and relatives.

Abstract of War Contributions of Schools Throughout Territory. Collected from school reports by Dr. M. Hollenbach. Records of schools and teachers on each island.

ISLAND OF HAWAII

Japanese Sentry Incident. Files of *Hilo Tribune-Herald*, October 29, 1939, November 15, 1945.

Life Magazine, November 13, 1939. Picture of Japanese warship in Hilo Harbor, showing "Salute the Sentry" notice.

Report by Lt. Col. Bryan on Japanese civilian activities prior to war, including Japanese national war bond sales, scrap-iron drives, purchase of bomber for use in China war, forwarding of soldier comforts to Japan, dual citizenship, etc. Notes on G-2 and F.B.I. investigations.

Honolulu Advertiser, January 24, 1939. Reports court injunction against sale of Japanese war bonds.

Honolulu Star-Bulletin, December 22, 1938, January 21, 1939. Japanese War Bond sales.

Nippu Jiji (Japanese language newspaper) November 6, 1938. Bond sales.

Report of J. Scott B. Pratt, manager, Kohala Sugar Plantation. Describes prewar organization for blackouts, emergency police, evacuation plans (with maps), demolition in case of invasion, census of local civilians, with their responsibilities. Hawaii Rifles (20th regiment), Mounted Troop, Kahua Ranch, etc.

Diary of L. S. McLane, manager, Paauhau Sugar Plantation. Record of events following December 7, 1941, on an outlying plantation of Hamakua coast.

Honokaa Plantation. P. Naquin, manager. Report by W. B. MacFarlane, assistant manager. Reports contribution to U.S.E.D. of labor and equipment, operations during wartime, evacuation plans, etc.

Hamakua Mill Plantation. W. F. Robertson, manager. Files on war activities, guarded areas, diversified crops, volunteer services, Red Cross activities, Hawaii Rifles.

Kaiwiki Sugar Company. Andrew Walker, manager. Report on war participation, civilian registration, home gardening, etc.

Onomea Sugar Company. R. Bryan, manager. Organization of defense units, patriotic contributions by local Japanese, relations with army, food and travel restrictions.

Report by A. T. Spalding, Island Co-ordinator. Covers general plantation co-operation with military, including transportation of Army and Marines, plantation scrap piles, air raid shelters, sugar storage, demolition plans, mill blackouts, Hawaii Rifles organization, 1st Regiment, Col. Spalding, commander.

Waiakea Mill Co. H. H. Padgett, manager. Co-operation with Army, blackout regulation, rest and rehabilitation program, 7th Air Forces.

Hilo Sugar Company. Reports on First Aid Stations, morale of Filipino laborers, labor difficulties, night-time fluming, contributions to military effort, etc.

Olaa Plantation. W. L. S. Williams, manager. Reports by Gilbert Hay, George Moir, and Guido Giacometti, with regard to home defense plans, alerts, evacuation, beach patrols, food storage, organization of civilians for invasion in Puna and Olaa districts. Report to Commanding General.

Laupahoehoe Sugar Company. R. A. Hutchinson, manager. Letters of thanks from military authorities for loan of plantation equipment and notification of next-of-kin in casualty lists. Registration for Food Production Committee of 1000 vegetable- and fruit-growers.

Files of O.C.D., Hawaii. W. H. Hill, director. University War Depository, Mrs. K. Stidham, director.

ISLAND OF MAUI

Minutes of Maui Planters' Association, Ray M. Allen, secretary. Deals with measures for co-ordinating work of all sugar and pineapple plantations for national defense, prior to and after December 7.

Maui News (Ezra Crane, editor). Valuable summary of war and preparedness items, e.g. report of Opinion Poll of Political Science — students, University class, March 1941. "Appease Japan," 4%; "Embargo or Boycott against Japan," 88%; "Send Fleet to Singapore," 8%; Japanese students' opinion conformed with general trends.

War-Time Public Relations. Judge Edna E. Jenkins, director. Questions and answers re individual wartime problems of Japanese, collected at meetings in schools and camps. War bul- letins for Filipinos, general orders translated and explained. An extremely interesting program in wartime relations and morale.

Alexander House Community Association. Statement by C. S. Childs, director. Covers island-wide co-ordination of U.S.O. activities. Recreation program for military.

"Boy Scouts and the War." Statement by Harold Stein, chief ex- ecutive. Twelve hundred Scouts organized for war duty on islands of Maui, Lanai, and Molokai. (Subject of special report.)

E. L. Damkroger. Statement re air-raid wardens, evacuation plans, military and civilian athletic programs. (Subject of special report.)

Hawaiian Commercial Sugar Co. F. F. Baldwin, manager. Instal- lation of water supply for air field, loan of mechanical equip- ment, electricity supplied, relations with military, land taken for military use — 3,827 acres.

Maui Agricultural Co. H. A. Baldwin, manager. Prewar defense activities, guards for utilities, manning observation posts, assist- ing O.C.D. plans for first aid, fire-fighting, trial alerts, supple- mentary hospitals, land for military use.

Lahaina Activities. Account by Mrs. J. T. Moir. Covers Red Cross training plans, organization, and history of 1st Battalion Maui Volunteers, etc.

Pioneer Mill Sugar Co. Statement and report by J. T. Moir, Jr., manager. Setting up of observation posts, evacuation plans, student help on plantation. Alien Internment Board. Japanese civilian co-operation.

Wailuku Plantation. Diary of Ray M. Allen, manager. Chronological record of war events in relation to civilian community.

War-Preparedness Committee. J. Walker Cameron, chairman; General Lyman, C. S. Child, Ray Allen, W. Walker, J. T. Moir, members.

Maui Emergency Food Production. Committee Reports, July 1941.

Files of Maui O.C.D. J. Walker Cameron, University War Depository.

ISLAND OF KAUAI

Report of Kauai O.C.D. Covers preparatory work of Disaster Council, January to December 1941.

Kauai Volunteers. Statement by Col. Paul Townsley, Lihue Plantation (Caleb E. S. Burns, manager). Deals with contributions of plantations for equipment, transportation, etc. Work of mounted troops at Kapaa, Koloa and Waimea.

Women's Motor Corps. Training, organization, and O.C.D. activities.

Japanese Morale Committee. Final Report. Organized under Charles Ishii, to enlist co-operation of Japanese community in national defense, through meetings and group discussions in all districts of island.

Provisional Police Plan for Kauai, Judge Philip L. Rice, co-ordinator. Series of memos and bulletins outlining plans for training, organization, and duties of special police. From February 1941 up to outbreak of war.

"Koloa Plantation Participation in the War Effort." Statement by Hector Moir, manager. Deals with prewar enrolment of provisional police, diversified crops. War home activities, civilian evacuation plans and camps.

Kilauea Plantation Diary. J. F. Ramsey, manager. Lists contributions to home defense before and after Pearl Harbor.

Kekaha Sugar Co. Statement. By Lindsay Faye, manager. Machinery, labor, etc., supplied to Army. Co-operation on military road building. Use of local resources, seed storage, etc.

McBryde Plantation. John Sandison, manager. Statement re diversified crops, home gardening, water, electricity, supplied to military.

Olokele Plantation. Log of plantation activities before and after December 7, 1941, in relation to home defense.

Waimea Plantation. Statement by Alan Faye, manager. Reports Red Cross activities (ambulance corps, first-aid classes), emergency guards, food storage plans, and dairy supplies, ranch work. Account of formation and activities of mounted troop, Kauai Volunteers.

Report by Miss Elsie Wilcox on U.S.O. and O.C.D. activities on island.

Files of *The Garden Island*. Prewar preparations. Issues of *Kauai War Daily*. C. J. Fern, editor.

Grove Farm Plantation Statement. By W. Alexander, manager. Contribution to war effort, water supplied to community, evacuation camps, food crops. Shelling of Nawiliwili Harbor, blackouts, etc.

O.C.D. Records, Kauai. C. J. Fern, director. University War Depository. Mrs. K. Stidham, director.

ISLAND OF OAHU

"Petition to Congress for Relief of Damages and Expropriation of Properties by U.S.A." Honolulu Plantation. (Stafford Austin, manager.) History of plantation since 1899, describing organization, production, refining, capital losses through expropriation of 2,428 acres for military purposes. War preparation measures, services during attack, hospital and clinic services, Red Cross activities, labor and equipment loaned.

Ewa Plantation. J. D. Bond, manager. Report on War Activities. Itemizes all services rendered, equipment and labor contributed to military forces after December 7, 1941.

Waialua Plantation. John W. Midkiff, manager. Correspondence File containing copies of letters from military re use of lands in maneuvers, etc. Lists of separate permits issued, and blanket permission to locate troops on the plantation. H.S.P.A. File No. 1239.

Waimanalo Report. George Bennett, manager. Deals with operations on December 7, and following Japanese attack.

Kahuku Report. James N. Orrick, manager. Record of War Cooperation. H.S.P.A. Files.

Waipahu at War. A pictorial history of Oahu Plantation's War Activities. Hans L. Orange, manager.

War Diaries. File of Diaries from Pepeekeo, Honomu, Hakalau, Paauhau, Hawaiian Agricultural Co., Ltd., Hutchinson Sugar Co., Ltd., Honolulu, Waimanalo, Wailuku, Olokele Plantation, (C. Brewer & Co., Ltd., agents.) University War Depository.

NOTE: The University of Hawaii War Records Depository contains documents relating to Hawaii at war, filed under 73 subject headings and 236 sub-sections. It also has on file 3,500 feet of microfilm of war records.